Is Jesus the Only Savior?

Is Jesus the Only Savior?

JAMES R. EDWARDS

WILLIAM B. EERDMANS PUBLISHING COMPANY
GRAND RAPIDS, MICHIGAN / CAMBRIDGE, U.K.

Wm. B. Eerdmans Publishing Co.
2140 Oak Industrial Drive N.E., Grand Rapids, Michigan 49505 /
P.O. Box 163, Cambridge CB3 9PU U.K.
www.eerdmans.com

Printed in the United States of America

12 11 10 09 08 07   10 9 8 7 6 5 4

Library of Congress Cataloging-in-Publication Data

Edwards, James R.
    Is Jesus the only savior? / James R. Edwards.
        p.   cm.
    Includes bibliographical references and index.
    ISBN 978-0-8028-0981-0 (pbk.)
    1. Jesus Christ — Person and offices.   2. Christianity and other religions.
    I. Title.

    BT203.E39   2005
    232′.3 — dc22

                                        2005040479

The quotation on pages 220-21 is from *All Rivers Run to the Sea* by Elie Wiesel, copyright 1996
by Elie Wiesel. Used by permission of Alfred A. Knopf, a division of Random House, Inc.

To

The RePhil Group

Contents

Contents

Contents

Preface

The purpose of this book, as its title suggests, is to consider whether Jesus is the only savior of the world. A constellation of factors, which I discuss in subsequent chapters of this book, has subjected the claim that Jesus is the only savior to suspicion and doubt. It has become fashionable to express such doubts in public venues. It is my impression that people are anxious about this question, and that they would breathe more easily if we could all agree that Jesus is *a* savior of the world, not *the* savior of the world.

A spate of books and articles and television specials is being produced on Jesus today, some Christian, some quasi-Christian, and some not at all Christian. These books and articles and specials are being read and viewed and talked about by a large number of Christians and church members. On this subject, at least, the boundary between people inside and outside the church is quite fluid.

Readers will discover my own conviction that Jesus is the only savior of the world. I do not intend my personal judgment on this matter to carry a great deal of weight, however. A question of the magnitude of Jesus as savior is too important to be decided by someone else's opinion. More important than who affirms or denies this question are the *reasons* for affirming or denying it. The purpose of this book is to consider the particular views and reasons that would make a judgment possible and meaningful, especially in light of the currents we are navigating at the beginning of the third millennium.

It is my hope that this book may be of help to two types of readers. Throughout its writing I have had in mind readers whose faith has been unsettled or stimulated by the views of Jesus expressed above, and who do not know where to turn either to hear the issues adequately framed or responded to. I would hope that the following pages would help such readers "find their sea legs." There is much more information, evidence, and reasoning in support of the trustworthiness of the New Testament and the truth of the gospel than many people are aware of, even those who have spent a lifetime in the church. I hope to show that "the faith that was once for all entrusted to the saints" (Jude 3) rests upon a solid foundation.

I also have a second group of readers in mind, one that does not adhere to any particular Christian claims, and that wonders if there is anything especially credible to be said for the besieged view that Jesus is the only savior. I know a fair number of people who have opted for what I believe to be a mistaken view of Jesus largely because they have not heard a plausible counter-position. I venture to hope that those who consider the case against Christianity closed may find it reopened in the pages that follow.

A number of the views of Jesus I wish to consider in this book argue that Christianity and Christians have been mistaken about Jesus all along, or that Christianity has become antiquated and needs to be changed in order to survive. I have tried to address these concerns. Yet this book is not about Christian history, neither celebrating its contributions nor seeking to defend its misdeeds. The specific deeds and misdeeds of Christians over the centuries will not answer the central question whether Jesus is the only savior. The substance of this book is devoted rather to the source of the faith, to the evidence and claims of the New Testament and early church, especially as they appear in contemporary perspectives.

The content of this book has begged for a certain style of book. A book on Jesus as savior is too important to be relegated to academia. Hence I have tried to avoid some things that are typical of the scholarly guild, and include some things that are not. Where possible, I illustrate concepts and ideas from my own experiences or those of others; footnotes have been kept to a minimum; technical terminology has been reduced, or clearly defined when no substitute seemed adequate; and biblical quotations have been cited from the New Revised Standard Version of the Bible, a respectable modern translation. On the other hand, a book on Jesus as savior is too important to be written simplistically or breezily. A reader interested in the subject of this book is not, I think, interested in a superficial treatment or pat answers. I have endeavored to make thoughtful reading also interesting reading.

I am grateful for the support I have received in writing this book. A summer 2002 research grant from the Weyerhaeuser Center at Whitworth College launched the project. Two students, Gabe Schmidt and Geoffrey Helton, rendered helpful research assistance, especially with interlibrary loan. I am grateful to the following friends who volunteered to read portions of the manuscript: Tom Crocker, Peter Fern, John and Jean Klopsch, Carol Larson, Josh Mikelson, and Drew Strait. I am especially grateful to Susan Fern, Brent Mitchell, Troy Onsager, Jerry Sittser, and my wife Janie, who plowed through the entire manuscript and made many wise and helpful suggestions.

I am blessed to work with academic colleagues who are willing to read and discuss drafts of our manuscripts. This book is dedicated to our Monday night RePhil Group — Jerry Sittser, Terry McGonigal, Keith Wyma, and Keith Beebe, members of the Religion and Philosophy Department at Whitworth College. Their vigorous comments and insights have made this a better book than it would have been without their faithful efforts on its behalf.

JAMES R. EDWARDS
Good Friday 2004

The Shore and the Current

Not many years ago a book on the subject of Jesus as the only savior might have seemed like one arguing that spouses should be faithful in marriage or that parents should provide for their children. Things so obvious needed no special pleading. That was not because everybody believed and practiced such things. There have always been and will be people who fall short of or reject theological orthodoxy, just as spouses fall short of marriage and parenting ideals or choose to ignore them. The difference between a generation ago and now is not the discrepancy between the ideal and the practice. We bring a different ethos to things like faith, good parenting, and citizenship than we did before. Such things used to be regarded as self-evident virtues, even public goods — regardless of the exceptions that occurred in a given heart or home. There was little encouragement or empowerment in church or marriage or state to question the perceived ideals, which were widely acknowledged, even if not always followed. Anything outside them was considered an aberration that might be tolerated, but not celebrated.

Stephen Carter, author of *The Culture of Disbelief: How American Law and Politics Trivialize Devotion*, speaks specifically to the changes that have occurred in this regard with respect to religion.

> In an earlier generation there was a healthy respect for what counted as religion. People might have been somewhat limited in their visions of what counted as religion, but there was a respect for it, and I think

that was true right across the political spectrum and up and down the social and economic ladder. That has changed. There is less respect for religion, less of an appreciation of it as an important force that can genuinely be the motive force in people's lives without being somehow a symptom of something neurotic. That's what's been lost.[1]

I do not interpret Carter's statement to mean that interest in religion has waned. What has been lost is respect for what we call "organized religion." Despite the loss of commitment to the established church, however, there is widespread interest in religious experience, spirituality, religious mentors, and so forth today. The difference is that people are responding to these phenomena in intensely individualistic and eclectic ways rather than along ecclesial lines.

The general respect (or deference) that people formerly showed toward religion has been replaced by wariness, even skepticism, toward religious orthodoxy. People listen to categorical claims in the name of religion and morality differently than they used to. A conversation about the subject of this book illustrates this change in attitude. "What are you writing about?" asked an acquaintance of mine. "I'm writing a book about Jesus as the only savior," I said. A slight frown began to form on the questioner's face. "Is that the right question?" he asked. I could tell the conversation was about to turn away from social courtesies. "I think so," I said. "In fact, I think it is the most important question in life to answer correctly." My acquaintance was of a different mind, and he informed me that Buddha, Krishna, and the Dalai Lama satisfy their followers as much as Jesus satisfies Christians.

Conversations of this sort are not at all unusual today. What seemed to me significant about this conversation was that my partner was a person whose vital statistics were woven into the fabric of the church. He was well bred and well read in the Christian tradition. Yet he was annoyed at the subject of Jesus as the only savior. That seems to me paradigmatic of the changing attitudes toward Christianity today.

1. From an interview with Stephen Carter, published in Huston Smith, *Why Religion Matters: The Fate of the Human Spirit in an Age of Disbelief* (San Francisco: HarperSanFrancisco, 2001), 122-23.

Mix-and-Match Religion

One of the major changes that seems to have taken place is that people have shifted religious authority away from creeds, traditions, and churches and assumed it themselves. People are less inclined today to defer to established religious authorities, and more inclined to express their own religious preferences. They are given a wide array of options when they buy a car or join a fitness center. Why shouldn't they enjoy the same with religion? The August 1998 issue of *Utne Reader* captured this spirit with its cover story, "Designer God: In A Mix-And-Match World, Why Not Create Your Own Religion?" The author of the story saw in religion *a la carte* potential for religious utopia. Readers were encouraged to channel surf among the endless options of religious possibilities, real and imagined, in hopes of achieving a spiritual state that, like mixing paint colors or formulating an exercise routine, was customized and calibrated for each individual.

On the subject of religion the *Utne Reader* speaks for more than the bohemian fringe. A 2002 Gallup survey discovered unprecedented interest, even hunger, in Americans in spiritual matters. Eight in ten Americans say they desire to experience spiritual growth in their lives, and over two thirds say they believe in the devil. Interest in spiritual matters should not be equated with interest in orthodox Christianity, of course. It includes exploration and experimentation in a circus of supernatural phenomena, such as parapsychology, channeling, and interest in extraterrestrial life, spirits of the dead, and demonology. Such eclecticism results in wild unlikelihoods: born-again Christians who also believe in channeling, and mainline church members wearing the symbols of other faiths around their necks. "Americans, little aware of their own religious traditions, are practicing a do-it-yourself, 'whatever works' kind of religion, picking and choosing among beliefs and practices of various faith traditions," says Gallup. People do not seem to know what they really believe, or why. The results are religious forms that are broad but not deep, emotionally intense but neither intellectually clear nor outwardly practiced. God is popular, the poll concludes,

3

but not primary in people's lives. They believe in God, but do not trust God.[2]

A 2001 Barna poll paints a similar picture. Eighty percent of members of the Evangelical Lutheran Church of America, the Episcopal Church, the Presbyterian Church (USA), and the United Methodist Church — all mainline Protestant denominations — believe that salvation can be earned by good works, and not, as the hallmark doctrine of the Protestant Reformation maintains, by faith alone. Only one third of the same sample believes that Jesus Christ was sinless. Even in the more theologically conservative Assemblies of God and Pentecostal churches the percentage rises to only about seventy percent on the sinlessness of Jesus. About one third of mainliners accept the accuracy and infallibility of the Bible; and when asked if they were "absolutely committed to Christianity," about one half said yes. The Barna Research Group concluded that American Christianity is suffering theological collapse. The primary commitments of church members seem to be to peace, the search for personal fulfillment, and the conviction that God judges no one.[3] That, as theologically literate readers will recognize, is essentially Deism: the idea that an all-powerful Creator God allows people, who by nature are good, to determine their private lives and eternal destiny.

Eclecticism — picking and choosing — is a defining element of our individual religious autonomy. People (at least in the West) are not adhering to faith traditions with theological consistency, nor do they feel a need to. Nor are they opting for one set of beliefs over another. They are freely syncretizing — mixing and matching beliefs that previously were thought incompatible and contradictory. An instance of this nonchalance in faith matters is the following letter written to an Episcopalian minister.

> I attend a Bible study group at church every Friday morning. To my astonishment, several of the women (pillars of the church) said [yester-

2. George Gallup, Jr., and D. Michael Lindsay, *The Gallup Guide: Reality Check for 21st Century Churches* (Loveland, Colo.: Group Publishing, 2002), 7-9.

3. Barna Poll on U.S. Religious Belief — 2001. http://www.adherents.com/misc/BarnaPoll.html.

day] that they not only didn't believe in the divinity of Jesus but they didn't believe in the Resurrection or most of what is written in the Gospels either!!! Yet they recite the Nicene Creed, take Communion and go through all the motions. How can they if they don't believe in Jesus Christ as the Son of God and our Savior?[4]

Faith seems to be regarded like a transformer toy that can be made into different objects: a robot, a truck, or some other gadget. An experience on a recent flight reminded me how wild these transformations can be. A woman was sitting across the aisle from me and knitting. She announced, "This is what I do in faculty meetings." "I sit in faculty meetings too," I replied, "but I don't know how to knit." "What do you teach?" she asked. "Religion," I said. Her voice went up as her knitting when down. "Are you a pastor?" "Yes, I'm a Presbyterian pastor," I said. She reached across the aisle excitedly to shake my hand. "I'm a Presbyterian Buddhist," she exclaimed. Not knowing exactly how to respond, I asked, "How does it work being both a Presbyterian and a Buddhist? Do you attend church?" "Sure," she said. "You know, to funerals and things like that."

This woman may well have been muddled in her faith, but others practice religious syncretism with great sophistication. A professor of world religions charts his spiritual pilgrimage from Catholicism, in which he was raised, through Hindu gurus, Zen masters, and a Sufi shaykh. "My Christian faith," he told me, "has been strengthened by their practices, and now I can comfortably attend Yoga class, a Zen retreat and a Christian mass without conflicting feelings."

What seems to have happened is that the concept of a personal God or of a historical Jesus has been replaced by an *idea* of God or of Jesus. And like any idea — that of freedom of speech, for example — ideas of God and Jesus can be interpreted differently. We reserve the final interpretation, at any rate, for ourselves, as the Rev. John Spong, an Episcopal bishop, indicates in an email column. Asked, "Is God a person?", Spong said this:

4. Fleming Rutledge, "It's About God," *Princeton Seminary Bulletin*, n.s., 23/3 (2002): 345.

Human language is so limiting. Again and again, when I talk about God I come back to what has almost become my mantra. I cannot tell anyone who God is or what God is. That is not within the capacity of any human being, no matter how pretentious a title that person may have. All any human being can ultimately do is to tell another human being how that person believes that he or she has experienced the Holy, the Transcendent, the limitless Other, or to use our more common word, God. Even when we seek to relate only our experience of God and not God, there is still the possibility that we are delusional.[5]

For Spong, then, God is not only an idea, but essentially a description of his feelings. Statements like, "I felt ashamed," or "I feel at peace," are, of course, valid descriptions of feelings. I do not think, however, that language about God necessarily intends to assert anything particular about the feelings of the speaker. Rather, like language about gravity or mathematics, for example, language about God aims to describe something independent of ourselves. The question is, to which category does God conform? Is God an idea or feeling that, like wet clay in our hands, has no fixed form; or is God a hard reality, of which some descriptions are more appropriate, and others less so?

Navigating the Current

Several years ago I was swimming off the beach of Morro Bay, California, and noticed to my dismay that the shoreline had changed. The shoreline had not changed, of course. A riptide was gradually carrying me out to sea, and my position with respect to the shore had changed. My dismay at Morro Bay was the result of an interplay between a constant (the shoreline) and a current (the riptide). This book is also about a constant and a current, and the frequently dismaying interplay between the two. I believe that the biblical testimony to Jesus as savior of the world is an unchanging constant, a fixed point. I hope to show that this

5. John S. Spong, "Bishop Spong Q&A," http://www.directionstoorthodoxy.org/mod/news/view.php?article_id=488.

belief is not an arbitrary belief — like belief in UFOs, for example — but a well-informed belief for which there is considerable evidence. I do not imagine, of course, that I can *prove* that Jesus is the savior of the world, or that the evidence I shall supply would supplant the need for faith. I shall argue, in fact, that *all* final judgments of Jesus are faith judgments. But they need not be uninformed, and certainly not ill-informed, faith judgments. Sound evidence is a step toward sound faith. One of my objectives in this book is to assure Christians and to inform seekers that there are sound reasons for taking the biblical witness to Jesus Christ seriously. I hope to show that the presumption of the credibility of Scripture is, evidentially speaking, an entirely justifiable presumption.

My first objective is thus to speak about the shoreline. My second objective is then to speak about the current. We do not observe the shoreline — the story about Jesus — from a fixed and immutable vantage point. No age does, and ours is no exception. We view the shoreline while being carried in a riptide of cultural values and assumptions. Unlike a river, a riptide is slow and generally imperceptible. It is easy to think yourself stationary in a riptide when in fact you are not. My second objective is to examine the riptide itself, that is, the contemporary movements that account for the interest in Jesus today and the widely differing opinions of him. These currents include Enlightenment rationalism and the scientific method, pluralism, moral relativism, postmodernism, the quest for peace, and the challenge of other religions. It is from the vantage point of these currents that we see the shoreline. We need to consider how they influence our understanding of the gospel, and particularly its central claim that Jesus Christ is the sole and sufficient savior of the world.

Our line of approach in this book will be as follows: The first two chapters define the current state of affairs as inherited from the Enlightenment and expressed most recently in the Jesus Seminar. In order to speak to the prevailing skepticism about Jesus as the savior in the first two chapters, we shall need to turn to the evidence of the New Testament itself. But before we consider *what* the New Testament says about Jesus as savior, we need to examine *whether* it is admissible evidence. That will be the subject of Chapter 3, which will investigate the reliability of the New Testament as a historical source; Chapter 4, which will consider what the New Testament says about Jesus; and Chapter 5, which will take up the question of Jesus' own self-understanding. The purpose of Chapters 3, 4, and 5 is to lay a credible foundation for the central task of the book, which is to consider the specific claims of the New Testament about Jesus as savior (the shoreline) from the perspective of the contemporary currents affecting our judgment about those claims (the riptide). Chapter 6 begins the central purpose of the book by a straightforward presentation of the New Testament evidence for Jesus as savior, and Chapter 7 considers that evidence from the perspective of pluralism. Chapter 8 considers the New Testament teaching of Jesus as savior from sin from the perspective of moral relativism, and Chapter 9 asks whether an all-encompassing proclamation of the gospel is viable in a postmodern world. The last three chapters consider the relevance of Jesus as savior for the question of peace (Chapter 10), and finally for other religions (Chapters 11 and 12).

The shoreline and the current provide the metaphors for our task. A person being carried by a current normally wants to find a way to navigate it, particularly if the current is going in undesired directions. I hope, therefore, to do one further thing in this book, and that is to give readers oars and anchors with which to ply the current. I believe that the Christian faith as expressed in the New Testament and earliest confessions of the church is not something that can merely survive the current, but actually harness it, as a sail seizes the energy of a powerful trade wind and propels its craft to new shores.

CHAPTER ONE

The Quest of the Historical Jesus

A book on the subject of Jesus, especially Jesus as savior, might seem to be of appeal only to Christians. If the subject were limited to baptism or bishops that might be true. But it is not true about Jesus. Television specials on Jesus are regularly aired by the major networks at Christmas and Easter. There are shelves of books on Jesus at bookstores, some of which have little to do with Christianity. Jesus is more popular in America today than in the 1950s, when far more people attended church. The more unorthodox America becomes, the more interest there seems to be in Jesus.

"The world has gone after Jesus," lament the Pharisees in the Gospel of John (12:19). Well, maybe not the world, but the historical Jesus is indeed a public phenomenon in the Western world. We are more likely to see a cover story or television special on Jesus than we are on any other figure from the past — and certainly from the distant past. The appeal of Jesus is by and large detached from the church and organized Christianity, however. The Jesus who interests the modern world is Jesus as a spiritual personality who is recoverable by scholars, historians, and social scientists, not the Jesus proclaimed from pulpits. The "Sunday-Jesus" is suspected of having been tarnished with legend and dogma.

We noted in the Introduction that religion and morality are often not thought of as objective realities that exist independently of our ideas about them, like Mount Everest or the law of gravity, for example, but as ideas that can be adapted to changing times. This same current of thought affects the modern understanding of Jesus as well. The purpose of this chapter is to identify one particular current that has shaped the quest for the historical Jesus for more than two centuries now. This current is the foundation of all scholarly investigations of the Bible, including investigations of Jesus. Like most foundations, it is underground, out of sight, and rarely seen. Occasionally, however, we catch a glimpse of the foundation. A professor at a leading university wrote in a popular Bible journal recently that the idea of God directly speaking to or intervening in the world was a view of "the Bible's premodern devotees." "For academic scholars," said the professor, "such an explanation violates the 'rules of the game' by invoking the supernatural."[1] Secular scholars, he continued, seek to account for events in the Bible, whether mundane or "miraculous," in the same way they account for events in any other period of history. They account for them by human causality, not by direct divine causality. There is the foundation in full view: the "rules of the game" do not allow God to break onto the field of play.

The Rules of the Game

The rules by which a game is played affect the outcome of the game, and the rule that all events must be accounted for by natural causes rather than by supernatural ones is technically known as naturalism. Naturalism goes back roughly to the time of the founding of the American Republic, to a movement we call the Enlightenment. The Enlightenment is usually remembered as the age that birthed the scientific method, representative democracy, and the industrial revolution. It birthed all three — and with them the modern world. The indelible mark of Enlightenment thinking was a shift in allegiance away from traditional authorities, such as kings and queens; social position and privilege; popes, prelates, and pastors; church decrees and dogmas. The ultimate court of appeal was no longer the old authorities, but the autonomous individual. The Enlightenment endowed the human spirit — each individual human spirit

1. W. H. C. Propp, "Who Wrote Second Isaiah?" *Bible Review* 19/5 (October 2003): 34.

— with the right to question every authority except the authority of reason and experience.[2]

The Enlightenment inaugurated an intellectual revolution in which the West is by and large still participating. For the first time since the ancient Greek Cynics, the Enlightenment made skepticism a virtue. But unlike the little-known Cynics, Enlightenment skepticism has become pervasive in Western thought. The program of the Enlightenment consisted in trying to establish the absolute grounds of objectivity and certainty, and to establish them by discounting everything that could not be understood in terms of human reason. By submitting all beliefs, including the previously-hallowed truths of morality and religion, to doubt and rational examination, the Enlightenment broke trail into the modern world, a world dominated by the values of discovery, invention, and the idea of progress. Personal liberties and rights were made the standard by which past conventions and traditions, whether social, political, economic, or religious, stood or fell. Where earlier ages placed their confidence in the old authorities or in God, the Enlightenment placed its confidence squarely in the autonomous individual, as embodied in unadorned, unencumbered, and iconoclastic figures such as Voltaire, Ben Franklin, and the American Minuteman. The Enlightenment called the human individual out from the wings to center stage. Human reason was the only altar before which one should bow. Not surprisingly, the human self became the most sacred thing in the world.

The commitment to human reason as a standard for truth and morality, and the values of discovery, questioning, invention, and individual autonomy are very appealing to me, and they must be to most people. Who but tyrants, the insane, and charlatans could object? The answer is that surely no one would object — if the above values were as straightforward as they appear. But here we must become Enlightenment individuals ourselves. When we read the fine print of Enlightenment "reason" with the glasses of Enlightenment skepticism we discover not a

---

2. Hans-Georg Gadamer, *Truth and Method* (New York: Seabury Press, 1975), 241: "It is the general tendency of the enlightenment not to accept any authority and to decide everything before the judgment seat of reason."

pure and independent reason, but a reason driven by definite constraints that affected its outcome.

Let me illustrate by telling a story. In the 1970s and 1980s I participated in several church visitations to then communist East Germany. After the fall of the Berlin Wall in 1989, an East German with whom I was fairly well acquainted asked me if I had not been working for the CIA. Surprised, I asked him why he thought so. "Your knowledge of German, your interest in our country, and your frequent visits and many contacts here have taught you more about East Germany than any American I know," he said. "I assumed you must be working for the CIA." What my acquaintance observed in me was what he expected of a CIA agent, and he chose to explain his observations in that light. It was, in one sense, a reasonable conclusion — although in this instance it was wrong. I did not work for the CIA, nor had I ever thought of doing so. My acquaintance did not consider that other conclusions might be even better explanations of the same observations. (The proper explanation of my "covert activities" was simply this: they were inspired by a commitment to witness to the oneness of the church of Jesus Christ in a divided Cold War world.)

The thinking of my East German acquaintance was driven by prior assumptions and constraints that caused him to interpret facts and observations in predetermined ways. Thomas Kuhn calls these constraints "paradigms"; we might liken them to intellectual houses that attempt to accommodate large families of data and ideas. There are as many paradigms as there are families of data. Racial profilers operate with a paradigm of suspicion against minorities. Men who suspect their wives of infidelity interpret otherwise normal acts in light of a paradigm of infidelity. Most cancer survivors contend with a paradigm of the inevitability of the recurrence of cancer; that is why they suspect aches and pains as a return of the dreaded disease. Paradigms provide explanations for common facts and data. People who rely on them are not irrational. But neither are they truly objective. They do not — or cannot — admit that the same facts and observations could be rationally accounted for equally well or better by other paradigms. A predetermined circle is drawn, and everything, whether it falls inside or outside the circle, is interpreted in light of it. In truly objective thinking, seeing is believing. In paradigm thinking, believing is seeing.

Now, back to the Enlightenment. The reason of the Enlightenment was paradigmatic reason, and the paradigm was naturalism. Naturalism is the philosophical belief that all phenomena can be explained either by material or scientifically provable causes. Committed to explaining all reality by means of the scientific method, the Enlightenment reduced all reality to naturalism, empiricism, and rationalism. Committed to naturalism as the sum of reality, the Enlightenment could not admit the possibility of a God (if there was one) who would "violate the laws of nature" by breaking into the natural order. Things that could not be explained by the scientific method — whether historical events, morality, human affection, or the existence of God — were explained *away* by it.

In a society in which skepticism was a sacred duty, one might expect everything associated with the Christian faith to have been jettisoned like a spent booster rocket. Much was jettisoned, including the authority of the church, Scripture, and divine revelation. In many respects, the Enlightenment signaled a twilight of the gods in the Christian West. Surprisingly, however, there were two important aspects of Christianity that were not jettisoned, although they were greatly altered.

The first was God. The Enlightenment did not dispense with the concept of God, although God was altered to resemble the laws of nature, as the Stoics much earlier had thought of the *Logos*, and the Neo-Platonists of the First Principle. Enlightenment thinkers were fond of referring to God in functional categories — Providence, Creator, Nature's God. God was thought of as a concept or idea, a facsimile of Reason that pervaded the universe and superintended its processes. The rational processes of the world corresponded to the God of Reason in the same way that a waterfall corresponds to the law of gravity. And just as there could be no contradiction between the law of gravity and a waterfall, there could be no contradiction between the way God works in the world and the way human reason works in the world. As rational creatures, human beings became partners of God and, insofar as they were ra-tional, even like God. Since God both embodied and conformed to reason, traditional ways of knowing God had to be discredited and discarded.[3] Revelation could no longer be regarded as an independent source of truth that superseded reason. The resultant view of God is known as Deism. Deism granted that God created the world, and through the laws of nature was the benefactor of the world. But the God of Deism could not and did not meddle in the world apart from the laws of nature.

The Quest Begins

The second aspect of Christianity not jettisoned by the Enlightenment was Jesus. But like God, the Jesus that survived was an abridgment of the New Testament Jesus. The Enlightenment donned critical investigation into the origins of the Bible and the life of Jesus with intellectual legitimacy. Indeed, if the effect of the Enlightenment on Christianity in general was like a sedative, its affect on the quest for the historical Jesus was like a steroid. The lion's share of this investigation was done in Germany. Only a fraction of the scholarship has been translated into English, but its magnitude is staggering. Indeed, it occupies a unique genre of research in the Western intellectual tradition. Two problems above all dominated the field of inquiry. One was the attempt to explain the relationships among the first three Gospels, the Synoptic Gospels, as they are called.[4] The question of the formation of the Gospel traditions was a dominant and defining post-Enlightenment intellectual enterprise. In the words of a scholar who devoted his life to the problem:

3. Andrew F. Walls, "From Christendom to World Christianity: Mission and the Demographic Transformation of the Church," *Princeton Seminary Bulletin*, n.s., 22/3 (2001): 321-22, observes that the influence of the Enlightenment on the liberal democracies of Western Europe "has proved one of the largest and fastest movements away from the Christian faith ever to have taken place; much faster, for instance, than that in the Middle East which followed the rise of Islam." Further, see Jacques Barzun, *From Dawn to Decadence: 1500 to the Present — 500 Years of Western Cultural Life* (New York: Perennial, 2000), 270-71 and 359-60, who speaks of God being forced "into respected retirement" by the Enlightenment.

4. "Synoptic" comes from the Greek *synoptikos*, "a seeing together." It refers to the Gospels of Matthew, Mark, and Luke, whose content, style, and sequence are comparable.

The critical analysis of the sources of the Gospels is justifiably regarded as one of the most difficult research problems in the history of ideas. . . . one can truly say that no other enterprise in the history of ideas has been subjected to anywhere near the same degree of scholarly scrutiny.[5]

Related to what became known as the "Synoptic Problem," but much better known, was a second intellectual enterprise of the Enlightenment, the "quest of the historical Jesus," to quote the English title (1910) of Albert Schweitzer's monumental study. Schweitzer was a German scholar who surveyed over 200 tomes written between 1750 and 1900 about the life of Jesus. *Leben Jesu Forschung* — investigation of the life of Jesus — became a virtual genre of literature.

The most important thing to understand about the quest of the historical Jesus is the term itself. When we hear the phrase "historical Jesus," we might think of something along the lines of "the Jesus who would have been recorded by a camcorder," for example. But in the Enlightenment paradigm, the expression meant the Jesus discernible by the historical methods of naturalism. Naturalism, as we have noted, is the commitment to explain all phenomena as results of causes that can be measured by the senses or conceived of rationally. Therefore, permissible evidence was limited to what could be known about Jesus by "the rules of the game" discussed above. The books surveyed by Schweitzer all assumed that the laws of nature are understandable by reason alone, and that God neither intervenes in them nor alters them. A distinction developed between the human Jesus of critical historiography and the divine Christ of the church. For the Enlightenment the real Jesus was not the supernatural Christ who was born of a virgin, performed miracles, and whose death and resurrection effected salvation of the faithful. That Jesus — the Christ of the church — was rejected. The Enlightenment Jesus, rather, emerged as an itinerant humanitarian who could be known by naturalistic historical research.

5. H.-H. Stoldt, *History and Criticism of the Marcan Hypothesis* (Macon: Mercer University Press/Edinburgh: T&T Clark, 1980), 1. For a comprehensive survey of the Synoptic problem, see D. L. Dungan, *A History of the Synoptic Problem. The Canon, the Text, the Composition, and the Interpretation of the Gospels* (New York: Doubleday, 1999).

Another way to put it would be to say that relevant knowledge about Jesus had to come "from below" rather than "from above." Knowledge "from above" has God as its direct source, and what comes directly from God must be primarily known by *revelation*. But revelation violates the "rules of the game" by invoking the supernatural, and the supernatural, as a way of knowing things and explaining their existence, was ruled out of bounds. Everything about the life of Jesus as recorded in the Gospels had to be accounted for "from below," in the same ways we would account for events in the life of Julius Caesar or Princess Diana. Miracles, naturally, had to be explained without reference to God, and various explanations were put forth to explain rationally all the miracles attributed to Jesus in the New Testament. The story of Jesus' walking on the water (Mark 6:45-52), to take one example, was usually explained as an optical illusion caused by Jesus' walking along the shore; or alternatively by Jesus' walking on a sandbar hidden in the Sea of Galilee. At any rate, the Gospel narrative that he actually walked on water could not be taken at face value.

The First Quest was supremely confident that human reason could, like a metal detector in an airport, cull out the contraband of legend and superstition in the Gospels and render Jesus compatible to a naturalistic worldview, safe and respectable. There are, however, significant flaws in this methodology. There are a great many things in life we presume true that cannot be verified either by naturalism or by the scientific method. All historical events, for example, fall outside scientific verification, since they can neither be controlled or repeated. When naturalism became the only standard by which Jesus could be judged, it had to dismiss very plausible evidence not compatible with the theory — somewhat like eliminating infrared and ultraviolet light from the spectrum because they cannot be seen by the naked human eye.

Consider the following summary of Jesus' life: He was a figure of *antiquity*, known primarily through *historical record*. According to his own self-understanding and the testimony of his followers, he stood in an *unshared relationship* with God. His contemporaries (opponents included) believed in his ability to perform *miracles*. His earliest followers believed that his death effected *forgiveness of sins* and *atonement* with God for those who received the gospel in faith. His followers believed he was *resurrected from the dead*. This is a sparse list of affirmations about Jesus compared to the New Testament or virtually any Christian creed. Nevertheless, each italicized affirmation was rejected by the quest of the historical Jesus because it could not be verified by scientific methodology. The rules of the game dismissed such evidence, regardless how plausible it might be, as supernatural and thus "unscientific." The Enlightenment was forced by its methodology to explain away the supernatural as legend, mistaken belief, symbol, or hallucination.

Quest II

Schweitzer's *Quest* summed up over a century of debate on the historical Jesus, but it did not end debate. It had the opposite effect, in fact. It stimulated theology (and popular culture to some extent) with an interest in the historical Jesus that has ebbed and flowed ever since. One of the flows surfaced in the 1950s and 1960s, again primarily in Germany. It fell short of the passion of the first Quest, but it added a new card to the deck of *Leben Jesu Forschung*. The new card was not Enlightenment rationalism in the service of naturalism, as in the First Quest, but the role of the church in the formation of the Gospels. In the first half of the twentieth century radical New Testament scholars such as Martin Dibelius and Rudolf Bultmann doubted that much could be known for certain about the historical Jesus, apart from the fact that he existed. Nor were they particularly interested in pursuing what little might be known. They believed that the worldview of the New Testament was essentially "mythological," and that the Gospels, in particular, did not preserve the actual words of Jesus. Jesus, rather, was essentially a personification, a mascot perhaps, of the convictions and proclamation of the early church. An American scholar in the 1960s voiced the project of "demythologizing" thus:

> Clearly, the New Testament portrayal of Jesus is essentially mythological. Statements about his preexistence, divine sonship, virgin birth, contacts with angelic and demonic forces, supernatural powers, sacri-

ficial death, resurrection, ascension, second coming, and the like are appropriate to the first-century mythological world views of Jewish apocalypticism and Hellenistic gnosticism but not to a twentieth-century scientific world view.[6]

This description more or less characterizes the ground rules of critical biblical scholarship in the 1960s and 1970s. Not everyone, of course, who taught or studied theology in those decades would have necessarily agreed with the above statement, but the statement sets forth the new rules by which the game was generally played. In this view, Jesus' expressed purpose of giving "his life a ransom for many" (Mark 10:45), for example, or the many statements in John's Gospel about Jesus' relationship with the Father, were beliefs of the *early church* that were attributed to Jesus. Neither they nor anything like them could be traced back to the historical Jesus, however. This approach to the Gospels operated on the assumption that the written Gospels were composed of brief identifiable *forms* of oral tradition. The attempt to recover the early oral forms was called "form criticism." Form critics believed that the real Jesus of history was forever obscured beneath these forms. The real Jesus — again, the Jesus that would have been picked up by a camcorder — was no longer recoverable by critical historians. What could be known for certain was only what the early church believed about Jesus, which was preserved in isolated and residual forms in the canonical Gospels.

A leading exponent of the Second Quest, Hans Conzelmann, described the enterprise this way:

> Only a small portion of the reports in the Gospels preserves reliable information about Jesus. The chief part of such reports are the product of the Christian community. An anonymous entity, the "community," took the place of Jesus. As far as Jesus' own self-consciousness goes, we know next to nothing.[7]

6. W. O. Walker, Jr., "Demythologizing and Christology," *Religion in Life* 35 (1966): 69-70.
7. H. Conzelmann, "Das Selbstbewusstsein Jesu," *Beiträge zur evangelischen Theologie* 65 (München: Christian Kaiser Verlag, 1974): 30.

Ernst Käsemann, another exponent of the Second Quest, echoed Conzelmann.

> It was the belief of Jesus that, in his word, the *basileia* [kingdom] was coming to his hearers. Does this mean that he understood himself to be the Messiah? The only way of dealing briefly with this question is simply to express at this point one's own personal opinion. I personally am convinced that there can be no possible grounds for answering this question in the affirmative. I consider all passages in which any kind of Messianic prediction occurs to be kerygma [proclamation] shaped by the community.[8]

In the view of the Second Quest, the real Jesus might be compared to a simple beam of light, more or less like any other beam of light. But when directed to a prism, the beam of light was refracted into a spectrum of colors. The early church was this prism, and the "colors" (that is, the supernatural aspects) of Jesus recorded in the Gospels were due to the prism, not to the beam of light. The early church transposed its views onto Jesus in the four Gospels, and thus the Gospels tell us not who Jesus was, but what the church believed him to be. In so doing, the hypothesis concludes, the early church obscured for the most part the real Jesus from historical recovery.

Quest III

A more vigorous surge of interest in the historical Jesus arose in the late 1980s. The first two Quests were European and primarily German, the endeavors of liberal Protestantism. The Third Quest, however, has been dominated by North Americans. It includes not only Protestants, Catholics, and Jews, but also people of unorthodox religious commitments, and of no religious commitment. The philosophical naturalism charac-

8. E. Käsemann, "The Problem of the Historical Jesus," *Essays on New Testament Themes*, trans. W. J. Montague, *Studies in Biblical Theology* 41 (Naperville, Ill.: Alec R. Allenson, 1964), 43.

teristic of the first two Quests is still presupposed in the Third Quest, but there are again new cards in the deck of the Third Quest. The chief innovation of the Third Quest is the attempt to understand the historical Jesus through the lenses of the social sciences, cross-cultural anthropology, and the ideology of liberation. The latest Quest is not primarily interested in what Jesus has to teach about theology, and it is also less rationalistic than the First Quest. Its chief interest is in the sociological and anthropological conditions that influenced Jesus.

Quest III acknowledges that Jesus was indebted to the Jewish Wisdom tradition. His parables, above all, reveal that he was a chief exponent of wisdom in Israel. Above all, the Third Quest sets Jesus and the New Testament squarely within the context of first-century Judaism. To argue that the historical Jesus should be interpreted within a Jewish context might seem self-evident to many readers today. Nevertheless, the tendency of the first two Quests was to separate Jesus from his Jewish background, and sometimes even to denigrate it. The acknowledgement of the Jewish context of early Christianity is thus a welcome contribution of the Third Quest. The Third Quest aims to consider the Jesus-drama within a full, three-dimensional set. The Third Quest is as interested in the sociology of first-century Palestine as it is in Jesus, including investigations into the significance of the Jewish synagogue, the contrast between ruling urban elites in Jerusalem and landed laborers in Galilee, the role of women, Jewish family structures, rituals of purity and impurity, absentee landowners and the patronage system, the taxation system, and the temple cult in Jerusalem.

The value of any form of analysis depends on its ability to explain things. The Third Quest has shed considerable light on the social setting of Jesus and the early church. It has made a genuine contribution in furthering our knowledge of the social world of first-century Palestine. Nevertheless, to assume that a social setting — even a correctly perceived one — captures the meaning of a person in it is like supposing that a job résumé captures the essence of a person. Résumés are good at conveying *what*, but they inevitably fall short of portraying *who*. Stage sets are necessary, but on their own they cannot replace plot or actors in a play. C. S. Lewis was right in saying that a Christianity that concentrates on contextual matters to the exclusion of essential matters leaves out all that is specifically Christian.[9] Most Christians will naturally affirm that Jesus was a peasant Jew, movement founder, overcomer of social barriers, opponent of the Sanhedrin, healer, ecstatic, sage, and so on. But they will not find anything in that list that explains the significance of Jesus in *their* lives. When such a list is packaged and marketed as the sum of the matter, the result is a sociological stick figure, a Jesus who is simply the product of an environment. In striving to give a three-dimensional context of Jesus' life, the Third Quest has left us, curiously, with a flat, two-dimensional Jesus.

In the next chapter we shall look at the most publicized front of the Third Quest, the Jesus Seminar. But before doing that let us summarize, briefly, the ground we have covered so far. We began by saying that the modern understanding of Jesus dates from the Enlightenment. The Enlightenment extracted both God and Jesus from the realm of the church, and sought to redefine each according to naturalistic standards of thinking, that is, according to what could be known and believed about them apart from reference to the supernatural, to ecclesiastical pronouncements, and to creeds and confessions. Three Quests of the historical Jesus followed, or evolved, from this starting point. The First was a Herculean endeavor attempting to explain especially the miraculous in the Gospels by a form of rationalism *limited to the paradigm of naturalism*. The Second Quest continued in this naturalistic current, but concentrated on investigating how the interests of the early church may have influenced the resultant picture of Jesus in the Gospels. The Third and latest Quest, still operating under naturalistic assumptions inherited from the Enlightenment, has shifted emphasis away from the influence of the church to the influence of the social environment of first-century Palestine on Jesus. The Second Quest made Jesus more or less a personification of the beliefs of the early church, whereas the Third Quest makes him largely a product of a complex of social factors. The three Quests have focused on three different objects of investigation — the miracu-

9. See his discussion of the historical Jesus in *The Screwtape Letters* (New York: Macmillan Paperbacks Edition, 1973), Chapter XXIII.

lous in the Gospels, the role of the early church in the formation of the Gospels, and the influence of social factors in the life of Jesus. Yet all three have been approached from the methodological perspective of naturalism.

CHAPTER TWO

The Jesus Seminar

Three Pictures on a Wall

Let me begin this chapter with an illustration. Imagine three pictures hanging on a wall. The first is a photograph of Jesus, the second a portrait of Jesus, the third an abstract, indistinct painting of a human figure. These pictures represent three different ways of conceiving of the historical Jesus. The photograph represents a literalistic approach that believes the Gospels deliver an exact, photographic likeness of Jesus. The portrait represents critical scholarship that, while recognizing that the Gospels present the life of Jesus from the perspective of faith, sees the portrait of Jesus standing in trustworthy continuity with the Jesus of history. The abstract painting represents a skeptical vein of scholarship. In this view, the Jesus of the Gospels is not a trustworthy representation of the historical Jesus but an abstraction of him, the real historical Jesus being essentially unrecoverable. The figure in the third frame is non-representational, and thus the "meaning" or representation of the object must to a greater or lesser extent be supplied by each viewer.

I believe that all views of Jesus can be generally reduced to one of the three frames (with the exception of the very few who deny the existence of the historical Jesus). It will be my purpose in this book to argue that the portrait in the second frame is the most reasonable and scientific way to understand the New Testament presentation of Jesus. Since I am not writing for an audience that believes in the literal accuracy of every jot and tittle in the Gospel accounts, I shall not undertake a refutation of the Gospels-as-photographic-likeness-view. I personally believe — and I shall give a number of reasons for my belief in this book — that there is essential agreement among the Gospels on the life of Jesus. There are, however, details in each that seem impossible to harmonize with the other three. These details are neither great in number nor in importance, but acknowledging them places me outside the literalist-fundamentalist camp. At any rate, the fundamentalist view of Jesus and the Gospels rejects forms of "higher" (or critical) biblical scholarship, and I shall employ these throughout this book in defense of the second portrait perspective. These critical methodologies, when reasonably employed, provide quite compelling support for the intellectual defensibility of the biblical portrait of Jesus.

This leaves the third frame of the abstract, non-representational figure. As we saw in the last chapter, the first two quests for the historical Jesus concluded that the New Testament portrait of Jesus is a distortion of the real Jesus of history. Moreover, they contended that the real Jesus of history is practically unrecoverable, largely lost in history. Given that conclusion, the First Quest tried to salvage Jesus as a moral teacher. One thinks, for instance, of Thomas Jefferson, third president of the United States and a classic proponent of the First Quest, who pared his New Testament down to a collection of the sayings of Jesus.[1] A forty-six page patchwork primer of morality was all that was left, and Jefferson entitled it *Philosophy of Jesus.*

In the Second Quest, too, Jesus remained an abstract figure. The influential German New Testament scholar Rudolf Bultmann put forth a program of "demythologization," by which he attempted to liberate Jesus from the constrictions of Jewish apocalyptic.[2] Bultmann believed that the worldview of the New Testament was an obsolete one that had

---

1. C. B. Hunter, "Jefferson's Bible: Cutting and Pasting the Good Book," *Bible Review* 13/1 (1997): 38-46.

2. "Apocalyptic" derives from the Greek word for "revealed" or "unveiled," and refers to a genre of Jewish literature belonging to the time period from 200 BC to AD 100 that claimed to reveal future events.

been replaced by modern science. His goal was to salvage a Christ-figure who could mediate existential authenticity to modern individuals.[3] If Jefferson's Jesus was an Enlightenment moralist, Bultmann's was a modern existentialist. In both Quests scholarship produced a Jesus that conformed to the ideal of the age. The more abstract the figure, the more one can see in it what one wants.

The Jesus Seminar

And what of the Third Quest? As noted in the last chapter, Quest III is more varied than the first two. A number of scholars — John Meier, N. T. Wright, Larry Hurtado, Craig Evans, Ben Witherington III, and Luke Timothy Johnson among them — have produced works of erudition and careful scholarship that have appreciably enhanced our understanding of the historical Jesus. But this group of scholars has been overshadowed, at least in the public eye, by the Jesus Seminar, a highly publicized think tank of scholars that has met since 1985 to attempt to determine the authenticity of the words and deeds attributed to Jesus in the Gospels. Seminar members cast ballots on each saying or deed attributed to Jesus in the Gospels, including the *Gospel of Thomas,* a collection of sayings attributed to Jesus that was first discovered in 1945 at Nag Hammadi in Egypt. The *Gospel of Thomas* is widely thought to represent a Gnostic interpretation of Christianity, but the Jesus Seminar contends that it contains more authentic sayings than do the four canonical Gospels.[4] Their system of voting works like this: a red ballot indicates that a given statement (or something like it) was spoken by Jesus; a pink ballot, that a statement resembles something Jesus might have said; a gray ballot, that although the ideas may be close to those of Jesus, the statement did not originate with him; and a black ballot a definite negative, that the state-

3. R. Bultmann, *Jesus Christ and Mythology* (New York: Scribners, 1958).

4. Gnosticism encompassed a variety of movements in the early centuries of Christianity that proclaimed salvation based on superior knowledge (Greek *gnōsis*) of spiritual things. A number of Gnostic sects produced Gospels in which Gnostic teachings were attributed to Jesus.

ment derived from later tradition. Statements are assumed black until proven otherwise.

The labors of the Jesus Seminar have resulted in the "Scholars Version" of the New Testament, a translation that shuns pious phraseology in favor of "the common street language of the original."[5] Moreover, the result of the voting has been a sensation for the media. Eighty-two percent of the words attributed to Jesus, according to the Seminar, were not actually spoken by him. Only one statement in the Gospel of Mark (considered by most scholars to be the earliest and most reliable Gospel) is judged to have come with certainty from Jesus: "Give to Caesar what is Caesar's, and to God what is God's" (Mark 12:17). As for the Gospel of John, "the Fellows of the Seminar were unable to find a single saying they could with certainty trace back to the historical Jesus." For the Seminar, "the Fourth Gospel is alien to the real Jesus, the carpenter from Nazareth."[6]

What is novel about the Jesus Seminar is not its low opinion of the historical reliability of the Gospels. Our review of critical biblical scholarship since the Enlightenment, especially in its more radical forms, reveals that similar conclusions have been reached for the past two and one-half centuries. The novelty of the Seminar consists rather in its public relations expertise and marketing savvy. The Jesus Seminar has made an end run around the sequestered scholarly guild of biblical scholars and made Jesus into a media event on television talk shows and specials at Christmas and Easter.

Hand-in-hand with its media profile is the Seminar's iconoclasm toward church, faith, and creed. "The Christ of creed and dogma can no longer command the assent of those who have seen the heavens through Galileo's telescope," boasts the Seminar. The "old deities and demons" have been swept from the skies. Academic scholarship (particularly its own) is heralded as a chivalrous knight dispelling the darkness and oppression of the church. "The refuge offered by the cloistered precincts of faith gradually became a battered and beleaguered position" until "bibli-

5. R. W. Funk et. al., *The Five Gospels: The Search for the Authentic Words of Jesus, A New Translation and Commentary* (New York: Macmillan Publishing Company, 1993).

6. Funk, *The Five Gospels*, 10, 33.

cal scholarship rose to the challenge and launched the tumultuous search for the Jesus behind the Christian façade of Christ."[7] The Jesus Seminar wants "to break the church's stranglehold over learning" and to free Jesus from the "tyranny," "oppression," and "blindness" of his Babylonian captivity. The Apostles' Creed, asserts the Seminar, "smothers the historical Jesus" by imposing on him the heavenly Christ-figure of later Christian conviction.[8] The Seminar promises to dispel the age of darkness with the untrammeled light of scholarship and reason.

We are made to feel as if we have been freed from a dungeon. The Jesus Seminar has turned the wine of myth into the cold water of reality. The result is a Jesus who was an itinerant Jewish peasant teacher who challenged the urban establishment in Jerusalem. Like Buddha or a Cynic philosopher, he espoused a subversive view of traditional wisdom. He both preached and practiced radical egalitarianism in social relations. He gathered a group of followers and formed them into a movement that, like himself, had no messianic or eschatological expectations. Unlike the First Quest, many scholars of the Third Quest consider Jesus to have been a healer. True, his healings were not genuine miracles. Their essence, rather, lay in changing the psychological states of people by trances or by the power inherent in Jesus as a spirit-person. The actual physical conditions of people, however, were not altered. Jesus, in other words, healed people without curing their illnesses. Real miracles in the sense that most people understand the term did not occur. John Crossan, a leader in the Jesus Seminar, asserts that "miracles are not changes in the physical world so much as changes in the social world." At any rate, Jesus "did not and could not cure" actual diseases.[9]

According to Crossan, the résumé of the real Jesus of history is a far cry from the Gospel records of him. Crossan believes that Jesus did not call twelve apostles because a group that large could not have traveled in rural Galilee. The triumphal entry into Jerusalem and the cleansing of the temple did not happen either. The first was a later scribal addition,

---

7. Funk, *The Five Gospels*, 2.
8. Funk, *The Five Gospels*, 7, 24.
9. *Jesus: A Revolutionary Biography* (HarperSanFrancisco, 1994), 82.

and the second was a later story symbolizing the destruction of Jerusalem. Nor was there a Last Supper (since it is absent in the hypothetical Q source and the *Gospel of Thomas*).[10] To be sure, Jesus was crucified, but as a suspected political subversive, not as a messianic pretender. At any rate, his death had no atoning significance, nor was he resurrected from the dead. Crossan believes the accounts of the resurrection of Jesus arose by free associations of the early church on the scapegoat theme of Leviticus 16. The body of Jesus, insists Crossan, was in all likelihood eaten by dogs, as were the bodies of other victims of crucifixion.

Criteria of Authenticity

In broad strokes, such are the conclusions of the Jesus Seminar. On what basis does a group of scholars come to conclusions at such variance from the historical source they are investigating? That is the question to which we now turn. The answer to this question is both more instructive and more interesting than the conclusions themselves. The Seminar employs three general principles when considering whether a saying or an act attributed to Jesus in the Gospels is authentic. The first is the principle of *uniqueness*, meaning that a statement with no parallel in either Judaism or Hellenism probably did not arise from either, and may go back to Jesus. The second is the principle of *difficulty*, meaning that difficult sayings are more likely to be authentic, since they are less likely to have been fabricated by the early Christians who wrote the New Testament.

The last is the principle of *multiple attestation*, meaning that the likelihood of the authenticity of a statement increases according to the number of times it is attested in different sources or layers of tradition. For the Jesus Seminar, a biblical claim about Jesus cannot be accepted as reliable unless it is paralleled in a source outside the New Testament — say, in the *Gospel of Thomas*, or in an early Christian or Jewish tradition. The

---

10. "Q" (from the German *Quelle*, "source") is a presumed written or oral source for teaching material, mostly, common to both Matthew and Luke, but not Mark. The Jesus Seminar believes Q to be the earliest and most reliable record of the real Jesus.

Jesus who emerges after this criterion has been applied looks quite similar to the charismatic sage and wonder-worker reported by the first-century Jewish historian Josephus.[11] Observant readers will note that this methodology favors claims *outside* the body of evidence being examined. In fairness to the criterion, this is doubtlessly intended to offset allegedly exaggerated claims about Jesus from early Christians. Nevertheless, in principle the methodology seems a dubious test of historicity — rather like writing the history of a city by discounting everything the local newspaper said unless it were corroborated by *Newsweek* or CNN.

Let us take an instance from the Gospels and see how these criteria apply. I choose a point of no great theological consequence — whether Jesus was literate — so that readers will follow a chain of reasoning rather than react to a conclusion that offends cherished theological conviction. John Crossan believes that Jesus was illiterate. This, of course, contradicts the New Testament, for there we are told that Jesus read from Isaiah before preaching in the synagogue of Nazareth (Luke 4:16-20). Crossan puts forth the following argument for his conclusion: He begins by saying that according to Mark 6:3, Jesus was a *tekton*. The most common English rendering of *tekton* is "builder," or "carpenter," but Crossan takes the term not as a description of a trade, but as a description of a group of low-caste peasant expendables. He then states that 95-96% of Jews in first-century Palestine were illiterate; hardly any of the remaining 4-5% would have come from this low class. Here, then, is his

---

11. *Antiquities* 18.63-64: "About this time there lived Jesus, a wise man, if indeed one ought to call him a man. For he was one who wrought surprising feats and was a teacher of such people as accept the truth gladly. He won over many Jews and many of the Greeks. He was the Messiah. When Pilate, upon hearing him accused by men of the highest standing amongst us, had condemned him to be crucified, those who had in the first place come to love him did not give up their affections for him. On the third day he appeared to them restored to life, for the prophets of God had prophesied these and countless other marvelous things about him. And the tribe of the Christians, so called after him, has still to this day not disappeared." If this entire account is authentic, then Josephus' attestation to Jesus exceeds considerably the Jesus of the Jesus Seminar. But if, as many scholars suspect, the references to Jesus as the Messiah and his resurrection from the dead derive from later Christian scribes who copied Josephus, then Josephus and the Seminar paint a similar picture of Jesus.

conclusion: "[The stories that Jesus was literate] must be seen clearly for what they are: Lukan propaganda rephrasing Jesus' oral challenge and charisma in terms of scribal literacy and exegesis."[12]

I argue that Crossan is wrong on this point, and here are my reasons why: All Greek-English lexicons render *tekton* as "carpenter," a reference to a trade, not to a social class.[13] Moreover, we know that manual labor was *not* a derogatory distinction in Jewish Palestine, in contrast to Crossan's insinuation that it was. The Mishnah, for example, places the teaching of a manual trade to one's son on a par with teaching him Torah.[14] Obviously, in the Jewish world anything analogous to Torah was clearly honorable. Now, it is hard for me to imagine that the commandment to teach one's son Torah would result in a 95% illiteracy rate among the Jewish population. Consider the Jewish literature produced by the Roman period: not only the entire Old Testament, but also the New Testament, Apocrypha, Pseudepigrapha, the Dead Sea Scrolls, Josephus, the Bar Kokhba literature, the Mishnah, and the Oxyrhynchus Papyri. These are immense bodies of literature; in the last, the Oxyrhynchus Papyri, some fifty thousand documents exist! Would a literary achievement so extensive have been produced for a 3-5% reading population? Further, if Crossan were right about Jesus' illiteracy, why would Luke have intentionally lied about it? After all, if 95% of the population were illiterate, there would be no reason to make Jesus literate.[15]

---

12. *Jesus: A Revolutionary Biography* (HarperSanFrancisco, 1994), 24-26.

13. See, for example, Frederick W. Danker, *A Greek-English Lexicon of the New Testament and Other Early Christian Literature*, 3d ed. (Chicago: University of Chicago Press, 2000), 995.

14. "A man should always teach his son a cleanly craft" (*Qiddushin* 4:14); "At five years old [one is fit] for the Scripture, at ten years for the Mishnah" (*Aboth* 5:21); "Above all we pride ourselves on the education of our children, and regard as the most essential task in life the observance of our laws . . ." (Josephus, *Against Apion* 1.60); "[The Law] orders that [children] be taught to read, and shall learn both the laws and the deeds of the forefathers . . ." (Josephus, *Against Apion* 2.204).

15. See A. Millard, "Literacy in the Time of Jesus," *Biblical Archaeology Review* 29/4 (2003): 37-45, who concludes that "writing and reading were widely practiced in the Palestine of Jesus' day." Further, G. Dalman, *Jesus — Jeshua: Studies in the Gospels*, trans P. Levertoff (New York: KTAV, 1971), 36-37, leaves virtually no doubt that Jesus was literate.

Readers will have to decide for themselves which chain of reasoning claims better evidence and reasoning. But I should note that my defense of the New Testament testimony that Jesus could read is made, incidentally, entirely on critical and historical grounds. Nowhere did I resort to dogmatic opinion that "the church teaches" or "I believe that."

The Hidden Assumptions of the Jesus Seminar

Allow me to conclude with a revealing story. The Jesus Seminar is considered by many to be objective, with no agenda other than to describe Jesus in the same way we might describe, for example, Alexander the Great or another figure from ancient history. But the fact is that the Seminar is interested rather in recasting Jesus within the framework of a *new* religious creed. This unspoken agendum became clear to me in the spring of 2000 when Robert Funk, founder and chief architect of the Seminar, visited Cambridge University in England. I was on sabbatical in Cambridge at the time and I attended Funk's presentation on Jesus in the J. B. Lightfoot room, redolent of Cambridge scholars and dons. At the close of his lecture Dr. Funk appealed for what he called "a new orthodoxy." He then introduced a pastor traveling with him to provide a personal testimony to the value of the Seminar's understanding of Jesus, for him personally and for his ministry.

I was surprised that Funk used "orthodoxy" and "personal testimony" in his presentation. "Orthodoxy" and "personal testimony" are, after all, not scientific terms. They are religious terms — terms very similar to the ones that Funk and the Jesus Seminar take such delight in debunking in the *The Five Gospels*.[16] "Orthodoxy" derives from the combination of two Greek words meaning "the correct way to think about something so as to glorify God." "Orthodoxy" and "personal testimony" belong to the vocabulary of the church rather than to the vocabulary of scholarship and the academy. They are not achieved by rational inquiry alone. Rather, they depend in some measure on *faith* responses. Funk's

16. See note 5 in this chapter.

choice of terms seems to speak for the other Quests as well. Conclusions about Jesus are not determined by unbiased scientific evidence, in other words, but by prior convictions and personal beliefs. These convictions, as we have seen in our review of Enlightenment rationalism, are not the conclusions of scientific reasoning; they are the *presuppositions* that drive the reasoning!

If that is true — and Robert Funk's appeal for a "new orthodoxy" indicates it is — then a purely "historical Jesus" recovered by scientific inquiry is unattainable. All reconstructions of Jesus contain a measure — a healthy measure, I would maintain — of presuppositions and prior convictions from those who make them. The conclusions of the Jesus Seminar about Jesus — indeed, anyone's conclusions about any figure of history — are ultimately questions of faith based on the best evidence possible. That being the case, the proper question to ask is which reconstructions best fit the evidence we possess. That is the question to which we turn in the next three chapters.

CHAPTER THREE

How Reliable Is the New Testament as a Historical Document?

The first two chapters made us aware of the historical skepticism to which the New Testament has been subjected since the Enlightenment. The aim of the next three chapters is to attempt to address this skepticism. Our ultimate objective, of course, is to answer the question whether Jesus is the only savior of the world. In order to answer this question we need to examine the specific claims that the New Testament makes of Jesus, and what, if anything, can be known about Jesus' own self-understanding. Those two examinations are the subjects of Chapters 4 and 5. But before we examine the evidence about Jesus we need to ask a prior question, namely, is the New Testament a credible source of information about Jesus? A particular belief, after all, is only as valid as the evidence for it.

We need to be clear about what falls within the purview of this chapter and what does not. The question of the historical reliability of the New Testament as a source for knowledge of Jesus is not the same thing as proof that Jesus is the Son of God, or that his death on the cross is of saving significance for the world. The value of the New Testament as a source of knowledge about Jesus can be argued on the same basis that we would consider any other historical source of knowledge, namely, by comparing it with other sources of evidence from the same era. That is the subject and purpose of this chapter. But even if the New Testament appears to warrant a high degree of historical credibility, as I believe it does, that does not mean that the faith statements it makes can be proven. The statement, "I believe Jesus Christ is the savior of the world," can be shown to be a reasonable statement on the basis of the evidence for it, but it cannot be proven, any more than a man can prove his love for a woman, or a student can prove her commitment to the cause of justice. Statements of this order lie beyond absolute rational proof. They lie beyond such proof not because they are contrary to reason, but because they exceed reason. But this is to get ahead of ourselves. Our objective in this chapter is, first, to consider the historical reliability of the New Testament; and second, to argue that if the New Testament can be shown historically reliable where it can be compared with other historical sources of its era, then it is worthy of a presumption of reliability at points where comparisons do not exist.

The Nature of the New Testament

Our first task is to understand what kind of document the New Testament purports to be. If the New Testament is essentially a myth, for example, then readers are entitled to interpret the myth with subjective freedom and latitude. Many classic religious texts are myths. The Hindu *Bhagavad Gita* is a myth, as are the stories of the gods and goddesses of ancient Greece and Rome. Myths do not intend to be actual history, and consequently if a myth makes any claim to "truth" it must be truth in some sense other than historical factuality. Likewise, if the New Testament is essentially a collection of sayings, teachings, and propositions, then readers are again invited to interpret those propositions by other than historical criteria. The *Dhammapada* is a collection of Buddhist sayings and traditions. The *Analects* are likewise a collection of Confucian sayings. The merits of such sayings and teachings can be debated on philosophical, religious, and moral grounds, but, like myths, they make no claim to state historical fact. Or, perhaps the New Testament claims to be a record of something that did happen, but for which there is no historical evidence. The Book of Mormon is an example of this kind of religious text. According to the Book of Mormon, America was settled and colonized by two races of peoples, the first from the era of the

Tower of Babel (Genesis 11); and the second from Jerusalem in the seventh century B.C. It further believes that after his resurrection, Christ himself ministered briefly in America. These three claims are asserted by the Book of Mormon as putative historical claims, but there is no evidence for them, either archaeological or historical.

Many people think of the New Testament as falling into one of the above categories. That is, they imagine it to be a religious text about which people hold various opinions, but that the opinions, like opinions about *Alice in Wonderland,* for example, are not subject to historical investigation. People who think of the New Testament in this way will be surprised to learn that the New Testament does not purport to be a timeless myth, or a collection of moral and spiritual sayings, or a putative historical story for which there is no evidence. The New Testament claims to be a genuine history of and witness to a divine intervention of God in a human person, Jesus of Nazareth, for the purpose of saving the world. The earliest Christians invited their hearers to examine the historical evidence for this claim, beginning with their own testimony: "what we have heard, what we have seen with our eyes, what we have looked at and touched with our hands . . . we declare to you" (1 John 1:1-3). Evidence for the claim far exceeded themselves, however. The apostle Paul claims that the resurrected Jesus appeared to more than five hundred persons at one time, and he provides names of some of the witnesses (1 Corinthians 15:6). Those are historical claims, and there is no evidence that they were disputed. The New Testament claims to be a revelation of God within history, and that is the standard by which it deserves to be judged.

New Testament 101

The crucifixion of Jesus occurred in A.D. 30, plus or minus a year or two. We know this because the Gospel of Luke records that Jesus began his ministry "in the fifteenth year of the reign of Emperor Tiberius" (3:1). Tiberius became Roman emperor in August, A.D. 14, and according to the method of computation in Luke's day, the fifteenth year of Tiberius's reign would have commenced in autumn A.D. 27.[1] According to the Gospel of John, Jesus was crucified in Jerusalem on his third annual Passover pilgrimage to Jerusalem, which would have been in A.D. 30. This date falls within the overlap of the reigns of Pontius Pilate, the Roman governor of Palestine (A.D. 26-37); Herod Antipas, the Tetrarch of Galilee and Perea (4 B.C.–A.D. 39); and the High Priest Caiaphas (A.D. 18-36), all mentioned in Luke 3:1-2. The date also fits with the testimony of the Roman historian Tacitus that Jesus was "executed by sentence of the procurator Pontius Pilate when Tiberius was emperor."[2]

The writing of the New Testament documents began no later than twenty years after the crucifixion of Jesus, near the year 50. The letters of the apostle Paul were the first to be written, between roughly A.D. 50 and A.D. 65. Matthew, Mark, and Luke, the first three Gospels, and the book of Acts appear to have been written between A.D. 65 and 85, and the Gospel of John shortly after the latter date. The majority (and probably all) of the documents that comprise the New Testament were thus completed and in circulation by the close of the first century. We know this because two early Christian writers, Clement of Rome (A.D. 96) and Polycarp (A.D. 120), quote from nearly all of them. These basic facts prove, first, that the New Testament documents, and particularly the Gospels, were written relatively close in time to the events they record; and second, that the New Testament documents were produced within the lifetimes of people who were witnesses to the events described in them. Historical credibility is directly related to proximity to the events described, and participation of authors in the events described. The New Testament thus satisfies the two most important criteria of historical reliability.

---

1. Any portion of a regnal year was counted as an entire year. Tiberius began his reign in August, A.D. 14, at the end of a regnal year. His second regnal year would have begun in autumn of the same year. Hence, his fifteenth regnal year would have begun in autumn, A.D. 27.

2. *Annals* 15.44.

Are the Manuscripts on Which the New Testament Depends Reliable?

The vast majority of people who read the Bible are unaware of the superior manuscript evidence for the text of the New Testament. The question of the reliability of the text of the New Testament depends, in large part, on two factors. First, earlier manuscripts will, generally speaking, claim a higher degree of authority, since they stand in closer proximity to the events related. A second criterion is that the greater the number of manuscripts, the greater the probability of accuracy. On both of these counts the New Testament claims far more manuscripts, and far earlier manuscripts, than any other ancient writing. With regard to number of manuscripts, there are some five thousand extant Greek manuscripts of the New Testament, in whole or in part. Moreover, these manuscripts stand in much closer proximity to their source documents than do other ancient manuscripts.

In order to appreciate the significance of this evidence, consider the following comparisons. Caesar's *Gallic War*, which was written between 58 and 50 B.C., has only ten manuscripts of worth, the oldest dating from nine hundred years after Caesar. Tacitus's *Histories*, written about A.D. 100, and his *Annals*, written slightly later, depend on only two manuscripts, one ninth-century and one eleventh-century. Thucydides' *History*, written in the 5th century B.C., depends on eight manuscripts, the earliest of which dates to A.D. 900, fourteen centuries after the date of composition.[3]

The manuscript evidence supporting the New Testament text is, by contrast, vastly superior. Consider the following. The two most important and complete manuscripts of the entire Greek Bible, known to scholars as Codices Sinaiticus and Vaticanus, date from the fourth century A.D. — within three centuries, at the most, of the writing of the New Testament. The Chester Beatty papyrus (known as p[45]) of the Gospels is earlier yet, dating from the third century; and the same papy-

---

3. See F. F. Bruce, *The New Testament Documents: Are They Reliable?* (Downers Grove, Ill.: InterVarsity Press, 1973), 16-17.

rus[4] of Paul dates to about A.D. 200, within a century and a half of Paul's authorship. Two further papyri, the Geneva Bodmer papyrus (p[66]) and the Barcelona papyrus (p[67]), date to about A.D. 200. The oldest single New Testament manuscript, a fragment of John 18:31-33, dates to A.D. 130, no more than forty years after John penned the Gospel.

This large number of early manuscripts puts the text of the New Testament into a class by itself. F. F. Bruce writes that "No classical scholar would listen to an argument that the authenticity of Herodotus or Thucydides is in doubt because the earliest [manuscripts] of their works which are of any use to us are over 1,300 years later than the originals."[5] The text of the New Testament has far more manuscripts, which are much closer to the originals' date of composition, than any comparable document. The text of the New Testament is without qualification the best-attested text of any document in ancient history. If the New Testament text cannot be trusted, I cannot imagine how any ancient text could be trusted.

How Reliable Are Hand-Copied Texts?

Prior to the invention of moveable type in the fifteenth century, all written documents were reproduced and transmitted by human hands. Modern reliance on mechanical and electronic print leads many people to suspect that texts copied by hand were highly susceptible to error. This is a legitimate question. After all, none of the autograph copies of any of the books of the Bible is still in existence. All the originals have perished by one means or another. We are dependent on later copies of the originals for our knowledge of the text of the New Testament. How can we know whether copyists, either knowingly or mistakenly, altered the New Testament documents they transmitted?

4. Papyrus was an early form of paper made from cross-hatching the splayed stems of papyrus plants, which were especially plentiful in the Nile marshes. The plural of papyrus is papyri.
5. *The New Testament Documents,* 16-17.

38

The accidental discovery of the Dead Sea Scrolls at Qumran in 1947 has demonstrated the remarkable accuracy of ancient Jewish scribes. The Scrolls were apparently produced by a separatist Jewish sect known as Essenes. Immediately prior to the invasion of the Roman legions under Titus in A.D. 70, the Scrolls were hidden in a series of caves above the Qumran settlement at the northwest end of the Dead Sea. The Scrolls can thus positively be dated to A.D. 70, at the latest. The Essenes were annihilated by the Romans, and their scrolls remained unknown and undisturbed until their discovery in 1947. The Scrolls contain portions of every book of the Old Testament except for Esther, although the only complete Old Testament book is a beautifully preserved parchment (fine leather) manuscript of the book of Isaiah. Prior to the discovery of the Dead Sea Scrolls, the oldest manuscript of Isaiah was the famous Leningrad Codex, produced in about A.D. 1000. The discovery of the Dead Sea Scrolls allowed scholars the unique opportunity of comparing two scrolls of the same text that were separated by a thousand years of hand copying. With the exception of a few minor spelling variations, the Leningrad Codex was virtually identical to the Isaiah scroll of Qumran produced a millennium earlier. The result confirmed that both Jewish and Christian scribes undertook the copying of sacred texts as a religious duty, and produced remarkably accurate copies. The discovery of the Dead Sea Scrolls was proof positive that long centuries of hand copying had not falsified the Old Testament.

Prior to the discovery of the Dead Sea Scrolls in 1947 it was not unusual to hear skeptics assert that biblical texts had undoubtedly undergone alteration and even falsification in centuries of hand copying. The discovery of the Scrolls has laid this argument to rest. No reputable scholar today doubts that the text of any New Testament book is in material agreement with its authorial wording. The wealth of manuscripts of the New Testament, their unparalleled proximity to the life of Jesus, and the faithfulness of scribes in copying biblical texts combine to ensure that the text of the New Testament is, with the exception of minor disagreements, virtually identical with its original source documents.

How Do Historical Details in the New Testament Compare with Ancient History?

The New Testament mentions many historical persons and events that are also attested by non-Christian Jewish and Roman writers. A complete survey of these instances would require a book in itself, but we can mention several that are typical of the various historical overlaps that occur between the New Testament and ancient historical sources. In some instances, a reference in a secular historical source helps date a New Testament event. For example, Acts 18:12-17 records that Paul was hauled before a Roman court in Corinth "when Gallio was proconsul of Achaia." A proconsul was the ruler of a senatorial province in the Roman Empire.[6] Gallio, a brother of Seneca, the Roman philosopher, is mentioned in references in Seneca, Dio Cassius, and Pliny the Elder. Prior to 1905, however, the exact dates of his proconsulship were not known. In that year an inscription of the Emperor Claudius (Roman emperor from AD 41-54) was discovered in Delphi, indicating that Gallio ruled Achaia from July 51 to August 52. This inscription anchors Paul's appearance before Gallio to that time period.

In other instances a secular source can verify a biblical story that by itself might seem legendary. In Acts 12:20-23, the death of Herod Agrippa I (10 B.C.–A.D. 44), the grandson of Herod the Great, is recorded in grotesque and, on the face of it, highly improbable terms. Because Agrippa allowed himself to be revered as divine, Acts tells us that "an angel of the Lord struck him down, and he was eaten by worms and died." Curiously, the Jewish historian Josephus not only corroborates this ghastly account, but embellishes it. According to Josephus, when Agrippa failed to decline the flattery of the people in calling him a god, he immediately saw an omen of God and "felt a stab of pain in his heart. He was gripped in his stomach by an ache that he felt everywhere at once

6. There were two kinds of provinces in the Roman Empire. Senatorial provinces were older, more established, and more peaceful. As their name implies, were overseen by the Roman senate. Newer provinces that lay on the frontier and were prone to revolution were overseen directly by the Roman emperor, and thus called imperial provinces. Palestine was an imperial province.

and that was intense from the start. . . . Exhausted after five straight days by the pain in his abdomen, he departed this life in the fifty-fourth year of his life and the seventh of his reign."[7] The account of Josephus not only dates Acts 12:20-23 to A.D. 44, the year of Agrippa's death, but it corroborates his dramatic demise.

The Main Characters of the New Testament

The above two examples give a clue to the care that New Testament writers devoted to routine historical detail.[8] Let us now turn to a more important question. What do we learn about the main characters of the New Testament from historical sources outside the Bible?

A character of obvious importance is John the Baptist. According to Mark 6:14-29, John was imprisoned by Herod Antipas, son of Herod the Great, for condemning Antipas's marriage to his half-sister, Herodias. Mark reports that John, after being incarcerated for an undisclosed length of time, was beheaded by Antipas at the ancient equivalent of a stag party. The narrative of John's death in Josephus is remarkably similar to Mark, and told in even greater detail.[9] Josephus, too, calls him "John the Baptist"; emphasizes the effect of John's eloquence on the crowds; reports that John was exemplary in his piety toward God, and in his call for justice toward others. All these details agree with the New Testament portrait of John. And, like the New Testament, Josephus reports that John was arrested, imprisoned, and executed by Antipas. The main differences between the New Testament and Josephus are those of perspective: the New Testament emphasizes the moral charges John brought against Antipas, whereas Josephus stresses the political fears he aroused in Antipas.

Josephus also mentions Jesus.[10] In a passage slightly shorter than his

7. *Antiquities of the Jews* 19.343-52.

8. For further corroborations of New Testament history by archaeology, see "The Short List: The New Testament Figures Known to History," *Biblical Archaeology Review* 28/6 (2002): 34-37.

9. *Antiquities* 18.116-19.

10. *Antiquities* 18.63-64.

account of John the Baptist, Josephus mentions that Jesus was wise, a worker of wondrous deeds, and a renowned teacher who won over many Jews and Greeks. Josephus notes that Jesus was arrested by Pontius Pilate, condemned, crucified, and that "the tribe of Christians" did not die out but actually grew after his death. In these basic points Josephus agrees with the New Testament portrait of Jesus. Surprisingly, his account also includes references to Jesus as Messiah, and to the fact that he was raised from the dead, according to the word of the prophets. These last two references remain the source of a longstanding controversy among scholars whether Josephus, a Jew, believed Jesus to be the Messiah who was raised from the dead, or whether these two articles were added by Christian scribes who copied Josephus. Apart from these two points, however, no reputable scholar doubts the veracity of Josephus's account. The account of Josephus is a short but faithful summary of the Gospel accounts of Jesus, at no point of which does he disagree with the Gospels.

Not surprisingly, there is fuller testimony to Pontius Pilate, Roman governor of Judea from A.D. 26-37. A dedicatory inscription discovered in the coastal city of Caesarea Maritima in 1961 mentions Pilate as a prefect of the Emperor Tiberius in Palestine, exactly as the New Testament records. Combining the stories of Pilate in the Gospels with those of Josephus[11] and Philo,[12] we see a picture of a ruler who was insensitive, inflexible, and capable of executive brutality, as we see in Luke 13:1-2, for example. Anyone who reads Josephus's and Philo's accounts of Pilate will recognize the figure who callously surrendered Jesus to scourging and crucifixion.[13]

Let us look briefly at two other leading figures in the New Testament. The first is Herod the Great, ruler of Palestine at the time of Jesus' birth. Josephus's profile of Herod as competent, but paranoid, ruthless, and cruel underscores the much briefer glimpse of Herod in the New

---

11. *Antiquities* 18.55-87; *Wars of the Jews* 2.169-77.

12. *Embassy to Gaius* 299-304.

13. For a discussion of Pilate in the Gospels and in Josephus and Philo, see J. R. Edwards, *The Gospel According to Mark*, Pillar New Testament Commentary (Grand Rapids: Eerdmans, 2002), 454-56.

Testament.[14] Herod married ten different wives in all, killing at least two of his wives and three of his own sons out of jealousy. He killed the grandfather of one wife, and he drowned the brother of another wife in his swimming pool in Jericho. He seized the robes of the high priests so they could not officiate. A ruler of such paranoia and cruelty was entirely capable of ordering the deaths of baby boys in Bethlehem less than two years of age (Matthew 2:16).

Our last personality is the high priest at the time of Jesus' ministry, Joseph Caiaphas, who was reelected high priest for eighteen consecutive years from A.D. 18 to 36, and before whom Jesus was interrogated prior to crucifixion. In 1990 a bulldozer uncovered by accident an ancient burial site in Jerusalem. An ossuary at the burial site was inscribed, "Joseph Son of Caiaphas."[15] By all accounts, this is the same individual mentioned in the New Testament. Caiaphas, along with his father-in-law Annas, belonged to an elite family dynasty that wielded great influence in the Jewish Sanhedrin.[16] The New Testament concurs on the high priesthood of Caiaphas, and displays, along with Josephus, a rare understanding that the father-in-law was actually the moving force behind his son-in-law's policies.[17] This historical nuance reveals the degree to which the New Testament reflects important subtleties behind common historical facts of first-century Judaism.

The New Testament's knowledge of Judaism far exceeds the intimate chief priestly family circle, of course. The New Testament happens to be the only source of knowledge of a splinter group of Jewish nationalists known as the Herodians (Mark 3:6; 12:13; Matthew 22:16). It is also the chief source of knowledge about Jewish scribes (or lawyers), who comprised one of the most influential offices in Second Temple Judaism, but who go unmentioned in both Josephus and Philo.

14. For Josephus's unabridged and lengthy treatment of Herod, see *Antiquities* 14.158–17.199.

15. An ossuary was a stone box containing bones of deceased persons.

16. The Sanhedrin, the seventy-one-member ruling Jewish council, was presided over by the high priest.

17. *Antiquities* 18.35. On the collaboration of Annas and Caiaphas in the New Testament, see Luke 3:2; Matthew 26:57; John 11:49; 18:13, 24, 28.

The New Testament, a Primary Historical Document

The events described in the New Testament intersect nonbiblical sources at many points not mentioned in this brief survey. But the pattern we note in this chapter is paralleled in the many instances we have not noted: where the New Testament can be compared with other historical sources, it compares favorably with them; and in some instances — such as the Herodians and scribes, to mention but two — it is more complete than other ancient sources. We should further note that the New Testament is as credible with Roman and Greek sources (as we shall see in Chapter 7) as it is with Jewish sources, which were closer to its historical ambience. The historical framework of the New Testament is not only corroborated by Jewish and pagan sources. It is, in fact, *the* primary source document for first-century Palestine.

As we noted at the outset of this chapter, this does not mean that the faith claims of the New Testament are proven. What it does mean is that those faith claims are set within a historical context that can be repeatedly verified. Given that fact, it seems reasonable to assume that the New Testament writers would be equally trustworthy in other parts of their story. A personal example may help to illustrate this relationship between fact and faith. A number of years ago I ran out of money while on vacation. I made a long-distance telephone call to my home bank requesting money to be wired to me. The teller with whom I spoke said she would transfer me to the bank president, who would consider my request. Fortunately, the president had some acquaintance with my family. After I explained my predicament, the president asked me to name and describe my father's family members. I gave the names of my grandmother and grandfather, and the names of my two aunts, one of whom had died. Convinced that I was who I said I was, the president approved the transfer of money from my account.

I had not, of course, proved my identity. Someone else could have known my father's family information and used it to draw money illegally from my account. The bank president and I both knew that I could not, in fact, prove my identity on the phone. He did the next best thing. He predicated his judgment on matters that could not be verified by my responses on matters that could be verified. It was the reasonable thing to do on his part — and it was right.

When we consider the claims of the New Testament about Jesus of Nazareth, we stand with the bank president. We must make decisions about which we cannot have absolute proof. But the decisions must be made, so we do the next best thing. The fact that the New Testament is a credible historical document should, at the least, prejudice us in favor of believing whatever claims cannot be historically verified.

It is to those claims that we now turn.

CHAPTER FOUR

What Can We Know about the Jesus of History?

In the first two chapters we discussed cultural currents that many people find unnerving with regard to the acceptance of historic Christian beliefs, particularly those regarding Jesus' role as savior. Those who have followed the arguments so far may imagine the currents, whether Enlightenment naturalism or modern forms of pluralism and relativism, too strong to row against. They are stiff currents, to be sure, but they are not impossible to navigate. I intend to show in this chapter and in the next that there are any number of solid points — rocks of fact and strong trees of argumentation — that are holding firm against these currents, and indeed dividing and diverting them. I wish to appeal to these points of evidence in order to argue that there is a reasonable and trustworthy line of continuity between the Jesus of history and the portrait of Jesus we find in the New Testament.

The Scandal of Equating Jesus with God

I wish to begin by directing our attention to a remarkable fact. In order to appreciate this fact we need to remember that the first Christians were Jews. These included the Twelve Apostles called by Jesus, and the earliest converts to "the Way," as it was first called (Acts 9:2). For at least five years after the crucifixion of Jesus, and perhaps as long as ten years afterward (that is, until A.D. 35-40), the Way remained a Jewish movement confined to the temple in Jerusalem and to synagogues within perhaps a hundred-mile radius of the temple. During this period there were already several thousand Jewish converts to the Christian movement (Acts 4:4). This early allegiance of a large number of Jews to the Christian gospel is very significant, because the cardinal tenet of Judaism was and is monotheism. Monotheism is the belief in one God only, as recorded in the *Shema*, "Hear, O Israel: The Lord our God, the Lord is one" (Deuteronomy 6:4). Jews were instructed by divine decree, in other words, to seek only one God, and to accept no contenders to this one God and this God's commandments.[1]

Something unheard of in Judaism happened to these Jewish converts. They began to think and speak of Jesus in ways that either compromised or rivaled their monotheism — at least in the eyes of Jews who had not converted to Christianity. To the best of our knowledge the most ancient Christian confession was "Jesus is Lord," as already attested in the early Aramaic expression *maranatha*, "Lord, come!"[2] Now, the Greek word for "Lord," *kyrios*, could be used in Jesus' day as an honorific title for people (meaning "Sir") or for God. The British use of "lord" and the German use of *"Herr"* function similarly today. We know for certain, however, that when the early Christians said *maranatha*, they were appealing to a divine Lord, not a human one. According to Acts 2:24-25, less than two months after Jesus' crucifixion Peter preached a Pentecost sermon to Jews in which he quoted Psalm 16:8, "I saw the Lord always before me, for he is at my right hand so that I will not be shaken." The remarkable thing about this quotation is that Peter applies "the Lord," which in Psalm 16:8 refers exclusively to Yahweh, directly to the resurrected Christ.[3] Peter did something that had never been done in the Old

---

1. For a full discussion of the Shema, see H. L. Strack and P. Billerbeck, *Kommentar zum Neuen Testament aus Talmud und Midrasch*, 6 vols. (Munich, 1922-1961), 4/1.189-207.

2. 1 Corinthians 16:22; *Didache* 10:6. See also Romans 10:9; 1 Corinthians 12:3; Philippians 2:11.

3. "Jesus is Lord," or "Lord Jesus" is rooted in the language of early Jewish Christianity (Acts 2:36; 7:59; 10:36), including baptismal formulas (Acts 8:16). See O. Cullmann, *The Christology of the New Testament*, rev. ed., trans. S. Guthrie and C. Hall (Philadelphia: Westminster Press, 1963), Chapter 7. Cullmann (contrary to Bousset) ar-

Testament or intertestamental period: he transferred nomenclature for Yahweh to a human being.[4]

The apostle Paul did the same thing in his letter to the Philippians. Isaiah 45:23 solemnly affirms that Yahweh alone is to be worshipped, "To me every knee shall bow, every tongue confess." In the famous hymn to Jesus Christ in Philippians 2:10-11, however, Paul applies the Isaiah quotation to *Jesus:*

> so that at the name of Jesus
> every knee should bend,
> in heaven and on earth and under the earth,
> and every tongue should confess that Jesus Christ is Lord.

This is utterly unprecedented in Judaism. Nothing of the sort had ever been said of Abraham or David, Moses or Elijah. "What is perhaps the most stridently monotheistic passage in the Old Testament" is quoted not with reference to God but with reference to Jesus Christ.[5] The confession "Jesus is Lord" affirmed that the resurrected Jesus was not only alive and with God, but that he was the object of the church's faith and even its prayer.[6] The scholar Larry Hurtado rightly recognizes that "the

---

gues that the confession is not an invention of the Hellenistic church but of the early Jewish Christian community: "There is no reason at all, then, for contesting the fact that the very earliest community called Jesus 'the Lord'. He was considered the invisible Lord who rules his church and appears in worship among the brothers . . . although at the same time he sits at the right hand of God and rules the whole world" (208). Further, "*Kyrios Christos* probably comes therefore from the language of the original community at Jerusalem" (A. D. Nock, *Early Gentile Christianity and Its Hellenistic Background* (New York: Harper Torchbooks, 1964), 33. In the most recent and most comprehensive investigation of the early church's devotion to Jesus since Bousset, Larry Hurtado declares that "[Lord Jesus] goes back to the devotional life of Jewish Christian circles" (*Lord Jesus Christ: Devotion to Jesus in Earliest Christianity* [Grand Rapids: Eerdmans, 2003], 20-21).

4. Murray J. Harris lists and discusses thirteen Old Testament passages referring to Yahweh that are directly applied to Jesus by New Testament writers. See *Three Crucial Questions about Jesus* (Grand Rapids: Baker Books, 1994), 88-92.

5. Hurtado, *Lord Jesus Christ*, 73.

6. See M. Karrer, *Jesus Christus im Neuen Testament* (Göttingen: Vandenhoeck & Ruprecht, 1998), 342-45. Already in the second century Celsus, a pagan despiser of

most striking innovation in earliest Christian circles was to include
Christ with God as recipient of cultic devotion." He asks, "What might
have moved Christian Jews to feel free to offer to Christ this unparalleled
cultic devotion?" He answers, rightly, that no reason can be supplied for
their doing so except that "they felt *compelled by God*" to do so.[7]

How did early Jewish Christians who confessed Jesus as Lord understand that confession in relation to the *Shema,* that "The Lord our God,
the Lord is one"? Confession of Jesus would have posed no problem if Jesus were thought to be a prophet, priest, king, or even Messiah. Each of
those titles and offices already existed in the Old Testament. None compromised God's singular nature because, although each was an exalted
office, none was more than a human being. Even the Messiah, the most
exalted figure in Judaism, was understood to be entirely human, "a human born of humans," as Justin Martyr, the second century church father, records the Jew Trypho asserting.[8] In fact, in the Old Testament the
Messiah is never unequivocally called Savior.[9] In the New Testament,
however, Jesus was believed not only to fulfill each of the roles and offices of prophet, priest, king, Messiah, but to exceed them. Moreover, he
was frequently called Savior, which in the Old Testament was a title used
almost exclusively of God.

To be sure, in calling Jesus "Lord" the New Testament does not identify the exact relationship of Jesus to God. The resolution of that ques-

---

Christianity, attacked the fledgling faith for its worship of Jesus: "If [Christians] worshipped one God alone, and no other, they would perhaps have some valid argument
against the worship of others. But they pay excessive reverence to one who has but
lately appeared among men, and they think it no offence against God if they worship
also His servant." Celsus clearly regarded worship of Jesus as an offense against monotheism. Origen, the third-century church father, countered that Jesus and the Father
are one, insisting, "we do not worship any other besides Him who is the Supreme God"
(Origen, *Against Celsus* 8.12; also 8.14).

7. Hurtado, *Lord Jesus Christ,* 72 (italics in original).

8. *Dialogue with Trypho* 67.2

9. *Exegetical Dictionary of the New Testament,* s.v. *sōtēr.* There are, however, allusions
to this effect in Zechariah 9:9 and 4 Ezra 13:26. The Servant of the Lord who would
bring salvation to the ends of the earth in Isaiah 49:6 is not identified with the Messiah
in Jewish tradition.

tion would require several centuries of the subtlest debates in Christian history. Not until the Council of Nicea in 325 was the Trinity defined as "three persons in one substance." But even in the first century Christians asked the question of the relationship of Jesus to God. The opening chapter of Hebrews preserves evidence that in attempting to account for Jesus' uniqueness, some early Jewish Christians considered the possibility that he was an angel. Even that sublime status ultimately failed, however, because angels are not human as was Jesus, nor can they die and be resurrected. The oldest written record leaves an inescapable fact: from the earliest proclamation of the Christian gospel, Jesus was called "Lord" because he said and did things that in the history of Israel had only been attributed to God. From the outset of the Christian tradition, in other words, believers began thinking and speaking of Jesus in the same ways that they thought and spoke of God.[10]

Anyone can see the problem these first Christians were creating for themselves, for as Jews they were fully committed to belief in only one God. This is demonstrated by the apostle Paul, among others, who continued to affirm the oneness of God in concert with the *Shema* (see, for example, Romans 3:30; 1 Corinthians 8:6).[11] Although Jewish and later Muslim antagonists would accuse Christians of polytheism — of holding Jesus to be a second God — the New Testament and all subsequent Christian tradition vigorously denied the charge of polytheism and steadfastly affirmed monotheism. The earliest Jewish Christians — Paul, Mark, Matthew, John, and the authors of the Epistle to the Hebrews and 1 Peter — insisted that as the Son of God, Jesus was God humanly present, "the image of the invisible God" (Colossians 1:15). Herein lay the conflict, indeed the scandal, for in asserting that Jesus was Lord and God the early church did not intend to surrender its commitment to monothe-

10. See the material gathered in support of this point by L. Hurtado, *One God, One Lord: Early Christian Devotion and Ancient Jewish Monotheism* (Philadelphia: Fortress Press, 1988), 93-128.

11. G. Fee, in *The First Epistle to the Corinthians*, New International Greek Testament Commentary (Grand Rapids: Eerdmans, 1987), writes: "Although Paul does not [in 1 Corinthians 8:6] call Christ God, the formula is so constructed that only the most obdurate would deny its Trinitarian implications" (375).

ism. *Kyrios Iesous,* "Jesus is Lord," seems flagrantly to compromise the inviolable confession of all Jews that only Yahweh is Lord.

This confession is revealing because it appears to jeopardize the foundational convictions of those who made it. This heightens its value in the mind of the critical historian because it is not the kind of thing Jews would naturally invent. The first Christians, in fact, would have been extremely loath to proclaim Jesus as Lord because of the problems that proclamation necessarily involved. The divine Lordship of Jesus was certainly not a natural or logical outflow of Judaism. Judaism did not demand the confession "Jesus is Lord," and in the end it could not tolerate it. Exactly how intolerable the confession was for Jews is apparent from the church father Justin Martyr. During "the Jewish war which lately raged," wrote Justin, "Barchochebas, the leader of the revolt of the Jews, gave orders that Christians alone should be led to cruel punishments, unless they would deny Jesus Christ and utter blasphemy."[12] Justin was referring to the Bar Kokhba Revolt, the second revolt of the Jews against Rome in A.D. 132-135. Justin wrote close enough to the Revolt to refer to it as "lately," i.e., around A.D. 140. His proximity to the event heightens the historical reliability of his report. Justin's reference puts a razor's edge on the issue that defines the Christian gospel. For Bar Kokhba, a Jew, the confession of Jesus as Lord blasphemed monotheism; for Justin, a Christian, a denial of Jesus as Lord imperiled monotheism, for it denied God himself.

Was the Early Church Responsible for the Scandal?

In an attempt to explain the oddity of monotheistic Jews holding Jesus to be God — or something very close to God — radical New Testament scholarship as far back as Schweitzer's *Quest of the Historical Jesus* adopted what has become known as "the assumption of discontinuity." Basically, the assumption of discontinuity hypothesizes that Jesus was not proclaimed Son of God and savior of the world until Christian missionaries

12. *First Apology* 31.

penetrated the Gentile world. As long as the Christian movement remained in the orbit of Judaism, Jesus was simply viewed as a prophet, perhaps even as Messiah. (Remember that in first-century Judaism, the expected Messiah was considered a human being, not the divine figure it became when Christians applied the title to Jesus.) When the gospel was preached to non-Jewish Gentiles, the hypothesis continues, Jesus needed to be upgraded to a savior figure, equal to the divine figures of Greco-Roman mythology, such as Hercules, Dionysus, Augustus, and the scores of extraordinary figures who were elevated to divine status. The proper term to describe this elevation is "apotheosize," to make someone godlike. The theory further posits that Jesus was not God incarnate, nor did he believe himself to be, nor did his early Jewish followers believe him to be. The deification of Jesus, according to the hypothesis, developed probably at least a decade or more after the death of Jesus in order to make his image competitive with and attractive to the Hellenistic hero-cults. In short, the hypothesis posits that the historical Jesus was an outstanding human figure, but nothing more, whereas Jesus as the divine Son of God was a later embellishment that arose by catering to Gentile expectations.[13] In other words, although the New Testament does, in fact, proclaim Jesus as Lord, that proclamation is an invention of the first Christians rather than a fact about the historical Jesus.

This hypothesis has dominated more than a century of critical New Testament scholarship. Before showing its implausibility, a word needs to be said about the idea of something "dominating more than a century" of thought. In democratic societies, where majority opinion determines political realities, we are tempted to imagine that majority opinion determines truth as well. Statements like "Most doctors recommend . . ." or

13. This hypothesis has been maintained with little variation for nearly a century. In 1919 E. Lohmeyer could write, "It was then the religious forms of the Hellenistic world that caused the content of Jesus' human life to be elevated to a symbol of divine essence" (*Christuskult und Kaiserkult* [Tübingen: Mohr/Siebeck, 1919], 22-29). In 1998 M. Karrer put it this way: the Hellenistic development led "to a virtual paganizing of Christianity. On heathen turf, the brakes of Israelite monotheism gave way. Removed from its sources, the exaltation of Jesus to deity developed of its own accord" (*Jesus Christus im Neuen Testament,* 330).

"Experts agree" carry great weight in democratic societies. Among the criteria of verification, however, majority opinion is on the low end of the scale, and rightly so. It is virtually immaterial how many people are of a given opinion; what is important is how *informed* their opinion is. One knowledgeable judgment is worth more than a hundred uninformed opinions.

Here is a case in point. We still hear it said today that until Copernicus everyone thought the world flat. That is untrue, however. In the third century B.C., Eratosthenes, director of the famous library at Alexandria (Egypt), performed an experiment on lengths of shadows at two different locations at the same time, from which he concluded that the earth was a sphere rather than a disk. He further calculated the earth's circumference to be approximately 25,000 miles — which is within 100 miles of its actual size! Eratosthenes was remarkably correct in both his theory and calculations. Nevertheless, for eighteen long centuries his work was forgotten or regarded as fanciful until proven true by Magellan's circumnavigation of the globe.[14]

The point, obviously, is that truth is not determined by popular vote. There are seasons in which error is embraced by multitudes and truth is held by few. The widespread publicity of Christianity's cultured despisers, as the German theologian Friedrich Schleiermacher called them, should not be seen as a vindication of their cause. The various Quests are rooted in the assumption of naturalism, the philosophical belief that we live in closed system in which everything that happens can be accounted for by prior empirical phenomena. This assumption eliminates from the outset the possibility of Jesus being God, for naturalism asserts that God (if God exists) does not break into the natural order, and is thus irrelevant to it. If Jesus could not have been God, then he must have been a human being more or less like all human beings. For those committed to naturalism, the assumption of discontinuity offers the most plausible explanation to account for two conflicting pieces of data, (1) that Jesus was not God, although (2) his followers proclaimed that he was.

14. See Carl Sagan, *Cosmos* (New York: Random House, 1980), 14-15.

At this point we must employ the art of scholarly criticism by showing the utter untenability of the above thesis. The assumption that early Christians desired to apotheosize Jesus to make him like or equal to other Greek gods has been tirelessly repeated in New Testament scholarship. One is reminded of the story of a pastor who wrote the following note in the margin of a sermon: "Weak point, speak loudly!" The loud and long rehearsal of the apotheosis hypothesis cannot compensate for its weaknesses. Peter Stuhlmacher of Tübingen, Germany, is correct in saying, "Although scholars continue to repeat this viewpoint, it remains an abstraction of research that the texts and historical probability contradict."[15]

The first strike against it is that a number of pagan philosophers of the second and third centuries, including Galen, Celsus, and Porphyry, regarded the apotheosis of Jesus as God's Son and savior as an insurmountable problem. A wise man Jesus was, to be sure, but nothing more. His purported miracles and resurrection from the dead were dismissed as superstition. Porphyry was particularly offended by the exclusive nature of Christian revelation, its insistence that no one could come to God except through a man who lived at a specific time and place. What about people who lived before Jesus, or had no knowledge of him? The inability to answer such questions satisfactorily was seen as a refutation of an "unreasoning faith." The arguments of these cultured pagans against the Christian gospel sound quite modern. The doctrine of the Incarnation and the proclamation of Jesus as Son of God, in other words, in fact alienated many of the Gentile intellectuals to whom the hypothesis suggests it should have appealed.[16]

The hypothesis meets with equal problems from the Jewish side of the equation. The suggestion that early Jewish Christians proclaimed Jesus as Son of God, thereby compromising their salient belief in monotheism, in order to gain acceptance by Gentiles, whom they regarded as

---

15. *Jesus of Nazareth — Christ of Faith*, trans. S. Schatzmann (Peabody: Hendrickson, 1988), 24.

16. See Robert Wilken, *The Christians as the Romans Saw Them* (New Haven and London: Yale University Press, 1984), 68-163.

sinners (Galatians 2:5) and idolaters (Romans 1:23), is wildly improbable. It fails to explain why Jewish Christians held fast to confessional articles of much less importance, such as kosher food observance, the practice of circumcision, and observance of the Sabbath. According to Acts 10:14, the apostle Peter was unwilling to break Jewish food laws even when commanded to do so by a divine vision! How plausible is it that he and others of his culture would adhere adamantly to food laws, yet willfully abandon a foundational understanding of God by exalting a human being to godlike status? Anyone who understands Jews and Judaism, ancient or modern, finds this nearly impossible to imagine.

Again, the hypothesis that pious Jews such as Peter and the early church promoted Jesus as Lord and God in order to appeal to the Gentile world rests on the assumption that they emulated the Gentile world, including its polytheism. But observant Jews most certainly did not emulate the Gentile world; they by and large disdained it. The Mishnah and both the Palestinian and Babylonian Talmuds leave no doubt about this. So does the New Testament in its sporadic but unambiguously negative references to Gentile polytheism (Acts 17:22-23; 1 Corinthians 8:5). We cannot imagine pious Jews emulating Gentile polytheism, even for the sake of promoting Jesus as savior. We know of no other instances when Jews surrendered creedal formulas or moral practices to what they regarded as disdainful Gentile preferences and practices. There is certainly no evidence that they did so in proclaiming Jesus in the Gentile mission. Martin Hengel, perhaps the greatest living scholar of Christian origins, is correct in saying,

> The discrepancy between the shameful death of a Jewish state criminal and the confession that depicts this executed man as a preexistent divine figure who becomes man and humbles himself to a slave's death is, as far as I can see, without analogy in the ancient world.[17]

The idea that the early church fabricated a portrait of Jesus that eventually resulted in the Nicene formulation of "true God of true God" from a

17. *The Son of God: The Origin of Christology and the History of Jewish-Hellenistic Religion* (Philadelphia: Fortress Press, 1976), 1.

historical Jesus who was simply a first-century Jew about whom little was known, and who was either uncertain or confused about his identity, is a highly improbable — and unadvised — leap of faith. It is not surprising that an imposing line of biblical scholars has opposed it for nearly two centuries.[18]

Is the Portrait of Jesus in the Gospels Trustworthy?

Is there any way of knowing whether the Jesus presented in the Gospels stands in continuity with or discontinuity from the Jesus of history? Was the Jesus tradition simply a quantum of raw data that, like wet clay, had no meaning until shaped by the early church? Or did the person and mission of Jesus have an inherent meaning that the early church sought to preserve, proclaim, and interpret? Did the early church freely invent stories and sayings and attribute them to Jesus, or did it preserve and guard a tradition that it considered inviolable? How did the early church define itself in relation to the Jesus story? Did the early church create the Jesus of the Gospels, or conserve the historical Jesus in the Gospels?

The various Jesus Quests discussed in Chapters 1 and 2 operate on the assumption that the Jesus of the Gospels is, to a greater or lesser extent, a creation of the early church.[19] The Quests assume that the Gospels are not fact-based interpretations of the historical Jesus, but rather freely invented stories and sayings that reflected the needs and experiences of the early church. There are considerable data, however, that argue decidedly against this assumption. Some of what we might call the

18. Adolf Schlatter, Martin Kähler, Julius Schniewind, Joachim Jeremias, Leonhard Goppelt, F. F. Bruce, I. H. Marshall, Raymond Brown, Otto Betz, Peter Stuhlmacher, Birger Gerhardsson, Martin Hengel, Bruce Metzger, Ralph P. Martin, D. A. Carson, N. T. Wright, Craig Evans, Donald Hagner, Craig Keener, Ben Witherington III, Luke Timothy Johnson, Craig Blomberg, and many others.

19. Several studies of Jesus in the Third Quest are happy exceptions to this, however. The works of N. T. Wright, Luke Timothy Johnson, Craig Evans, and Ben Witherington III, among others, are correct in seeing the Gospels as preservations of the Jesus tradition, not a creation of it.

"quality controls" are matters of fact, and others are common sense. Together they form a convincing case that the early church did not wildly invent "Jesus material," but rather exercised a high degree of faithfulness in its transmission of the Jesus tradition.

First, one of the most important quality controls over the Gospel tradition was the fact that *eyewitnesses* were still alive when the tradition was being formed. These eyewitnesses functioned as gatekeepers and custodians "of the faith that was once for all entrusted to the saints" (Jude 3). The importance of this fact is not so apparent when we read only the four canonical Gospels in the New Testament, which paint similar portraits of the character and mission of Jesus. Anyone who ventures into the many stories about Jesus that circulated outside the circle of eyewitnesses and after their deaths, however, will readily appreciate the sobriety of the portrait of Jesus in the Gospels. In the extra-canonical Gospels the most fanciful and bizarre caricatures of Jesus arise. These stories are preserved in great numbers in the New Testament Apocrypha and Nag Hammadi libraries, which were largely the product of Gnostic communities and beliefs, dating primarily from the second century. It is in these later Gospels that one sees the wild inventiveness that is wrongly suspected of the early church.[20]

These apocryphal works present a Jesus who, for the most part, resembles the Jesus of the four canonical Gospels in name only. Primarily this is due to the influence of Gnosticism, a movement that gained prominence in the second century and that taught that spiritual knowledge and secret revelation were necessary for salvation. This secret revelation was called *gnosis,* which in Greek means "knowledge." A large number of the extra-canonical Gospels were falsely attributed to New

20. On the exaggerated legends of the apocryphal Gospels, see Origen, *Against Celsus* 3.46. For collections of apocryphal and gnostic Gospels, see *New Testament Apocrypha,* rev. and ed. W. Schneemelcher, trans. R. McL. Wilson (Cambridge: James Clarke & Co./Louisville: Westminster/John Knox Press, 1991/1992). *The Nag Hammadi Library in English,* ed. J. Robinson (New York: Harper & Row, Publishers, 1977). For an informed and skillful critique of the attempt to rewrite the story of Christian origins from the perspective of the gnostic Gospels, see Philip Jenkins, *Hidden Gospels: How the Search for Jesus Lost Its Way* (New York: Oxford University Press, 2001).

Testament apostles in hopes of gaining legitimacy and wider acceptance among non-Gnostic Christian churches. Unlike the Jesus of the New Testament, the Jesus of the extra-canonical Gospels usually does not travel or perform miracles or healings. He is, rather, a sedentary teacher and sage who expounds on esoteric matters and speaks in riddles and symbols. Further, the emphasis on the ethical dimensions of faith characteristic of the Jesus of the canonical Gospels is usually absent from the Jesus of the New Testament Apocrypha and Nag Hammadi documents. Rather, this Gnostic Jesus speaks enigmatically about topics typically associated with the then-popular philosophies of Platonism and Neo-Platonism, such as divine emanations, androgyny, secret knowledge and enlightenment, the achievement of perfection, the evil of sex, and the superiority of the male principle over the female.

The Jesus of the canonical Gospels and the Jesus of the New Testament Apocrypha and Nag Hammadi are different individuals, and the differences between them are virtually irreconcilable. The Jesus of the Apocrypha and Nag Hammadi is deeply introspective and speculative. Readers are left pondering what his occult symbols and ethereal thoughts mean, never certain whether they understand him rightly — or if there even is a right understanding. The apocryphal *Acts of John* is typical of the many Gnostic renditions of Jesus' life. The narrator of the story, supposedly the apostle John, says that as he walked with Jesus his own feet left footprints in the sand, but the feet of Jesus did not. Sometimes, he says, he grasped for Jesus and felt a solid body, and other times "when I felt him, his substance was immaterial and incorporeal, and as if it did not exist at all." If this sounds unlike the Jesus of the canonical Gospels, it is because the *Acts of John* is the product of a community far removed from the eyewitnesses responsible for the New Testament. It represents a second-century strain of Gnosticism, in which the gospel — even the crucifixion — is transformed into symbol and illusion, and in which the proper understanding of the symbols is the prerequisite of salvation.[21]

---

21. See *New Testament Apocrypha*, ed. E. Henneke, W. Schneemelcher, R. McL. Wilson (Cambridge: James Clarke; Louisville: Westminster/John Knox Press, 1992), 2.152-212. The quotations above come from sections 93 and 101-2.

The Jesus of the canonical Gospels, on the other hand, leaves footprints in the sand. People who reached out to him clutched flesh and blood. They encountered a teacher whose stories and sayings tended to be simple, hard-hitting, and inescapable, not vague, open-ended, and unknowable. Indeed, the problem is that we often know *exactly* what he means. His compassions were broad and surprising, as were his incisive judgments. The Jesus of the canonical Gospels is a relational and rational human being who shunned ostentation and sensation and impressed his contemporaries with his personal integrity and authority. In comparison to the many wonder workers of the Greco-Roman world — and particularly his namesake in the gnostic Gospels — the Jesus of the New Testament has an inherently believable quality to him.

A second factor that ensures reliability in the Jesus tradition is the *methodology of rabbinic teaching.* Jewish rabbis required of their disciples careful listening and observation in order to attain the highest possible degree of understanding and accuracy in transmitting their teachings. Like the great Jewish rabbis and sages, Jesus employed didactic techniques that aided retention and transmission of material among his disciples. These included picturesque speech, alliteration and assonance, rhythmic phrases, parallelisms, symmetrical arrangements, and above all, parables. In the rabbinic tradition disciples were taught to memorize, repeat, and recite (and often write) their masters' teaching exactly and accurately, and they were rewarded for doing so. Novelty, expansions and additions, and free interpretations were neither taught nor rewarded. The Swedish scholar Birger Gerhardsson has devoted a lifetime to investigating the art and techniques of rabbinic instruction, many of which Jesus employed. The early church, he rightly argues, was as zealous in guarding the Jesus tradition as the Jewish rabbis were in guarding the Torah tradition. "There is historical justification, based on sound historical judgments, for concluding that there is an unbroken path which leads from Jesus' teaching in *meshalim* [picturesque sayings] to the early church's methodical handing on of Jesus texts, a transmission carried on for *its own sake.*"[22]

22. B. Gerhardsson, *The Origins of the Gospel Tradition* (Philadelphia: Fortress Press, 1979), 77 (emphasis in original).

To be sure, Jesus did a number of things typical Jewish rabbis did not do. He called his disciples, for example, whereas traditional rabbis were chosen by their disciples. Too, Jesus was sharply critical of the rabbinical tradition, the "tradition of the elders," as he called it, because he believed it substituted human interpretations for the original intent of the law (Mark 7:1-23). In Jesus' day, "rabbi" was probably not the established title that it would later become following the destruction of the Jerusalem temple in A.D. 70 when the rabbinic schools were formally founded under Rabbi Johanan ben Zakkai.[23] Although Jesus was often recognized and addressed as rabbi, in his distinctive teachings and actions, and particularly in his self-understanding vis-à-vis Torah and God (as we shall see in chapter 5), he far exceeded the characteristics of any known Jewish rabbis.

A third factor that argues in favor of the Jesus tradition in the canonical Gospels is the presence of *embarrassing material* in them. At first thought the presence of problematic statements would seem to jeopardize the authenticity of a historical document. But further thought argues otherwise. A document containing information exclusively favorable to those responsible for it should probably be suspected of some degree of falsification. On the other hand, information that compromises the character and reputation of the agents responsible for a document will normally be taken as a sign in favor of authenticity. People who are hatching a story will not, as a rule, include information that might cause you to question them.

The New Testament contains a fair amount of information you would not expect to find in it. Consider the statement of Jesus in Mark 9:1, "There are some standing here who will not taste death until they see that the kingdom of God has come with power." The plain sense of that claim was not fulfilled in Jesus' lifetime, nor has it been since. A prediction that does not transpire raises a question about the reliability of the one who said it. If the early church were inventing sayings and putting

23. See G. F. Moore, *Judaism in the First Centuries of the Christian Era* (New York: Schocken Books, 1958), 1; and M. Hengel, *The Charismatic Leader and His Followers*, trans. J. Greig (New York: Crossroad Publishing Company, 1981), 43-44.

them in the mouth of Jesus, we cannot imagine that it would have risked discrediting itself by making Jesus predict events that apparently never came to pass. On the other hand, if the early church was committed to preserving the words of the historical Jesus, it is not unreasonable to assume that it would include a statement, despite its interpretational difficulties, simply because Jesus said it.

Similarly, in Mark 13:32 Jesus says that "neither the angels in heaven, nor the Son, but only the Father" knows the day or hour of the return of the Son of Man. According to this statement, Jesus did not know when the Son of Man would return in glory. It is very difficult imagining early Christians inventing a statement that ascribes ignorance to one whom they considered Lord. The presence of this rather humbling statement in the Gospels can only be accounted for, it seems to me, on the assumption that Jesus actually said it. Its very difficulty is a guarantee of its authenticity.

The Gospels preserve material that is compromising to the disciples as well as to Jesus. In Mark 8:14-21 Jesus berates the disciples for their failure to understand his teaching: "Do you still not perceive or understand? Are your hearts hardened? Do you have eyes, and fail to see? Do you have ears, and fail to hear? And do you not remember?" Or, consider the sharp rebuke against Peter, eventually to become the chief apostle, when he threatened to impede Jesus' mission: "Get behind me, Satan!" (Mark 8:33). These examples are all taken from the Gospel of Mark, considered by most scholars to be the earliest of the Gospels. Omission of such material — and there is more that could have been omitted — would have resulted in a more flattering picture of both Jesus and the disciples. But such material was not omitted. Even more remarkable, the people responsible for its inclusion in the record are the ones most compromised by it. The presence of such compromising material argues decidedly against inventiveness on the part of the early church. The presence of embarrassing material in the Gospels is most reasonably explained by the early church's commitment to transmitting an unexpurgated record of Jesus, even when doing so reflected poorly on the disciples and even on Jesus himself.

Further Evidence in Favor of the Historicity of the Gospels

We noted earlier that a ruling assumption behind radical skepticism in Jesus studies is that the early church projected its own words and themes onto the Jesus of the Gospels, much like a ventriloquist projects his or her voice onto a puppet. If this were the case, the Gospels would tell us something about the early church, but we would learn little if anything about the historical Jesus. There is considerable evidence, however, that argues against what we might call the ventriloquism hypothesis. The absence of parables outside the Synoptic Gospels is a prime example. If the early church projected its own speech forms and themes onto the Jesus of the Gospels, we should expect to find parables in evidence in the early church. We do not. In the book of Acts, in all the New Testament epistles, and in early Christian literature outside the New Testament, including the works of the apostolic fathers, we do not find parables. Parables did not characterize the early church. If they did not characterize the early church, they could not have been projected by the early church onto Jesus. Some sixty parables are attributed to Jesus in the first three Gospels alone, however. This extensive and distinctive feature of Jesus' teaching cannot be accounted for by the projection theory. The parables of Jesus can be far more reasonably accounted for by the explanation that they originated with the historical Jesus himself.

Further evidence against the ventriloquism hypothesis is found in the content of Jesus' teaching. The Gospels record that Jesus preferred to refer to himself as "Son of Man," and that the dominant theme of his teaching was "the kingdom of God." Consider the following statistics in relation to these two expressions: "Son of Man" occurs eighty-one times on the lips of Jesus in the Gospels, but apart from one reference in Acts (7:56), and two in Revelation (1:13; 14:14), it vanishes from usage in the early church. Similarly, "kingdom of God" (or "kingdom of heaven") occurs eighty-five times on the lips of Jesus in the Synoptic Gospels, but only five times in the New Testament epistles and the book of Revelation. It is nearly impossible to affirm the ventriloquism hypothesis in the face of these statistics, since themes so characteristic of Jesus are virtually absent from the vocabulary of the early church. Reason would argue that "Son of Man" and "the kingdom of God" derived from Jesus, not from the early church.

Evidence against the ventriloquism hypothesis also arises from a comparison of the New Testament epistles with the New Testament Gospels. If the early church projected its interests back onto Jesus when the Gospels were composed, we should expect to see a high degree of harmony between Paul's words and themes, and those of Jesus. But we do not see this. Even to first-time readers of the New Testament, the *disharmony* between Paul's themes, vocabulary, and manner of writing, and the words of Jesus in the Gospels, is manifestly clear. The building blocks of Paul's letters are grace, justification, righteousness, reconciliation, law, flesh, Spirit, the church, sin, faith, dying and rising with Christ, and other conceptual understandings of the Christian faith. These building blocks are rare or altogether absent in the Gospels. Particularly the first three Gospels depict Jesus speaking in concise figures of speech, puns, pithy proverbs, picturesque poetic forms, and parables. His thematic accents fall on the kingdom of God and particularly God as *his* Father; the centrality of his person for every aspect of life; the supremacy of his teaching over Torah; an ethic more rigorous than Torah (yet featuring a willingness to forgive that was uncharacteristic of Torah); and sober reminders of the coming judgment of God. These themes, as well as the forms in which Jesus delivered them, are not characteristic of Paul. The themes and speech forms not only of the apostle Paul but also of the leading members of the early church are not projected onto the Jesus of the Gospels. The harmony between Paul and Jesus demanded by the ventriloquism theory is absent.

The apostle Paul was himself aware of these differences, and made a concerted effort to distinguish his opinion from divine revelation. His ruling on divorce is a case in point. When Paul was asked for his judgment on divorce — a subject on which Jesus had earlier spoken — he differentiated carefully between instructions from Jesus and his own opinions (1 Corinthians 7:10, 12, 25). In other words, in express contrast to the ventriloquism hypothesis, Paul avoided projecting his judgments onto Jesus. Surely divorce was not the only subject on which he did so.

We know from Paul's own testimony that his apostleship was viewed disapprovingly by some of the Twelve and other leaders of the church in Jerusalem following his conversion to the faith (Galatians 1:11–2:10; 1 Corinthians 9). It is hard to imagine that he would risk jeopardizing his precarious standing with the pillars of the church by playing loose with the Jesus tradition. In carefully distinguishing between his judgments and those of Jesus, Paul was surely conforming to a practice expected of all early church leaders.

Perhaps the most clinching argument against the supposed inventiveness of the early church relates to "the Gentile question." According to the book of Acts and the New Testament epistles, the preaching of the gospel to Gentiles, and their admission into the church, was *the* burning question in the early church. Could Gentiles be saved without first becoming Jews? And if so, on what basis? If the early church actively projected its agenda onto the portrait of Jesus in the Gospels, this issue would have to appear. Indeed, one would have to say that if the Gentile issue does not appear, the projection theory as a whole should be abandoned. Anyone who reads the Gospels, however, knows that the Gentile question — at least in the way it is framed in Acts and the epistles — is conspicuously absent from the Gospels. Had the early church actively engaged in framing "Jesus material" according to its needs and interests, surely it would have developed sayings on the Gentile question and projected them into Jesus' mouth in the Gospels. We should expect to see statements attributed to Jesus about circumcision, food laws, and the acceptance of Gentiles, as we see statements about such issues in Acts 15 and Romans and Galatians, for example. The absence of such material from the Gospels argues strongly in favor of their historical reliability.

We can, in fact, demonstrate from the similar portrait of Jesus in the canonical Gospels that in them the Jesus tradition was handled with integrity. A majority of scholars today believes that the Gospel of Mark was the first Gospel to be composed and that it was used as a source for both Matthew and Luke. Even if one does not accept the theory of Markan priority, there is obviously some other literary relationship in evidence among the first three Gospels. When the Synoptic Gospels are compared side-by-side it is apparent that, despite differences due to the distinctive purposes of each Gospel writer, the portrait of the historical Jesus is in broad agreement. At any rate, nothing comparable to the wild divergences in the extra-canonical Gospels occurs in the canonical Gospels. There are no stories of an erratic and bad-tempered little Jesus as found in the *Infancy Narrative of Thomas;* no cloudy discourses on monads, eons, and perfections from a Gnostic Jesus as in the *Apocryphon of John;* no tirades against sex and eating meat from a Torah-bound Jesus as in the *Gospel of the Nazoreans;* no embellished legends about the birth and annunciation of Mary as contained in the *Protoevangelium of James.*[24]

The Roar of a Cowardly Lion

The purpose of this chapter has been to show that internal evidence within the New Testament itself argues in favor of the veracity of the New Testament portrait of Jesus. The evidence for trusting the historical reliability of what the Gospels say about Jesus is considerable. Indeed, there are more and betters reasons for trusting what the Gospels say about Jesus than for doubting or denying what they say of him. And so the overall case against the reliability of the New Testament portrait of Jesus presented in the three Quests is less daunting than it first appeared. Like the roar of the Cowardly Lion in *The Wizard of Oz,* the roar of the radical skeptics of the first three Quests turns out to be a rather pathetic roar.

The various quests for the historical Jesus have been built on the twin pillars of the assumption of discontinuity and the projection hypothesis. Both assumptions, it turns out, fail the litmus tests of history, reason, and probability. The Jesus of the Gospels cannot be accounted for by apotheosizing him in order to gain Gentile favor. Nor is the Jesus

24. The idea that Christians invented sayings and put them into the mouth of Jesus in the canonical Gospels is as old as Celsus, the second-century detractor of Christianity. In answer to this allegation, Origen, the third-century church father, asserts: "Of a truth [Christians] were not guilty of inventing untruths, but such were their real impressions, and they recorded them truly." It was not Christians who falsified the Gospels, maintains Origen, but unorthodox individuals in the second century, including Marcion and the gnostic Valentinus (*Against Celsus* 2.26-27).

of the Gospels a mere mouthpiece of the early church. We are left with a dilemma we cannot dodge — at least not if we want to be evenhanded with the New Testament testimony to Jesus. The unsettling fact remains: early Jewish Christians thought and spoke of Jesus as they thought and spoke of God. This startling reality can best be accounted for — indeed I should say it can *only* be accounted for — by inferring that their beliefs and speech about Jesus were governed by the desire to be faithful to the earthly Jesus that they or their teachers had known. Their beliefs, as we have seen, caused them considerable theological problems. Nevertheless, the evidence we have submitted in this chapter is the most logical and satisfying explanation of the most distinctive and governing characteristic of the New Testament and the early church, the confession that "Jesus is Lord."

To be sure, this is not absolute proof that he is Lord. We mentioned in the last chapter that *all* historical reconstructions of Jesus contain some measure of faith. The lines of reasoning I have followed in this chapter contain elements of faith as well. All lines of reasoning do. The question is simply whether the steps of faith one must inevitably take in considering the New Testament evidence regarding Jesus seem warranted by evidence and reason. To return to the argument of Chapter 3, if the Gospels are trustworthy where they can be checked against history, they should be considered worthy of a presumption of trustworthiness at those points where they cannot be checked. The cumulative weight of the evidence considered in this chapter, especially when considered in its historical context, claims a very high degree of historical probability.

CHAPTER FIVE

Did Jesus Consider Himself God?

Can the New Testament witness to Jesus be trusted? We would be well-advised by the evidence and reasoning in the last two chapters to place our bets on it. The Gospels are simply not what we would expect to find if the early church were perpetrating a hoax. There is a further question that must be raised, however, before we consider whether Jesus was the only savior of the world. The question is simply, *What did Jesus think himself to be?* After all, the early Christians who wrote the New Testament could have been mistaken — honestly mistaken — about his identity. That would make the New Testament the more deceptive, because an honest error can normally be argued more persuasively than a deliberate fraud.

Let us begin our discussion of Jesus' self-understanding by considering the most distinctive feature of Christianity — its devotion to Jesus in confession and worship. No other religion even comes close to elevating its founder to the same degree that Christianity elevates Jesus. Moses, Muhammad, Buddha, Confucius, Lao Tzu, Nanak, Black Elk — none of them appears in a creed next to their faith's supreme God or ultimate reality. Yet Christianity's first confession, composed shortly after Jesus' crucifixion, was atomic in its brevity: "Jesus is Lord." Language reserved in the Old Testament for God was applied directly and without apology to Jesus in the New Testament. Within twenty years of Jesus' death the apostle Paul spoke of Christ as the one "in whom all the fullness of God was pleased to dwell," as "the image of the invisible God," the very agent of creation and salvation "in whom all things in heaven and on earth were created" (Colossians 1:15-20). Those words identify the purpose, work, and even nature of God inseparably with Jesus. Not only was Jesus referenced with God, he was also *worshipped*. God is, of course, most frequently worshipped in the New Testament, but the God worshipped is now identified expressly as "the God and *Father of our Lord Jesus Christ*" (2 Corinthians 1:3; Ephesians 1:3; 1 Peter 1:3). A number of prayers in the New Testament are addressed simply to "the Lord."[1] In many instances this "Lord" should probably be understood as God. But given the fact that early Christians already referred to Jesus as Lord, the term may not have excluded Jesus. At any rate, there are isolated instances in which Jesus is clearly the object of prayer, as in the martyr's prayer of Stephen in Acts 7:59-60. The New Testament preserves several instances in which Jesus during his ministry received reverence due to God, and several more in which he is worshipped in his exalted state.[2] From the earliest days of the church, Jesus was at the center of its devotional life. Early Christian art portrays Christians praying in a cruciform stance — the form of Jesus on the cross. Believers were baptized in the name of Jesus, and they celebrated their most sacred meal by partaking of bread and wine meant to represent the body and blood of Jesus. They even "sang a hymn to Christ as if to a god," wrote a confounded Pliny to the Emperor Trajan early in the second century.[3]

The practice of devotion, worship, and prayer to Jesus says as much — if not more — about what the early Christians thought of Jesus as do their verbal formulations.[4] The verbal formulations in confession and

---

1. See, for example, Acts 1:24-25; 9:10, 13, 15-17; 22:17-19; 1 Corinthians 1:2; 16:22; 2 Corinthians 12:8; Revelation 22:20.

2. For Jesus' earthly life, see Matthew 14:33; 21:15-16; 28:9, 17; and John 20:28. The exalted Jesus is worshipped in Ephesians 5:19; Philippians 2:9-11; Revelation 5:8-9, 12-14. See Murray J. Harris, *Three Crucial Questions about Jesus* (Grand Rapids: Baker Books, 1992), 72-75.

3. *Epist.* 96; see Howard Kee, *The New Testament in Context: Sources and Documents* (Englewood Cliffs: Prentice-Hall, 1984), 44-45.

4. On worship and devotion to Jesus in the early church, see Larry Hurtado, *Lord Jesus Christ: Devotion to Jesus in Earliest Christianity* (Grand Rapids: Eerdmans, 2003), 134-53.

creed were unstoppable, however. In the fourth century we find Jesus confessed and glorified as the Most High God:

> Lord, the only begotten Son, Jesus Christ
> Lord God, Lamb of God, Son of the Father.
> Who takes away the sins of the world, have mercy on us.
> Who takes away the sins of the world, hear our prayer.
> Who sits at the right hand of the Father, have mercy on us.
> For you alone are holy,
> You alone are Lord,
> You alone are the Most High, Jesus Christ.[5]

Thus began the tradition of devotion to Christ that continues to this day. The crucial thing to note in this tradition of devotion is that the creeds may grow in length and number, but they do not grow in magnification of Jesus Christ. That is to say, we do not find an evolutionary trend to elevate Jesus in the creedal tradition of Christianity. "Jesus is Lord" already says the most profound and startling thing, that the name uniquely attributed to God in the Old Testament, "Lord," was from the very inception of Christianity attributed to Jesus. True, the creeds attempt to *define* the nature and mission of Jesus more closely, but they do not increase it. Christian creeds do not impute an increasing significance to Jesus Christ, in the way, for example, that Mahayana Buddhism made a historical human Gautama into a divine Buddha; or in the way that St. Francis has been embellished in Christian legend and hagiography. The Christian creeds, on the contrary, are like the undulating lines of geese in flight seeking to conform to a V-pattern. They do not seek to invent something, but to conform to something already given. The statements that Christians make about Jesus Christ are not intended to create a faith but to explicate a faith; not to enhance the historical Jesus but to stand in continuity with the historical Jesus.

And therein lie the two questions to which this chapter is devoted:

---

5. *Latinitas Christiana: Ein lateinisches Lesebuch mit Texten aus der Geschichte der christlichen Kirchen*, ed. K. von Rabenau, 2 vols. (Berlin: Evangelische Verlagsanstalt, 1978), I.11 (my translation from Latin).

why does Christianity alone exalt its founder to the status of God; and did the first Christians — and do Christians today — have any way of knowing whether their statements about Jesus re-present Jesus' own self-understanding?

The Self-Consciousness of Jesus Is the Key

We have already demonstrated the improbability of the prevailing thesis of naturalism that Jesus was a religious genius who was later divinized in order to make him competitive in the free-market pantheon of apotheosized Greeks and Romans. How, then, did the early church, dispersed in space and time throughout the ancient Mediterranean world, arrive in concert at the conviction that Jesus was the unique and saving Son of God?

According to the testimony of the New Testament, the source of its conviction lay not in the ingenuity of the early church but in the self-consciousness of Jesus. The claim that the Gospel writers manipulated the earlier tradition in order to produce an exaggerated Christology does not survive critical examination. The interpretation that the first Christians put upon the life, ministry, and death of Jesus does not appear to have originated in their minds at all, but in the mind and heart of Jesus. It was Jesus' self-consciousness that accounts for their confession of him. His self-consciousness is the best and only adequate explanation of the Christology of the Gospels and epistles of the New Testament. The editing of the New Testament writers did not exaggerate and complicate the record, but rather simplified the record by making reasonable deductions from and summaries of the plethora of witnesses to Jesus. The one interpretive key capable of providing an adequate explanation of what the early church experienced in the Jesus event is that he was, and knew himself to be, God's Son and savior.[6]

---

6. See Sir E. Hoskyns and N. Davey, *The Riddle of the New Testament* (London: Faber and Faber, 1968), 114. Further, "No New Testament writer could think of Jesus as the Greeks thought of Prometheus. We must therefore conclude that Jesus himself did not

The immediate problem with this conclusion is that the New Testament gives little direct information about the self-consciousness of Jesus. Although this complicates our investigation, it is not a surprise, because the New Testament was composed before the genre of psychological or introspective literature. The first work in Western history to qualify as such would be Augustine's *Confessions*, which was written some three centuries after the writing of the New Testament. Moreover, the many ancient biographies and stories of heroes that were contemporaneous with and similar to the Gospels in the New Testament were not interested in introspective and psychological wellsprings of thought and behavior. They were interested in the concrete teachings or actions of their protagonists. That is exactly what we find in the New Testament, and especially in the Gospels. In this respect, the New Testament conforms to the literary canons and ethos of its day.

The quest for Jesus' self-consciousness is further complicated by the fact that, so far as the New Testament record goes, Jesus never said, "I am God." At the same time it must be noted that a number of passages — indeed more passages than scholars often admit — record the New Testament writers either affirming or implying something very close to Jesus' deity.[7] This state of affairs may be dissatisfying from a modern point of view, but it is scarcely surprising considering the profound allegiance to monotheism in Judaism. Had Jesus made an outright claim to deity he would have compromised his ministry and message among both Jews and Romans, and supplied grounds for his immediate arrest and execu-

---

think of his life and death as a human achievement at all. Language descriptive of human heroism is entirely foreign to the New Testament. The event of the life and death of Jesus was not thought of as a human act, but as an act of God wrought out in human flesh and blood, which is a very different matter. The event was conceived of as a descending act of God, not as the ascending career of a man who was successful in the sphere of religion. . . . The concrete event, which was Jesus of Nazareth, was for them the sphere in which God had effected a mighty action for the salvation of men" (175-76). Similarly, O Betz, "Die Frage nach dem messianischen Bewusstsein Jesu," *Novum Testamentum* 6 (1963): 37: "The Messianic consciousness of Jesus provides the key to understanding his earthly work" (my translation).

7. John 1:1; 1:18; 20:28; Romans 9:5; Titus 2:13; Hebrews 1:8; 2 Peter 1:1; 1 John 5:20.

tion by both groups. In the Jewish world, the claim to deity was blasphemous, and blasphemy was a capital offense. But it must also be remembered that the Romans themselves reserved for Jewish Messianic pretenders the same punishment they meted out to revolutionaries and bandits.[8] It is not surprising that Jesus was careful in his self-disclosures.

A Window into Jesus' Soul

Although the New Testament does not provide a great deal of information about Jesus' self-understanding, it leaves a discernible trail of implicit evidence and insights into his self-consciousness. The trail was clear enough to convince Jesus' opponents to try him for blasphemy. "'According to our law,' said the Jewish council, '[Jesus] must die, because he claimed to be the Son of God'" (John 19:7; also 10:36). This testimony against Jesus comes from the Gospel of John, which typically ascribes divine titles and attributes to Jesus more freely than do the other Gospels. Independently of John, however, the Gospel of Matthew preserves the same charge in nearly the same wording when the chief priests taunted Jesus at the crucifixion, "He trusts in God. Let God rescue him now if he wants him, for he said, 'I am the Son of God'" (Matthew 27:43).

What gave the contemporaries of Jesus the impression that he understood himself to be the Son of God? The answer lies in the way he presented himself in his teaching, ministry, and overall bearing. Perhaps the most explicitly revealing window into Jesus' self-consciousness came from his own self-description.

> At that time, Jesus said, "I praise you, Father, Lord of heaven and earth, because you have hidden these things from the wise and learned, and revealed them to little children. Yes, Father, for this was your good pleasure. All things have been committed to me by my Father. No one

8. E. W. Stegemann and W. Stegemann, *The Jesus Movement: A Social History of Its First Century,* trans. O. C. Dean Jr. (Minneapolis: Fortress Press, 1995), 166: ". . . the Roman governors treated these movements [those of false messiahs and false prophets] in the same way as they did revolutionaries and social bandits."

knows the Son except the Father, and no one knows the Father except the Son and those to whom the Son chooses to reveal him." (Matthew 11:25-27//Luke 10:21-22)

The importance of these verses has been widely recognized by scholars, and aptly they have been described as "perhaps the most important verses in the Synoptic Gospels."[9] In the Greek text, "all things" is emphasized by its placement at the beginning of the sentence. Jesus is the steward of God's agenda. He is thus the heir of a full self-revelation of the Father. As the Son of God, Jesus is the solitary recipient of direct revelation from God, whom he exclusively calls *my* Father. In Judaism, true knowledge of God was believed to be the possession and privilege of the rabbis, and through them, of Israel.[10] How remarkable, in contrast, is Jesus' declaration here. In asserting that "no one knows the Father except the Son," he is not asserting simply greater knowledge than the rabbis, but *unique and incomparable* knowledge of God. Jewish rabbis received their knowledge of God from Torah and the rabbinic tradition; Jesus received his directly from the Father.[11] The Father reveals to the Son what others, the rabbis included, cannot know. Jesus testifies that conclusive knowledge of God and God's will are channeled through the agency of the Son, for "no one knows the Father except the Son and those to whom the Son chooses to reveal him." This prayer of Jesus is a self-witness to his unique status as both receiver and revealer of divine truth. "Between Father and Son there exists a perfect mutual understanding so unique, that any other person could participate in the complete knowledge of the Father only

9. A. M. Hunter, "Crux Criticorum — Matt. XI.25-30, A Re-Appraisal," *New Testament Studies* 8 (1961/62): 241. Further discussions of the passage can be found in J. Jeremias, *The Prayers of Jesus*, trans. J. Bowden (Philadelphia: Fortress Press, 1978), 45-52; I. H. Marshall, *The Origins of New Testament Christology* (Downers Grove: InterVarsity Press, 1976), 115; R. P. Martin, *New Testament Foundations* (Grand Rapids: Eerdmans, 1975), I.291-98.

10. A. Schlatter, *Der Evangelist Matthäus: Seine Sprache, sein Ziel, seine Selbstständigkeit* (Stuttgart: Calwer Verlag, 1948), 384.

11. S. Byrskog, *Jesus the Only Teacher: Didactic Authority and Transmission in Ancient Israel, Ancient Judaism and the Matthean Community* (Stockholm: Almquist & Wiksell International, 1994), 283.

through the medium of the Son."[12] Bruce Metzger refers to Jesus' relationship with God as "unshared Sonship": "Jesus claims not only that he alone stands in special relation to God, but also that he is the only one through whom one can be brought into a similar relationship."[13]

Rabbi Jesus — in a Class by Himself

For a long time it has been an axiom in New Testament scholarship that no Jewish rabbi could or did speak of himself as prominently as did Jesus, or assume of himself prerogatives so closely approximating those of God. This view has now been successfully refuted, in part by the Dead Sea Scrolls. The Scrolls preserve the words of an enigmatic figure known as the Teacher of Righteousness who separated himself distinctly from the community to which he brought deliverance. The Teacher repudiated his opponents as people of deception, who deviated from the covenant. By contrast, the Teacher remained resolute and faithful, regarding himself as standing in a special relationship to God. "You exhibit your power in me and reveal yourself in me with your strength as perfect light," he confessed to God. The Teacher was also seen as one through whom God revealed himself for the benefit of greater Israel: "Through me you have enlightened the face of the Many, you have increased them, so that they are uncountable, for you have shown me your wondrous mysteries." Fully conscious of his godly endowments, the Teacher of Righteousness asked, "What flesh is compared to this?" (1QH 12.16-29).

A select group of Jewish rabbis shared equally high estimations of themselves. One of them was Hillel, perhaps the greatest of rabbinic sages. Hillel was alive when Jesus was born, and his most illustrious

---

12. G. Dalman, *The Words of Jesus Considered in the Light of Post-Biblical Jewish Writings and the Aramaic Language*, trans. D. M. Kay (Edinburgh: T&T Clark, 1909), 283. Further, "He who stands in so uniquely close a relation to God is the only possible mediator of the kind, and also at the same time the absolutely reliable revealer of the whole wealth of the divine mysteries."

13. B. M. Metzger, *The New Testament: Its Background, Growth, and Content*, 3rd ed. (Nashville: Abingdon Press, 2003), 180.

protégé was Saul of Tarsus. Hillel shocked his contemporaries by applying biblical quotations that referred to God to himself. "If I am here, everything is here; if I am not here, what is here?" (*b. Sukk.* 53a). These quotations from the Teacher of Righteousness and Rabbi Hillel evince that, like Jesus, some rabbis spoke so prominently of themselves as to offend their contemporaries.

Nevertheless, Jesus' self-consciousness was even more exalted than theirs, or that of anyone like them. The Teacher and Hillel were mediators of God's word, to be sure, but the word they mediated was essentially the word that God mediated to Israel through Torah. They taught and acted as representatives of *all* Jewish people. In these respects they were dissimilar to Jesus. According to the testimony of the Gospels, Jesus had no equals, and his authority was not interchangeable with anyone else's. We know of no other Jewish rabbi who differentiated himself and his message so distinctly from Torah and the rabbinic tradition. In one very important text from the Dead Sea Scrolls (known to scholars as 4QMMT), the Teacher of Righteousness puts himself over against other Torah teachers, but he does not place himself in the same category with God, as did Jesus.[14] Jesus, however, had the audacity to refer to himself as the one and only teacher in the vast Jewish tradition contained in the Mishnah and Talmud.

> But you are not to be called rabbi, for you have one teacher, and you are all students. And call no one your father on earth, for you have one Father — the one in heaven. Nor are you to be called instructors, for you have one instructor, the Messiah. (Matthew 23:8-10)

The prominent Jewish scholar David Flusser summed up the difference between Jesus and the rabbinic tradition in this way:

> In the last analysis, there is a great difference between Hillel and Jesus. Hillel's self-understanding is not limited to his own person, but is typical for every person. Jesus' self-understanding of his unsurpassable bearing was, like Hillel's, always accompanied by humility and it avoided anything suggesting a "personality cult," but it was also

---

14. See Byrskog, *Jesus the Only Teacher*, 296.

bound up with the knowledge that his own person was not interchangeable with any other human being. He understood himself to be
'the Son', and as such to have a central commission and role in the
economy of God.[15]

This is not the claim of someone with Christian presuppositions,
but rather a judgment rendered as an objective assessment of the comparable historical data.

The Authority of Jesus' Teaching

When Flusser speaks of Jesus' "unsurpassable bearing . . . not interchangeable with any other," he is describing Jesus' consciousness of a
unique filial relationship with God. The word that best captured the essence of Jesus' identification with God is the Greek word *exousia*, meaning
"freedom," "right," "power," or "authority."[16] The *exousia* of Jesus permeated his speech, his ministry, his self-presentation, and his public bearing.

The primary way Jesus demonstrated his *exousia* was in the authority
with which he taught (Matthew 7:29; Luke 4:32). The crowds "were as-
tounded at his teaching, for he taught them as one having authority, and
not as the scribes," records Mark 1:22. The modern dismissal of Jewish
scribes as empty hypocrites is both unfortunate and mistaken. In reality,
their erudition was immense and their stature among the people was
legendary. Their prestige then would be analogous to that of profes-
sional athletes and rock stars today. They had memorized and mastered
huge portions of Scripture and the rabbinic traditions based on it, and
they were capable of rendering comprehensive judgments on matters
theological, legal, social, and political. In comparing Jesus' authority to
the scribes, the Gospels were scarcely drawing a straw man comparison,
but rather comparing Jesus to the members of an elite field.

15. David Flusser, *Entdeckungen im Neuen Testament. Band 1: Jesusworte und ihre
Überlieferung* (Neukirchen-Vluyn: Neukirchener Verlag, 1987), 215 (my translation).
16. See J. R. Edwards, "The Authority of Jesus in the Gospel of Mark," *Journal of the
Evangelical Theological Society* 37/2 (1994): 217-33.

Impressive as the scribes were, however, Jesus' teaching was more impressive. His teaching was not rooted, as was theirs, in the authority of Torah, but in his own authority, in "a personal quality given directly by God."[17] This fact did not escape his contemporaries (Mark 11:28), nor does it escape a modern Jewish scholar like David Flusser, who writes that Jesus "is the only ancient Jew known to us who not only proclaimed that the endtime was at hand, but at the same time that the new time of salvation had already begun."[18]

A striking example of the authority of Jesus' teaching was his presumption to reinterpret the Sabbath. "The Sabbath was made for humankind, and not humankind for the Sabbath; so the Son of Man is lord even of the Sabbath" (Mark 2:27-28). The establishment of the Sabbath was the crowning act of creation according to Genesis 2:1-3, succeeding even the creation of humanity. Sabbath observance was incumbent on Israel as a constitutive order of creation. The Sabbath ordinance was the longest and most pivotal in the Ten Commandments (Exodus 20:8-11; Deuteronomy 5:12-15).[19] Of all the nations Israel alone had been given the Sabbath, and Sabbath observance separated Israel from the nations and sanctified Israel in God's sight (*Jub.* 2:17-33). When Jesus declared *himself* to be master of the Sabbath — and even violated its ordinances by plucking grain (Mark 2:23-26) and healing on the Sabbath (Mark 1:21-28; 3:1-6; John 9:14) — he personally presumed the authority of the Creator God who instituted the Sabbath.

Equally striking was Jesus' posture as a teacher vis-à-vis Torah and Moses. Especially in the Sermon on the Mount, Jesus repeatedly cited teachings of Moses, and then superseded them with his own teachings, with the refrain, "You have heard that it was said to those of ancient times . . . , but I say to you." Jesus' authority over Torah exceeds anything taught by other Jewish rabbis. Samuel Byrskog calls him "a qualitatively unique teacher, . . . more confident than any rabbi or other human

---

17. Byrskog, *Jesus the Only Teacher*, 270-83.

18. *Jesus*, Rowohlts Bilmonographien 140 (Reinbek, 1968), 102 (my translation).

19. See P. J. Miller, Jr., "The Human Sabbath: A Study in Deuteronomic Theology," *Princeton Seminary Bulletin*, n.s., 6/2 (1985): 81-97.

teacher ever heard of."[20] Mosaic laws regarding murder, adultery, divorce, swearing false oaths, revenge, and hatred of enemies are referenced in Matthew 5:21-48. Pronouncements of Torah on these matters were accepted in Judaism as pronouncements of God. Unlike other rabbis, however, Jesus did not cite them as the final word on the subject. Jesus followed Torah pronouncement with a comma, as it were, and not with a period, as did the rabbis. Torah set the stage for something greater to follow that Jesus presumed to fulfill in himself. Whatever remained in force after Jesus, remained so only if validated by Jesus.[21] Jesus presumed to know the will of God behind the wording of Torah, and hence *the true intent of the law.* Jesus did not settle an argument by quoting Torah; he settled it by declaring, *"I say to you."* In each case he added something not stipulated in the original wording of Torah — usually, in fact, making the commandment more stringent. Any rabbi who presumed to alter Torah in like fashion would have cut himself off from the community of Israel. Jesus claimed to embody an authority superseding that of Moses, and anyone who claimed an authority above Moses had *ipso facto* set himself on a plane with God.[22]

His attitude toward Torah surfaced in a conversation with a man of means, confident in his wealth and fulfillment of Torah alike. "What must I do to inherit eternal life?" he asked (Mark 10:17). A typical rabbi would have directed him to Torah. For the rabbis, people were complete or perfect according to their degree of Torah observance. "The rabbinic scribes were so certain that a person possessed the ability to fulfill the commandments of God without fail, that in all earnestness they told people they were responsible to keep the whole Torah, from A to Z."[23] Jesus, however, did not question the man's Torah righteousness, nor did he advise him to pursue it further. He did not mention Torah at all. He

20. Byrskog, *Jesus the Only Teacher,* 281, 296, 307.

21. R. J. Banks, "Matthew's Understanding of the Law: Authenticity and Interpretation in Matthew 5:17-20," *Journal of Biblical Literature* 93 (1974): 226-42.

22. See E. Käsemann, "The Problem of the Historical Jesus," in *Essays on New Testament Themes* (1964), 42; Marshall, *The Origins of New Testament Christology,* 46-48.

23. H. L. Strack and P. Billerbeck, *Kommentar zum Neuen Testament aus Talmud und Midrasch,* 6 vols. (Munich, 1922-1961), 1:814-16 (my translation).

commanded him, rather, to sell his possessions, and "Come, follow me" (Mark 10:17-22//Matthew 19:6-30//Luke 18:18-23). Jesus called the man not to Torah but to himself, and this was unique in Judaism. We know of no Jewish rabbi who promoted himself above Torah in like manner. Jesus understood eternal life to be found not in Torah but in following and serving *him.* His teaching was not rooted, as was the scribes', in the authority of Torah but in a superior authority resident in himself, in "a personal quality given directly by God."[24]

The *exousia* of Jesus can be further shown from two aspects of his speech, long recognized as unique in rabbinic rhetoric. One was his use of the word *amēn.* "Amen" functioned as a liturgical response of affirmation of the worshipping community in Jesus' day, just as it does today.[25] Jesus, however, employed this common word, which means "it is true," or "it is worthy of belief," in a way it had never been used before as an emphatic preface to his teachings. The *amēn*-speech convention of Jesus, in the words of rabbinic scholar Joachim Jeremias, "is without any parallel in the whole of Jewish literature and the rest of the New Testament."[26] The Old Testament prophets had prefaced their pronouncements with "Thus says the Lord" as a guarantee of Yahweh's authority; but Jesus assumed that authority himself, with the words, "Truly I say to you." Some fifty times in the Synoptic Gospels, and half that number again in the Gospel of John, Jesus prefaces his statements with *amēn* to indicate that they are to be regarded as reliable and true. Their truth is not grounded in Torah, or even in God, but in *him.* Jesus "lays claim to an authority which does not need any outside justification."[27] "Amen," like the confession "Jesus is Lord," implies that the kingdom of God is uniquely present in Jesus' person.[28]

A second important aspect of Jesus' speech was his use of *abba* as a

---

24. Byrskog, *Jesus the Only Teacher,* 279-83.

25. See Strack and Billerbeck, *Kommentar,* 3.456-61.

26. Joachim Jeremias, *New Testament Theology* (New York: Scribner's, 1971), 35-36; so too, *Exegetical Dictionary of the New Testament,* s.v. *amēn; Theologisches Wörterbuch zum Neuen Testament,* s.v. *amēn.*

27. Marshall, *The Origins of New Testament Christology,* 45.

28. The *Theological Dictionary of the New Testament,* s. v. *amēn,* goes so far as to claim that *amen* contains "the whole of Christology *in nuce.*"

reference to God. Jesus' speech about God as Father reveals the heart of his filial consciousness. T. W. Manson is correct in saying that "the experience of God as Father dominates the whole ministry of Jesus from the Baptism to the Crucifixion,"[29] and hence is the source of Jesus' authority and filial consciousness. One of the oldest memories of the early church is that Jesus spoke of God personally and intimately with the Aramaic word *abba* (Mark 14:36; Galatians 4:6). *Abba* very likely lies behind most or all the references to God as "my Father" or "your Father" in the words of Jesus. *Abba* was thus at once the preferred and unique way for Jesus to speak of God. In the Gospels, "Father" never occurs in a Scriptural quotation, a narrative description, the discourse of any speaker other than Jesus, or in Jesus' words to his adversaries. That is, all references to God as Father come from Jesus, either in his prayers or in speech to his disciples.[30] Jesus' use of *abba* was unique among Jewish rabbis, for no evidence has yet been found in the literature of Palestine of "my Father" being used by individuals to address God. Jesus, on the other hand, not only addressed God confidently and securely, reverently and obediently, as *abba,* but he taught his disciples to do the same.[31]

We spoke earlier of the "unshared Sonship" of Jesus, and how it differed even from the prophetic consciousness of sages like the Teacher of Righteousness and Rabbi Hillel. Here is a statistic that confirms that difference. In the Synoptic Gospels there are fifty-one occurrences (excluding parallels) of "Father" in the mouth of Jesus. In twenty-nine instances Jesus speaks of God as "my Father," and in twenty-two he teaches the disciples about God as "your Father. Not once does Jesus include himself

---

29. T. W. Manson, *The Teaching of Jesus: Studies in Its Form and Content* (Cambridge: Cambridge University Press, 1963), 102.

30. R. L. Mowery, "From Lord to Father in Matthew 1–7," *Catholic Biblical Quarterly* 59/4 (1997): 642-56.

31. The foremost treatment of *Abba* remains J. Jeremias, *The Prayers of Jesus* (Philadelphia: Fortress Press, 1978), 11-65. Recent critiques of Jeremias (e.g., M. R. D'Angelo, "*Abba* and 'Father': Imperial Theology and the Jesus Traditions," *Journal of Biblical Literature* 111/4 [1992]: 611-30) modify his conclusions at isolated points but fail to alter his central thesis that there are (as yet) still no examples of the use of *Abba* for God in Jewish texts as early as the Gospels.

with the disciples in addressing God as "our Father."[32] Jesus' references to God as "Father" and "*abba*" preserve within the Gospel tradition a seminal memory of his unique filial consciousness. The Fatherhood of God was thus not a theological commonplace in Jesus' day, but the core experience of Jesus' deep metaphysical relationship with God, which was accessible to others via him alone.[33]

We have noted the divine authority with which Jesus taught, including the pronouncements on Sabbath and Torah, and his use of *amen* and *abba*. Let us remember that the great religious teachers of the world, including Buddha, Muhammad, and even the apostle Paul often differentiated among degrees of authority in their teaching. Some of their teaching was authoritative, and some negotiable. This is frequently in evidence in the sayings of the Buddha in the *Dhammapada,* and in the teachings of Muhammad in the *Hadith,* and in the teachings of the apostle Paul in 1 Corinthians 7, for example. The New Testament, however, does not present any teaching of Jesus that is negotiable or otherwise less than fully authoritative. Jesus taught not only the truth *of* God, but also the truth *from* God.

The Authority of Jesus in Supernatural Matters

One of the most profound expressions of the authority of Jesus was in presuming supernatural power unique to God. His presumption to forgive sins was one example of this.[34] According to Jewish tradition, forgiveness of sins was the exclusive prerogative of God.[35] Scribes, for example, did not presume to forgive sins. Even the long-awaited Jewish Messiah was not expected to forgive sins. The classical description of the Messiah in the apocryphal *Psalms of Solomon* 17–18 speaks of his righteousness, and even

32. The "Our Father" of the Lord's Prayer in Matthew 6:9 is an instruction of the disciples by Jesus.

33. See Manson, *The Teaching of Jesus,* 90-116.

34. Matthew 9:6; 11:20-24; 25:31-46; Mark 2:10; 8:38; Luke 5:24; 7:47; 10:13-15; 19:9-10; John 5:22; 8:11.

35. See Exodus 34:6-7; Psalm 103:3; Isaiah 43:25; Micah 7:18.

his sinlessness (17:36), but of the ability of the Messiah to forgive sins there is not a word. Jesus, however, presumed to forgive sins, and not only sins against himself. He pronounced forgiveness of sins against *others*. This is apparent in John 8:11, where Jesus forgave a woman caught in adultery even though her adultery was not against him. Again, in Mark 2:10-11, "'But so that you may know that the Son of Man has *authority* on earth to forgive sins' — [Jesus] said to the paralytic — 'I say to you, stand up, take your mat and go to your home.'" Jesus did not declare the man's sins forgiven in the name of God, but by his own *exousia* to forgive them.[36] In claiming to do so, he stood squarely in the place of God.

Another expression of Jesus' authority in supernatural matters was in the exorcism of demons. The Gospels record a number of gripping conflicts between the kingdom of God as present in Jesus and the dominion of Satan, between the one anointed with God's Spirit and those held captive by unclean spirits.[37] Since demonic powers were spiritual powers — albeit fallen ones — they were the first to recognize the supernatural mission and authority of Jesus, doing so even before humans did. Unlike other exorcists of whom we know, Jesus made no reference to formulas, mantras, secret techniques, or magical practices in his exorcisms. By the *exousia* resident in him and by the power of his word alone Jesus rebuked the fallen spiritual powers. Sometimes they sued for mercy: "What have you to do with me, Jesus, Son of the Most High God? I adjure you by God, do not torment me" (Mark 5:7). Sometimes they confessed him outright as "Son of God" (Mark 1:24; 3:11; Luke 4:41). Yet every encounter between Jesus and the demonic in the Gospels is a no-contest event. In both his word and work Jesus was endowed with the sovereign authority of God.

The confession of Son of God in the context of demon exorcisms is highly significant, for in the Old Testament only one individual — David, the Anointed of God (1 Samuel 16:13-23) — was known to drive out

36. J. D. G. Dunn, *Jesus, Paul, and the Law: Studies in Mark and Galatians* (Louisville: Westminster/John Knox, 1990), 27.

37. Matthew 8:16, 32; 12:28; Mark 1:25; 1:34, 39; 3:11, 15, 27; 5:8; 6:7, 13; 9:25; Luke 4:41; 8:29; 10:19; 11:20.

evil spirits. The line of David was designated by God to bear, at least in provisional form, the honor of divine sonship (2 Samuel 7:11-14). So when the demons confessed Jesus as the Son of God they were acknowledging his Messianic status as the fulfillment of the promise to David.[38]

The first parable in Mark's Gospel declares Jesus' power to vanquish Satan. "No one can enter a strong man's house and plunder his property without first tying up the strong man; then indeed the house can be plundered," said Jesus (3:27). The "strong man" refers to Satan, as the foregoing verses reveal, and the stronger man who plunders his stronghold is Jesus, the Son of God. Jesus did not snatch the imagery of subduing a strong man out of thin air. It came straight from the Jewish tradition. "Beliar [that is, the devil] shall be bound by [the Messianic high priest], and he shall grant to his children the authority to trample on wicked spirits" (T. Levi 18:12). The *Psalms of Solomon* likewise declare, "No one takes plunder away from a strong man" (5:3). These texts echo the prophetic vision of Isaiah:

> Can the prey be taken from the mighty,
>   or the captives of a tyrant be rescued?
> But thus says the LORD:
> Even the captives of the mighty shall be taken,
>   and the prey of the tyrant be rescued;
> for I will contend with those who contend with you,
>   and I will save your children. . . .
> Then all flesh shall know
>   that I am the LORD your Savior,
>   and your Redeemer, the Mighty One of Jacob.
>   (Isaiah 49:24-26)

Jesus audaciously applied to himself imagery that originally had been solely the prerogative of God as savior and redeemer. As Son of God and savior, Jesus did something *for* humanity before doing something *to* it. He liberated humanity from the power of evil so that he could proceed to restore it to the image of God.

---

38. O. Betz, "Die Frage nach dem messianischen Bewusstsein Jesu," 41.

The Authority of Jesus over Nature

One of the most common expressions of Jesus *exousia* can be seen in his miracles. Jesus' miracles were acknowledged by people who were not his followers. There is no hint of disbelief in the testimony of Josephus, the first-century Jewish historian, that Jesus was a "doer of remarkable deeds."[39] The Greek word for "remarkable," *paradoxos,* means "exceeding expectation," "out of this world." His miracles and exorcisms were even acknowledged by implacable adversaries. One of the six references to Jesus in the Jewish Talmud reports that he performed marvelous works.[40] The Talmud fully acknowledges that Jesus performed miracles, even though it attributes them to black magic in an attempt to discredit them.

The New Testament does not limit the healing effectiveness of Jesus (or in the name of Jesus) to instances where the psychological or emotional influence of the patient could be appealed to in order to aid healing. In some instances, such as the healing of lepers (Matthew 8:2-4; Mark 1:40-45; Luke 5:12-16), the disease was so notorious and ineradicable that Jewish rabbis thought of lepers as the "living dead,"[41] or "in no way different from a corpse."[42] Leprosy was a dreaded contagion that was generally regarded from the Old Testament onward as a divine punishment whose cure could only be effected by God (Numbers 12:10; 2 Kings 5:1-2).

Jesus healed persons whose participation, whether emotional, psychological, or religious, could have played no role in their healing. He healed illnesses at the request of third parties, such as the father of a sick boy (John 4:46-54), or the master of a servant (Matthew 8:5-13; Luke 7:1-10). In such instances the person healed had no contact with Jesus, and

---

39. *Antiquities* 18.63. The testimony of Josephus is quoted verbatim by the fourth-century Christian historian Eusebius, *H.E.* 1.2.7-8.

40. *b. Sabb.* 104b; *y. Sanh.* 25d. See *Encyclopedia Judaica* (1971), 10:14-17; R. T. Herford, *Christianity in Talmud and Midrash* (London: Williams and Norgate, 1903), 112-15.

41. Strack and Billerbeck, *Kommentar* 4/2:750-51; on leprosy in general, see 4/2:743-63.

42. Josephus, *Antiquities* 3.264.

presumably no expectation of him. In other instances Jesus healed people apart from their knowledge or will, such as the healing of the severed ear of the servant of the high priest (Luke 22:50-51). Most obvious were the several cases in which Jesus (or again, the name of Jesus) caused a dead person to be raised to life.[43] The only power possible to revoke the power of death is the power of God.

Jesus' miracles included power over forces of nature as well as illnesses. Jesus was reputed to have calmed storms (Matthew 8:23-27; Mark 4:35-41; Luke 8:22-25), fed crowds of people without the requisite food to do so (Mark 6:30-44; 8:1-10), and walked on water (Matthew 14:25; Mark 6:48; John 6:19). The descriptions of his *exousia* in several of these stories rewards closer consideration. In the calming of the storm in Mark 4:35-41, his "rebuke" of the wind and quieting of the waves (the Greek word used actually means "to muzzle") are phrased in the language of exorcism, recalling the power of God over chaos at creation (Genesis 1:2-3). And like the Genesis account of creation, both episodes are effected solely by the spoken word. Likewise, Jesus' walking on water in Mark 6:45-53 is described in a way that is reminiscent of Job 9:8 — that is, that Jesus walked where only God can walk. Jesus' self-designation in that event, "I Am," recalls the same expression for God's self-disclosure to Moses in Exodus 3:14.

The Authority of Jesus to Reorder Social Relations

Jesus' *exousia* expressed itself in a number of revolutionary social innovations. A rare indication of his unique self-understanding was that he expected no successors.[44] Moses looked forward to a prophet who would come after him (Deuteronomy 18:15-18); Elijah was sent to prepare the way for the Coming One (Malachi 3:1); and John the Baptizer proclaimed

---

43. Matthew 9:18-26; Mark 5:21-43; Luke 7:11-17; 8:40-56; John 6:40, 44, 54; Acts 9:40.

44. C. F. D. Moule, *The Phenomenon of the New Testament* (Naperville, Ill.: A. R. Allenson, 1967), 68ff.

that he would be followed by one stronger than himself (Mark 1:7). Jesus, however, never spoke of successors, heirs, or anchor runners in the relay race of salvation. The salvation that for his predecessors was still a future event, was for Jesus *at hand:* "The time has come. The kingdom of God is at hand" (Mark 1:15).

It was, moreover, at hand in himself. The roles of all who had gone before were roles of preparation. Jesus was the fulfillment. Once Jesus was present, the roles of Moses and Elijah and John were completed. This is discreetly symbolized in the Transfiguration narratives, where Elijah and Moses appear and testify to Jesus, and then depart, leaving Jesus alone with the disciples (Mark 9:2-8). So unique was Jesus self-understanding that he intended people to understand that their standing in God's reign depended on their standing with him:[45]

> Everyone who acknowledges me before others, I also will acknowledge before my Father in heaven; but whoever denies me before others, I also will deny before my Father in heaven. (Matthew 10:32-33// Luke 12:8-9; similarly Mark 8:38)

The authority of Jesus determined not only the call of individual disciples, but also the establishment of "the Twelve." The Dead Sea Scrolls provide an instructive backdrop against which to consider Jesus' establishment of the Twelve. The Qumran believers understood themselves as a spiritual remnant in the midst of faithless Israel and a temple desecrated by corrupt and apostate leaders. In the last days, however, they believed God would raise up the long-awaited Davidic heir who would restore the fallen tent of Israel and conclude a new covenant of salvation with his people (Ezekiel 34:25-26; 1QS 4:20-22; 5:20-21). The Davidic Messiah, in other words, would reconstitute Israel, and his doing so would signal the arrival of the kingdom of God.[46]

In choosing the Twelve, Jesus publicly fulfilled this ideal. The new community he created was signified by the number twelve, correspond-

---

45. J. Kremer, "'Sohn Gottes.' Zur Klärung des biblischen Hoheitstitels Jesu," *Biblical Literature* 46 (1973): 15; Marshall, *The Origins of New Testament Christology*, 50.

46. See O. Betz, "Die Frage nach dem messianischen Bewusstsein Jesu," 40-41.

ing to the twelve tribes of Israel (Matthew 19:28; Luke 22:29ff.). From a mountaintop, reminiscent of Yahweh's summons to Moses on Mount Sinai (Exodus 19:20), Jesus summoned the Twelve into a new community (Mark 3:13-19) and to a mission founded on a relationship with himself. Significantly, Jesus did not include himself in the Twelve. In establishing the Twelve he remained outside and above them in a way that was analogous to the relationship of Moses or God to the twelve tribes of Israel. Jesus conferred his authority on the Twelve and sent them out with dominion over demons (Mark 6:7-13). In the ordaining of the Twelve Jesus signified the reconstitution of Israel as the people of God.

One of the most unprecedented expressions of Jesus' *exousia* in social relationships was his compassion toward outsiders. Both the Mosaic and rabbinic traditions aimed to protect Israel from peoples considered alien and impure. But Jesus displayed an entirely different understanding of the people of God: rather than needing protecting from outside contagion, the redeemed community should be the contagion — healing and wholesome — that affected outsiders. Consequently, in his ministry Jesus accepted persons that Judaism did not embrace: lepers (Mark 1:40-45), tax collectors and sinners (Mark 2:13-17), and unclean Gentiles, including a woman from Israel's intransigent foe, Syrophoenicia (Mark 7:24-30).

The authority that the Gospels ascribe to Jesus is without parallel in Judaism. A skeptic might object that the above picture of Jesus is exactly what we would expect from Christian faith and tradition. Our evidence, however, has not been derived from creedal or dogmatic pronouncements, but by standards of authenticity that are applied to historical documents and arguments in general. A skeptic might further object that the attitudes and bearing of Jesus resulted from lunacy or insanity. If that were so, we would expect his contemporaries to have recognized the fact. With one possible exception (Mark 3:21), however, the people closest to Jesus — both friends and foes — did not draw that conclusion. His authority was too impressive and real to derive from insanity. His contemporaries acknowledged it as supernatural authority. The *exousia* of Jesus was the source of restoration, redemption, and salvation of those who encountered it. It was the legitimate and effective power of

God for salvation, a life-giving power that was not a burden to be borne but a gift freely given and forever enjoyed.[47]

Why Was Jesus Executed?

Not the least important piece of evidence for the Messianic self-consciousness of Jesus was that he saw his destiny to be determined in Jerusalem. The Gospels describe his resolve to go to Jerusalem as something willed and determined by God. The repeated use of "must" in the speech of Jesus, from the Greek participle *dei*, "it is necessary" or "it must happen," reminds readers that Jesus saw his journey to Jerusalem as an essential element in God's plan.[48] In the Old Testament Jerusalem was the city where God's name (that is, God's effective presence) dwelled (1 Kings 11:32), and from which salvation came (Psalms 14:7; 53:6). The City of David was where God was enthroned (Jeremiah 14:21; 17:12), and where the Messiah would be enthroned (Psalms 2:6; 110:1-2). Leaders in both the First (A.D. 66-70) and Second (A.D. 132-135) Jewish Revolts (the uprisings led by Menachem the Zealot and Bar Kokhba, respectively) sought to be enthroned in Jerusalem.[49] Jerusalem was the place where three inextricable realities in Jewish history and memory converged: the Messiah, the City of David, and the temple. Jesus' determination to go to Jerusalem was thus an expression of his commitment to fulfill his Messianic destiny. In Jesus' case, however, his Messianic destiny was not to be enthroned in glory, but to "undergo great suffering, and be rejected by the elders, the chief priests, and the scribes, and be killed, and after three days [to] rise again" (Mark 8:31). At the Passover in Jerusalem Jesus interpreted the bread and wine as symbols of his own body and blood and the fulfillment of his destiny.

It was in Jerusalem that Jesus was crucified. It is a remarkable fact

47. See T. Gillespie, "A Question of Authority," *Princeton Seminary Bulletin*, n.s., 24/1 (2003): 1-9.

48. Matthew 16:21; Mark 8:31; Luke 9:22; 17:25; 22:7; 24:26.

49. Josephus, *War* 2.433ff.; 4.575.

that we have no certain evidence of any other Jewish rabbis being sentenced to death by the Sanhedrin because of their beliefs. The Mishnah, an important source of present-day knowledge about Second Temple Judaism, records the sayings and confrontations of hundreds of rabbis over more than a two-century period, none of which resulted in the pronouncement of a death sentence by the Sanhedrin. The same is true of the Jewish historian Josephus, who covers not only Second Temple Judaism, but also the history of Israel preceding it. According to the Dead Sea Scrolls, the Teacher of Righteousness was persecuted and deposed, but it does not appear he was killed (1QpHab 11:4-7). His fate, at any rate, was the result of a power struggle with the Wicked Priest, not the result of his teaching. There were, to be sure, Jewish teachers and rabbis who were occasionally executed during this period. Both Herod the Great and Alexander Jannaeus are known to have executed Jewish leaders as suspected political or military rivals. During the Roman period, Jewish religious leaders such as Judas the Galilean and his son Menahem were likewise executed by Roman authorities because of their activities in movements we commonly associate with the Zealots. What we do not find in the entire history, however, is the pronouncement of a death sentence by the Sanhedrin on a Jewish religious leader because of either blasphemy or idolatry, the two explicit grounds for execution in Judaism.[50] One of the indisputable facts of the period, however, is that the Jewish Sanhedrin passed a sentence of death on Jesus, which was subsequently ratified and executed by the Roman governor.

It is widely, though mistakenly, believed that Jesus was arrested, tried, and executed as a Messianic pretender. We noted earlier that such individuals were hunted down and eliminated by Rome. That is certainly why the charge over Jesus' cross read "King of the Jews" (Mark 15:26). That he claimed to be the Messiah was indeed the *Roman* charge against Jesus, but

---

50. The only possible exception to this statement known to me involves a certain Ben Stada, whom the Talmud (*Shab.* 104b; *Sanh.* 67b) says was condemned to death and hanged because of witchcraft. Considerable uncertainty surrounds the name of Ben Stada in Jewish sources, however, including his confusion and apparent identification with Jesus of Nazareth. This uncertainty requires caution in making definite claims based on his case (see *Encyclopedia Judaica* 4:554).

it could not have been the Jewish charge, for according to Jewish law a claim of Messiah was *not* a criminal offense, and certainly not a capital offense. The claim to be Messiah, in other words, was not a blasphemous claim, since in Jewish thinking the Messiah was to be a human being who would not assume or challenge the prerogatives of God.[51] A person might be a fool for claiming to be the Messiah, but not a criminal. This was demonstrated by Bar Kokhba, the leader of the Second Jewish Revolt (A.D. 132-135), who openly proclaimed himself as the Messiah and was believed to be such by Rabbi Akiba.[52] There is no evidence that Bar Kokhba's claim was considered blameworthy by any of his contemporaries, not even after the revolt failed and Bar Kokhba's claims self-destructed.

We are left, then, with a puzzle. The Jewish authorities accused Jesus of blasphemy, but the claim to be Messiah was not considered blasphemous. We are not arguing that Jesus was not the Messiah, for as we have seen, a number of his actions point to the fact that he was. His calling of the Twelve has the symbolic hallmarks of reconstituting Israel (Mark 3:13-19); his presumption to judge Israel was consonant with Messianic expectations (Mark 10:35-40); as were his attempts to cleanse and reform the Jerusalem temple. The last action, in particular, was regarded in all strata of Judaism as a Messianic requirement.[53] As we have noted, however, Messianic pretension, even Messianic agitation, was *in Jewish law* not grounds for execution.

Why, then, did the Jewish chief priests press the Roman governor for

51. Justin Martyr referred to the Messiah as "a human born of humans" (*Dialogue with Trypho* 67.2).

52. Bar Kokhba struck coins depicting himself as a star rising above the temple. The Star of Judah (Numbers 24:17) was a traditional Messianic symbol. On the Revolt and his Messianic claims, see the material gathered in Schürer, *The History of the Jewish People*, 1:534-57.

53. The prophets believed the Messiah would transform the mountain of the house of the Lord into the mountain of the world (Micah 4:1ff.; Isaiah 2:1-5); the Qumran community expected the Davidic Messiah to rebuild the sanctuary (4QFlor 1:1ff.); the early Pharisaic movement spoke of the Davidic Messiah cleansing Jerusalem by sanctification (*Psalms of Solomon* 17:30); and the intertestamental literature spoke of the Messianic Son of Man gloriously renewing Jerusalem and the temple (*Sibylline Oracles* 414-33).

a death sentence against Jesus? The one ground that could account for the death sentence was the charge of blasphemy, that is, the claim (in some sense) to be God. The chief priest demanded to know of Jesus if he were the Christ, *the Son of the Most Blessed* (Mark 14:61).[54] "Son of the Most Blessed" was a reverential way to speak of God without pronouncing God's name, for fear of profaning it. The chief priest was asking Jesus if he was "the Son of God." According to Mark 14:62, Jesus not only affirmed the question, but proceeded to speak of himself as the Coming One who would judge the world with the power and glory of God. That amounted to a double claim of deity, for in the Old Testament the eschatological authority of judgment was reserved for God alone. The chief priest understood Jesus to be claiming something far in excess of being Messiah. As we noted at the outset of this chapter, he understood him to be claiming to be like God. In righteous indignation, the chief priest tore his garments and pronounced the sentence of blasphemy (Mark 14:63-65).

In ancient Judaism blasphemy was regarded as "stretching out one's hand against God" by impugning God's honor and holiness (*Sipre Deut.* 221 on Deuteronomy 21:22). God was blasphemed when, among other things, one ascribed divine powers to oneself or laid claim to divine dignity and position. This was clearly what the Sanhedrin understood Jesus to be ascribing to himself. As a consequence, the sentence of death, according to Leviticus 24:10-23 and Numbers 15:30ff., was irrevocable in their eyes.[55] At the historical core of Jesus' mission was his self-understanding as God's unique and beloved Son (so Mark 12:6). It was that understanding that was unmistakably perceived by the Sanhedrin

54. It is now clear that Jews could and occasionally did link the concepts of Messiah and Son of God in Second Temple Judaism. See 4Q246 where both terms are yoked at Qumran. See J. J. Collins, "The Messiah as the Son of God," in *The Scepter and the Star* (New York: Doubleday, 1995), 154-72.

55. *Exegetical Dictionary of the New Testament,* s v. *blasphēmia;* and P. Stuhlmacher, *Jesus of Nazareth — Christ of Faith,* trans. S. Schatzmann (Peabody: Hendrickson Publishers, 1988), 29-47. Stuhlmacher's argument that Jesus was sentenced and executed as a "religious deceiver," while true, seems to fall short of the crux of the problem for the Sanhedrin, namely that, in the words of the Fourth Gospel, he made himself God (John 10:33).

and that ultimately provided grounds according to Jewish law for his execution as a blasphemer.[56]

Jesus' Understanding of the Significance of His Death

A further window into Jesus' self-consciousness comes from his understanding of his own death. On select occasions Jesus gave insights that he understood his impending death as a sacrifice on *behalf of* humanity. The most important of these was reference to his death as a "ransom": "For the Son of Man came not to be served but to serve, and to give his life a ransom for many" (Mark 10:45). At the Last Supper he also interpreted the wine as symbolic of "my blood of the covenant, which is poured out for many" (Mark 14:24). Both of these passages appear to have originated with the historical Jesus.[57] They reveal that Jesus was conscious that his impending death should be interpreted according to the Old Testament paradigm of an atonement for sin. Jesus conscientiously assumed the role of the sacrificial Servant of Isaiah, whose "life is an offering for sin" (Isaiah 53:10) and who "bore the sin of many and made intercession for the transgressors" (Isaiah 53:12). And like the Servant, the vicarious atonement of Jesus would not be offered for Jews alone, but for all people, Gentiles included.[58]

56. A. Strobel, *Die Stunde der Wahrheit: Untersuchungen zum Strafverfahren gegen Jesus* (WUNT 21: Tübingen: J. C. B. Mohr [Paul Siebeck], 1980), 81ff. "In its core (Mark 14:61-62) we are confronted with a unique tradition, whose likely highly factual content is Jesus' own expectation of exaltation, voiced before the highest court of the Jewish people during this Passover period. The issue here is the historical core of the expectation and mission of Jesus."

57. See M. Wilcox, "On the Ransom-Saying in Mark 10:45c, Matthew 20:28c," in *Geschichte — Tradition — Reflexion: Festschrift für Martin Hengel zum 70. Geburtstag*, ed. H. Canick, H. Lichtenberger, and P. Schäfer, vol. 3: *Frühes Christentum* (Tübingen: Mohr/ Siebeck, 1996), 173-86.

58. See O. Betz, "Die Frage nach dem messianischen Bewusstsein Jesu," 43-48; and (with the exception of the articles by Morna Hooker) the collection of essays edited by W. H. Bellinger, Jr., and W. R. Farmer, *Jesus and the Suffering Servant: Isaiah 53 and Christian Origins* (Harrisburg: Trinity Press International, 1998).

The mission of the Servant of the Lord is more interchangeable with the mission of God than is the mission of any figure in the Old Testament. This is seen in Isaiah 43:3-4, for example, in which God offers a ransom for Israel's salvation.[59] The Israelite king, it is true, was often depicted as a savior in Israel. Thus, Saul was anointed by Samuel to "reign over the people of the LORD and save them from the hand of their enemies" (1 Samuel 10:1). But no king of Israel, indeed no other figure in Israel, offered a *ransom* for Israel — except for God and the Servant in Isaiah. The ransom offered by Jesus appears to fulfill both the mission of the Servant of the Lord and the mission of God. In presenting himself as a ransom (Mark 10:45) otherwise offered by God, Jesus ascribed to himself the conclusive act in the divine drama of salvation.

The Witness of the Gospel of John to Jesus' Messianic Self-Consciousness

So far we have bypassed the Gospel of John in this chapter. That is not for lack of evidence. On the contrary, John's Gospel preserves more numerous and explicit testimonies to Jesus' self-understanding than does the rest of the New Testament combined. We have held John until now so as not to prejudice the evidence of Jesus' self-consciousness outside John, for the Fourth Gospel shouts from the rooftops what elsewhere in the New Testament is whispered in the ear. It is now time, however, to consider what the Gospel of John says of Jesus' self-consciousness. What we find in John are clear explications of what is often only implied in the Synoptic Gospels.

At the heart of John's testimony to Jesus is Jesus' direct and unmediated relationship with the Father. Jesus comes from God (John 8:42), is the way to God (John 14:6-7), and is the eternal destiny of all his followers, whom he desires to be with him in heaven (John 17:24). Jesus' witness to the Father is without equal or rival; others who have gone before are thieves and robbers (John 10:8). Like Matthew 11:25-27 and

---

59. Stuhlmacher, *Jesus of Nazareth*, 33-35.

Luke 10:21-22, John speaks of Jesus' intimate and unshared knowledge of the Father, "as the Father knows me and I know the Father" (John 10:15). Knowing Jesus is knowing God (John 8:19), and eternal life is knowing God through Jesus: "And this is eternal life, that they may know you, the only true God, and Jesus Christ whom you have sent" (John 17:3).

In most religions the essential attribute of God is light. Jesus claims that essential attribute in the declaration, "I am the light of the world. Whoever follows me will never walk in darkness but will have the light of life" (John 8:12; 9:5). Like God, Jesus also claims eternality, "The Son remains forever" (8:35), for "before Abraham was, I am" (8:58). The implications of such statements were not lost on Jesus' opponents, who accused him of "making himself equal to God" (5:18).

The claims of Jesus were not an exercise in self-promotion, but rather the corroboration of the Scriptures that "testify on my behalf" (John 5:39), as the Father "who sent me testifies on my behalf" (8:19). In Judaism, God and Scripture were like the greater and lesser lights of creation (Genesis 1:16), beside which there was no third luminary. According to the Gospel of John, both testify to Jesus. From the unity of Jesus' being with God flows the integrity of his life. In John 5:19-23, works and attributes that are unique to God — the ability to raise the dead, the prerogative to judge humanity, the right to receive glory and honor — are ascribed to Jesus the Son. The work of Jesus is an extension of God and of the work of God, "for whatever the Father does, the Son does likewise" (John 5:19). God alone is qualified to judge the world, and yet that judgment is entrusted to Jesus (9:39). In the end, Jesus does not fail to accomplish the work the Father sent him to do, but on the cross exclaims, "It is finished" (19:30). The words of God are repeated and fulfilled in Jesus, as are the works of God.

Jesus is not a source of information about God, but the revelation of God: "when you have lifted up the Son of Man, then you will realize that I am he, and that I do nothing on my own, but I speak these things as the Father instructed me" (John 8:28). As both the word and work of God, Jesus defines true worship (4:23-24). He not only identifies the truth (18:37), he *is* the truth (14:6). This truth, for which the world thirsts, is an embodied truth as opposed to an abstract philosophical one. And the thirst is slaked in Jesus, "Let anyone who is thirsty come to me" (7:37). It is the will of Jesus to draw all people to God, and he does so, astoundingly, by drawing all people to himself (12:32).

Jesus is thus not only the identity of God, he is also the mission of God for the salvation of the world. Repeatedly in John we are reminded that the *Father sent the Son* for the salvation of the world (John 4:42; 5:34; 12:44-47). Apart from belief in Jesus people perish in their sins (8:24), because only Jesus is the shepherd who lays down his life for the sheep (10:15). As a consequence, the life that he shares with the Father is the same life he wills to give to the world: "I have come that they might have life, and have it abundantly" (10:10; 5:40; 17:2). As Jesus was raised from the dead, so too will he become the resurrection and life of those who believe in him (11:25-26).

This review of John's testimony to Jesus is far from exhaustive, but it is enough to demonstrate that it is impressive in boldness and exaltation. It is a more explicit witness to Jesus' filial oneness with God, but it is not a different witness from the Synoptic Gospels. In various ways the entire New Testament testifies that Jesus was uniquely empowered with divine *exousia*, and that his uniqueness is to be explained by his oneness *with* God.

The Particularity of Jesus' Relationship with God

To sum up, allow me to quote two modern critical scholars of unquestioned reputation on the question of Jesus' Messianic self-consciousness. The first is Raymond Brown:

> Did Jesus know that he had an identity which his followers later came to understand in terms of his being God? If he was God (and most Christians do agree on that), did *he* know who he was? I think the simplest answer to that is yes. Obviously there is no way of proving an affirmative answer because we do not have material describing all his life. Yet in the Gospel material given to us Jesus is always shown as be-

ing aware of a particular relationship with God that enables him to speak with awesome authority. There is never a scene in the Gospel portrait where he discovers something about himself that he did not know before. I realize that what I am saying runs against some popular views that would have Jesus discovering his identity at the baptism or some other time; but there is no evidence for such views. The baptismal scene is designed to tell the readers who Jesus is, not to tell him who he is.[60]

And secondly, this quotation from Martin Hengel, a preeminent scholar on the Jewish and Hellenistic backgrounds of the New Testament:

> Jesus' claim to authority goes far beyond anything that can be adduced as prophetic prototypes or parallels from the field of the Old Testament and from the New Testament period. [Jesus] remains in the last resort incommensurable, and so basically confounds every attempt to fit him into the categories suggested by the phenomenology or sociology of religion.[61]

The early church was not hasty in coming to a conclusion about the nature and work of Jesus of Nazareth. For the better part of three centuries it considered every conceivable category of religious phenomenology as a way of explaining the New Testament witness to Jesus. The fathers of the church were convinced that God was active in Jesus, but they were uncertain how. They correctly knew that the work of God is necessarily related to the being of God, and that both were present in Jesus. Was Jesus only apparently God, or like God, or part God, or half man and half God? If both divine and human natures were present in Jesus, how were they related? After centuries of consideration, and indeed almost reluctantly, the church concluded that to speak of Jesus in any

60. Raymond Brown, *Responses to 101 Questions on the Bible* (New York: Paulist Press, 1990), 99.

61. Martin Hengel, *The Charismatic Leader and His Followers* (New York: Crossroad, 1981), 68-69.

other way than as truly and fully God, and at the same time as truly and fully human, was to do injustice to the New Testament record — in spite of the logical problems that arose in doing so. Their conclusions summarize the evidence presented in this chapter, and answer the two questions that directed our inquiry: why Christianity exalts its founder above the founders of other religions; and whether that exaltation is true to Jesus' self-understanding. A panoply of evidence argues repeatedly and conclusively that Jesus understood himself to be "one being and substance with the Father," and that as such, he is rightly honored as God.

Taking Stock of the Argument

At this point in our study we are like trekkers standing on a hilltop. It may be helpful to survey the terrain we have covered so far, and what lies ahead. We began in Chapter 1 with the roots of naturalism in the Enlightenment, and showed how those roots influenced the quests for the historical Jesus that have continued to our day. Each of the three quests displays special accents. The First Quest was pursued along intensely rationalistic lines; the Second along the lines of form criticism (the theory that the church projected its agenda onto the picture of Jesus in the Gospels); and the Third along lines proposed by the social sciences. Despite their special accents, all three lines of thought follow naturalistic thinking, and are products of it. We followed this general survey by special consideration of the Jesus Seminar in Chapter 2, since it is the most publicized facet of the Third Quest. The purpose of the first two chapters was to set forth the state of modern Jesus studies, and to give readers an understanding of the methodologies that have resulted in such skepticism regarding the Jesus of the New Testament.

We then began to build a constructive response to this prevailing skepticism. In Chapter 3 we posed a foundational question, whether or not the New Testament, our source of information about Jesus, is a reliable historical document. We concluded that the New Testament satisfies to an unusually high degree the criteria of historical reliability, especially for an ancient document. Chapter 4 followed by arguing that the

New Testament does not, in fact, conform to the assumptions of naturalism that are projected on it. The first Christians, intensely committed to Jewish monotheism, had no reason to apply to Jesus of Nazareth categories that hitherto in Judaism had only been applied to God. Indeed, they had every reason not to. Nor can we imagine any reason for the disciples, who were responsible for transmitting the Jesus story, to paint such an unflattering picture of themselves — unless the picture were true. We noted that historical probability increases when the record does not serve the interests of those who preserved it. Modern skepticism has prodded us to dismiss historical and rational evidence that, on further consideration, seems ill-advised. An unbiased reading of the Gospels inclines us toward their historical reliability.

In the present chapter we shifted from the reliability of the New Testament to Jesus' own self-understanding. Our particular interest was whether the New Testament writers concocted (knowingly or not) a false picture of Jesus, or whether they were faithful to Jesus' own self-understanding. We peered into Jesus' self-understanding through various chinks in the record. Jesus was far from a typical first-century rabbi. In a plethora of ways — in word, deed, and bearing — he exuded a divine *exousia* or authority that impressed followers and opponents alike that he understood himself to speak and act for God, indeed *as* God. A considerable amount of information was amassed attesting to a trustworthy line of transmission from Jesus' self-understanding to the disciples, and from the disciples to the New Testament record of Jesus.

What have we gained? We have gained relief from a fear that the New Testament record is a fraud. Some doubts — like the fear of an unfaithful spouse, or that we are about to lose our jobs — can make us irrational. The brunt of the book so far has been to relieve us of crippling and besetting doubts. It is an enormous relief to see that the long shadow that naturalism has cast on the historical veracity of the Christian faith is cast not by flaws in the faith or in the record preserving it. The New Testament, as we have sought to demonstrate, withstands critical examination quite well — although we have noted points at which skeptical methodologies applied to it should be doubted. Our reasons for trusting the historical reliability of the New Testament look brighter than our reasons for complacent trust in the assumptions of naturalism. We are justified, if we choose, to reconsider — or perhaps consider for the first time — what the New Testament says about Jesus Christ with renewed confidence and intellectual credibility.

CHAPTER SIX

Jesus — the Savior of the World

The significance of Jesus Christ cannot be captured in a single title or image. No one formulation or template in the New Testament sums up the essence of Jesus. Christianity differs from many religions in this respect. Judaism summarizes its confession in the *Shema*, "Hear, O Israel: The LORD our God, the LORD is one" (Deuteronomy 6:4). Islam summarizes its faith in the *Shahadah:* "There is no God but Allah, and Muhammad is his prophet." Buddhists have the Four Noble Truths, and Sikhs the One True Name. The ability to distill a system of belief to a single thought or phrase is often seen as an indication of its substantiality — and as a harbinger of its success. Hence the proletarian mantra of communism, "From each according to his ability, to each according to his need"; or the slogan of Utilitarianism, "the greatest good for the greatest number." Christianity can, of course, reduce itself to a focal point in Jesus Christ, but it says many things about Jesus, some of which are quite subtle. These subtleties are troubling to some people. Intellectual subtleties appeal to us in some fields; that we can measure time in nanoseconds and study the intricacies of DNA are regarded as marvels of precision in physics and biology. But the same subtleties are regarded with suspicion in religion. Attempts to explain the Trinity or the relationship between predestination and free will are unpersuasive to most moderns. The debate over the relationship between the divine and human natures in Jesus is apt to strike many people today as proof that he was neither.

The purpose of this chapter will be to consider the distinct and multifarious ways in which the New Testament describes Jesus Christ, including some of their subtleties. We shall not only survey their fullness and comprehensiveness, however, but also consider why there are so many different witnesses to Jesus, and why no one of them succeeds in defining the essence of Christianity.

The New Testament refers to Jesus in searching and innovative ways. With regard to titles alone, Jesus is expressly called Teacher (or Rabbi), Prophet, High Priest, Servant of God, Messiah (or Christ), Son of David, Son of Man, Lord, Word, Savior, and Son of God. Each of these titles aims at identifying important characteristics of Jesus' nature and work. The last, Son of God, is the most comprehensive and important of all Christological titles. But even it, alone or combined with other titles, is incapable of a full and complete identification of Jesus.

The images and metaphors applied to Jesus abound in even greater multitude. Jesus is called the light, the way, the truth, the life, the new creation, the means of peace between humanity and God, a door, a gate, a root, a lion, a bridegroom, new wine, a rider on a white horse, the lamb of God, the head of the body or church, the new person, the true foundation, a high priest, a pure and royal garment, the last Adam, the reconciler, a schoolmaster, the author of salvation, the bread of life, living water, the true vine, the alpha and omega (the first and last letters of the Greek alphabet, respectively). And this is just a sampling. The early preachers, missionaries, and writers of the gospel ranged widely and imaginatively in search of word pictures, metaphors, and similes to give insight into the divine mystery present in Jesus. The New Testament witness to Jesus is like life forms in the tropics, teeming with evidence and examples, both explicit and implicit. No other individual in Scripture — not Abraham or Moses, not Elijah or David — claims a fraction of this interpretive enterprise, this hermeneutical passion. Why not a single rifle shot instead of the shotgun approach?

There is, of course, one other figure in Scripture whose names and titles, images and metaphors, word-pictures and similes rival those of Jesus. That figure is God. And therein, I think, lies the clue to the puzzle. The plethora of names and titles and images and metaphors that surround Jesus is evidence that, in attempting to elucidate the meaning of Jesus, the New Testament writers were facing the same challenge, and employing similar means, that their Jewish forebears did when they spoke of God.

New Creation in Christ

The earliest written witness to Jesus as savior comes from the apostle Paul, whose earliest letter dates from the late forties of the first century, no more than fifteen years after Jesus' crucifixion. "So if anyone is in Christ, there is a new creation: everything old has passed away; see, everything has become new!" (2 Corinthians 5:17). This celebrated Pauline text is actually the apostle's rendition of a text from the prophet Isaiah, "Do not remember the former things or consider the things of old. I am about to do a new thing; now it springs forth, do you not perceive it?" (43:18-19). In the passage alluded to by Paul, God is referred to in the most breathtaking exclamations: "I, I am the LORD, and besides me there is no savior" (43:11); "I am God, and also henceforth I am He . . . your Redeemer, the Holy One of Israel" (43:13-14); "I am the LORD, your Holy One, the Creator of Israel, your King" (43:15). This divine manifesto is the most unambiguous declaration of monotheism in the Old Testament. God is revealed not only as Israel's creator, but also as the only one capable of redeeming Israel — in this instance from Babylonian captivity. One is reminded of the policy of Rolls Royce: the only place in which a Rolls automobile can be repaired is in the factory where it was made. Similarly, the only one capable of redeeming Israel is Israel's maker. This sublime understanding of God was applied to Jesus by Paul, directly and without apology, within two decades of the crucifixion! To be "in Christ," avers Paul, is not simply to experience renewal and transformation, but to enter a new order of creation. The old world has passed away, and a new world stands open. In Jesus Christ, a person steps from the old world into the new world, from death to life, from corruption and decay to eternal salvation. Jesus Christ is likened to an act of divine creation, in which all things are new.

The idea of a second act of creation being effected in Jesus is reflected in a series of further New Testament passages. In Galatians 6:15, Paul writes, "for neither circumcision nor uncircumcision is anything; but a new creation is everything." In other words, the Torah practices and ethnic distinctions at the core of Judaism have been superseded not by greater practices or distinctions, but by a new creation: salvation by faith in Christ. In Ephesians 2:10 Paul speaks of the necessity of new creation in Christ as a prerequisite for living a moral life, "For we are what [God] has made us, created in Christ Jesus for good works." The Greek word for something that has been made, *poiēma*, occurs here and elsewhere in early Christian literature only in the sense of *divine* creation. The implication is that, prior to being created in Jesus Christ, persons exist in a state that is not divinely created or eternally destined. In a further passage, the bridging of the chasm of alienation between Gentiles and Jews in Jesus Christ is described by Paul as a new creation. God's purpose was to "create in himself one new humanity in place of the two, thus making peace, and reconcile both groups to God in one body through the cross" (Ephesians 2:15). The English translation of this passage is more ambiguous and less forceful than the original Greek, which indicates that the one who makes peace is Jesus Christ, not the renewed Gentile or Jew. In other words, the deepest and most chronic divisions of the world are reconciled by Jesus, not by human powers and resolutions. In two more passages believers are admonished to put on the new person of Christ much like they would put on a new set of clothes (Ephesians 4:24; Colossians 3:10). The clothing image signifies a personal transformation, a new human identity, a new creation. In the foregoing passages Paul speaks of the salvation of Jesus Christ in cosmic proportions. Being "in Christ," that is, living in a faith relationship with Jesus Christ, clothes one in a new personal identity, it creates the conditions for living a truly moral existence, and it reconciles the deepest divides in human existence and community. Being "in Christ" is nothing less than being crucified to the old world and being recreated in a new world (Galatians 6:14-15).

This new creation is merely the beginning of a host of additional images of Jesus as savior in Paul's letters. In 1 Corinthians 3:11 Paul adopts architectural terminology to speak of Jesus as savior: "For no one can lay any foundation other than the one that has been laid; that foundation is Jesus Christ." A foundation is the primary and essential part of a structure, upon which all subsequent stages of the structure are built. This statement not only asserts that Christ is the foundation of salvation; it asserts that apart from Christ there is no other foundation of salvation. In different terminology, in 2 Corinthians 11:3-4 Paul warns that anyone who proclaims another "Jesus" from the Jesus of the gospel is like the serpent who deceived Eve, luring her from life to death. This passage clearly implies that in Paul's day the historical Jesus was already being reimagined in all sorts of ways. That was perhaps inevitable; and as we saw in Chapters 1 and 2 of this book, such reimagining has continued with vigor and variety into our day. But Paul warns that these remodeled Jesuses are no longer able to save. They adulterate the saving integrity of the gospel, and they corrupt the minds of those who follow them. His message is similar in 1 Corinthians 15:1-2. Any "gospel" other than the gospel proclaimed by the church is vain and futile, not worthy of belief because it is not capable of salvation. In these texts written to the Corinthian church, Paul affirms that there is one foundation of salvation, one saving profile of Jesus, one true proclamation of the gospel. Those who deviate from this witness miss the mark of salvation.

Although early Christians did not succeed in distilling the gospel to a single phrase, the one that succeeds as well as any in capturing the essence of salvation is Romans 10:9-10: "If you confess with your lips that Jesus is Lord and believe in your heart that God raised him from the dead, you will be saved. For one believes with the heart and so is justified, and one confesses with the mouth and so is saved." Here we return to that oldest, most original and essential conviction of the church: "Jesus is Lord!" When that conviction becomes a public confession — remembering that the Jesus who is Lord is the Jesus who lived, died, and was raised by the power of God — then belief and proclamation combine to guarantee salvation.

This declaration finds an echo in a longer and equally absolute passage in Romans 3:9-20. Paul hammers home a half-dozen times that *no one* can achieve salvation on his or her own, for "all have sinned and fall short of the glory of God" (3:23). Paul then adds, ironically, that the very people condemned "are justified freely by [God's] grace through the redemption that came by Christ Jesus" (3:24). Paul must first demonstrate the impossibility of human righteousness as a basis for salvation in order then to declare the all-sufficiency of divine grace as the sole basis of salvation. It is important to recall who the recipients of this astounding pronouncement were. The collage of Old Testament texts assembled in Romans 3:10-18 addressed *Jews* — that is, people for whom rightness with God was understood in terms of moral righteousness. If a people distinguished by their concern for moral virtue could not rely on good works, then no one can; and if they need Jesus for salvation, then everyone does.

Jesus, Savior of Both Jews and Gentiles

Paul was not alone in emphasizing Christ's sole saving significance. Although Luke, to whom the books of Luke and Acts are both attributed, probably wrote slightly later than Paul, he anchors belief in Jesus as savior to the dawn of the apostolic era. The most notable example is the clarion affirmation of Peter and John that "There is salvation in no one else, for there is no other name under heaven given among mortals by which we must be saved" (Acts 4:12). The importance of this declaration cannot be appreciated without considering the context in which it was delivered. The setting is the apostles' defense before the Jewish Sanhedrin of their preaching in the name of Jesus. The Sanhedrin was the influential council of the Jews, dedicated to preserving the power and name of the Jewish faith in the face of Roman political, cultural, and military dominance in Palestine. Sensitive to issues of power and authority, the Sanhedrin was the zealous guardian of both the Jewish priesthood and temple. The Sanhedrin was an intimidating venue in which to argue that an upstart Galilean prophet, who had been executed by Rome at the instigation of the Sanhedrin itself, was the savior of the world. Before this powerful council Peter and John neither muzzled nor qualified their proclamation, however. They declared unambiguously ("Let it be known to all of you, and to all the people of Israel," 4:10) that although the Sanhedrin crucified Jesus, God raised him from the dead and established him, the one rejected by the authorities, as the capstone (4:10-11). The Greek words *kephalē gōnia* can mean either "cornerstone" or "capstone" (or perhaps "keystone"). It is a term of determinative connotation, meaning "first," "uppermost," or "end." The image comes from Psalm 118:22, and occurs in the New Testament only with reference to Jesus (Mark 12:10; Acts 4:11; 1 Peter 2:7). It includes the senses of both creation and consummation, singularity and indispensability.[1] The assertion that the power and authority of salvation was located neither in Judaism nor Rome, but unequivocally in Jesus, was a matter of the utmost conviction on the part of the apostles.

The importance of Acts 4:12 is further signified by the meaning of "no other *name*." In the ancient world, a name was not merely what someone was called, but rather the identification of the being or essence of its bearer. To the Jewish people, an idol could not properly have a "name," because it has no being to be represented by the name (Isaiah 44:9-21).[2] The "name" to which the apostles refer does not signify an event, but a *person*, in whom the authority and power of God was active for salvation. The saving activity of God was and is expressed in the name of Jesus Christ. The name of Jesus is thereby linked in the closest possible way to the name of God. "No other name" does not refer to a second name besides the name of God, but to the unity of God with Jesus Christ, signifying one name, one nature, one saving activity. The shared nature of God and Jesus is signaled in the most striking way by the custom of the early church to pray to God *in the name of Jesus*. When the apostles, as recorded by Luke, declared that "there is no other name under heaven given among mortals by which we must be saved," they meant that the name of Jesus Christ was the means through whom God's salvation is effected, and that apart from the name of Jesus Christ there is no salvation.[3]

1. *Theological Dictionary of the New Testament*, s.v. κεφαλὴ γωνίας.

2. See Owen Barfield, *Saving the Appearances. A Study in Idolatry* (London: Faber and Faber, 1957), 98.

3. See Adelheid Ruck-Schröder, *Der Name Gottes und der Name Jesus. Eine neutestamentliche Studie*, WMANT 80 (Neukirchen: Neukirchener, 1999), 259-72.

Luke is generally more sparing in his use of Christological titles than are the other New Testament writers. He nevertheless intended Jesus to be understood as God's unique saving mission in the world, as is evidenced by the infancy narrative at the beginning of his Gospel. In Simeon's speech in Luke 2:26-32, the baby Jesus is identified as the "Lord's Messiah" (v. 26) who has been sent as God's salvation (v. 30). Likewise, in Luke 1:67-79, Zechariah, prophesying in the Holy Spirit, celebrates John the Baptist as the forerunner of the *Lord* (v. 76). We see here another example of a title used exclusively of God in the Old Testament being applied without apology or equivocation to Jesus — indeed, to the infant Jesus — in the New Testament. In this child the God of Israel would bring redemption to the people, deliverance from their enemies, and knowledge of salvation. Hymns like Zechariah's can, of course, be found in the Old Testament, but there they refer solely to Yahweh. When such titles and language are transferred directly to Jesus, the conclusion is unavoidable: the salvation promised by God in the First Covenant was understood by the early church to be fulfilled by Jesus Christ in the Second Covenant.[4]

In Acts 4 and Luke 1, the evangelist Luke portrays Jesus as the expected savior promised to Israel. But this is not all. In the next chapter of this book we shall see that Luke portrays Jesus as the savior of the Gentile world as well. Luke 2 shows with undisguised irony that the savior of the world is not mighty Caesar Augustus, who presumes to "register all the world" (Luke 2:1), but rather the baby Jesus, lying in a feed trough. Luke leaves no doubt that Jesus of Nazareth is one and the same savior of both Jews and Gentiles.

4. In *Three Crucial Questions about Jesus* (Grand Rapids: Baker Books, 1994), 88-92, Murray J. Harris discusses thirteen Old Testament passages referring to Yahweh that are directly applied to Jesus by New Testament writers. They are Exodus 3:14 and John 8:58; Isaiah 44:6 and Revelation 1:17; Psalm 102:26-27 (LXX) and Hebrews 1:11-12; Isaiah 28:16 and Romans 9:33; 10:11; 1 Peter 2:6; Isaiah 8:12-13 and 1 Peter 3:14-15; Isaiah 45:23 and Philippians 2:10-11; Psalm 97:7 (LXX) and Hebrews 1:6; Psalm 102:25 and Hebrews 1:10; Joel 2:32 and Romans 10:12-13; Isaiah 40:3 and Matthew 3:3; Isaiah 8:14 and 1 Peter 2:8; Psalm 68:18 and Ephesians 4:8.

The Testimony of John

The Gospel and Epistles of John provide the supreme witness to Jesus as savior in the New Testament. The Fourth Evangelist gives Jesus the unequivocal title "savior of the world." God sent his Son into the world not to judge it, "but to save the world through him," says John 3:17. Again, "we have seen and do testify that the Father has sent his Son as the Savior of the world" (1 John 4:14). In the story of the woman at the well in John 4 the villagers of Samaria receive the witness of the woman and declare "we know that [Jesus] is truly the Savior of the world" (John 4:42). The source of their witness enhances its value. Samaritans were not Jesus' people; they were considered by Jews to be outsiders — unclean outsiders with whom "Jews do not share things in common" (John 4:9). Lesslie Newbigin rightly sees in this passage and others like it that it takes the world to teach Christians the meaning of Jesus as the savior of the world. "We cannot yet know what this truth means until the Lordship of Jesus has been manifested in the lives of all peoples and in all sectors of human living."[5] The confession of Jesus as savior *from* non-Jews means that Jesus is savior *of* non-Jews. "A Savior preached to Jews only might be a Savior available for Jews only, but a Savior preached to Samaritans was a Savior for non-Jews and therefore, by implication, a Savior for the world."[6]

The Greek word for "world," *kosmos*, in its original philosophical connotation, meant *totality*, the sum total of all things in the universe. The Hebrew equivalent of *kosmos* was the phrase "heaven and earth," by which the physical universe was signified. Cosmos, of course, also included the world of humanity.[7] It is striking that John should claim Jesus as savior of the world, because in the Fourth Gospel the *kosmos* is not thought of in a wholly favorable light. The world is often a place of darkness (John 1:5) and resistance to God (1:11), a place dominated by Satan

5. L. Newbigin, *Truth to Tell: The Gospel as Public Truth* (Grand Rapids: Eerdmans, 1991), 34-35.

6. F. F. Bruce, *Jesus: Lord and Savior* (Downers Grove: InterVarsity Press, 1986), 176.

7. R. Brown, *The Gospel According to John*, Anchor Bible Commentary (Garden City: Doubleday, 1966), I.508-9.

(14:30) and hostile to followers of Christ (17:14). The world would seem to be a place God would avoid, or even damn. The magnitude of God's love is demonstrated, however, by the fact that God sent his Son "not to condemn the world, but in order that the world might be saved through [Christ]" (3:17). In other words, God sent his Son not to save a good world, but to save a hostile world. When John declares that Jesus is the light of the world (8:12), or that he takes away the sins of the world (1:29), or is the savior of the world (4:42), John applies to the authority of Jesus the unlimited sphere of influence that can otherwise only be attributed to God. The world that God has made and superintends is the world that Jesus has saved.

Other terms and images reinforce Jesus' supremacy in John. Throughout John Jesus is likened to light, which, as we have noted before, is a universal metaphor for God. The two epochal discoveries in physics in the twentieth century — relativity theory and quantum mechanics — both revealed that light is the fundamental prerequisite of the universe. Too, modern physics reminds us how apt the metaphor of light is for God, for at the speed of light (186,000 miles per second) there is no longer time or space or separated events. Like God, light makes all things one. The biblical writers could not have known scientific facts like these, of course, but they accentuate the appropriateness of the metaphor of light as it is applied to Jesus by John. Jesus is the true light who has come into the world (John 1:9; 3:19), "the light of all people" (1:4). In one of John's signature "I am" sayings, Jesus says, "I am the light of the world" (8:12). To speak of Jesus as light is properly to speak of God, for "God is light, and in him there is no darkness at all" (1 John 1:5). John's equating of Jesus with God is elsewhere conveyed by the inseparability of Jesus and the Father. Whoever denies the Son cannot have the Father; and whoever confesses the Son has also the Father (1 John 2:22-23; 2 John 9). Jesus and the Father are one (John 10:30).

John's most prominent image for Jesus, however, is very simply that of life. A raft of references in John identify Jesus as both the source and essence of life.[8] In 1 John 1:1-4 Jesus is identified as the eternal life who ex-

---

8. John 3:35; 5:24-29; 6:37, 40, 47; 20:31; 2 John 9.

isted with the Father and who has been manifested to the world. References to Jesus as eternal life are epitomized in 1 John 5:11-12: "And this is the testimony: God has given us eternal life, and this life is in his Son. He who has the Son has life; he who does not have the Son of God does not have life." In the New Testament there are three Greek words for life: *bios, psychē,* and *zōē. Bios* refers to life in terms of years, accomplishments, wealth; it is life that can be counted and quantified. *Psychē* refers to life in terms of purpose, meaning, and volition. *Psychē* is often translated "soul," but its basic meaning is simply "person" or "personhood." These first two words for life refer to life in its quantitative and qualitative aspects, respectively. But the third term, *zōē,* is unique of God. In the New Testament, God is never said to have *bios* or *psychē,* but only *zōē. Zōē* is the life that characterizes God, and the life that God wills to impart to his people. All people participate in *bios* and *psychē* simply by virtue of being human. *Bios* and *psychē* are, to be sure, gifts of God in creation, which are inherent in all human life. But the third kind of life is not inherent to human life; not all people have it, and those who do have it receive it only as a gift of God through Jesus Christ. *Zōē* is life whose source is God, quintessential life, God-intended existence. The *zōē* of God is present in the world in the person of Jesus Christ, and only those who receive Jesus as God's self-manifestation receive *zōē,* the life of God.[9]

Zōē is the word used by John to describe the life brought by Jesus. John frequently couples *zōē* with the word "eternal," another attribute unique to God. The Greek word for "eternal," *aiōnios,* means "without end or limits," expressing positively and explicitly that the true nature of God is communicated in Jesus Christ, and that those who receive Jesus receive the essence of God. These and other texts remind us that John's Gospel "confronts its hearers time and again not with a multiplicity of truths taught by a wise man, but with what it understands to be the one Truth, the compelling, liberating power of the loving Word incarnate."[10]

---

9. See J. R. Edwards, "Life in Three Dimensions," *Touchstone* 6/3 (1993): 17-21.

10. Harold Attridge, "Genre Bending in the Fourth Gospel," *Journal of Biblical Literature* 121/1 (2002): 19.

The Cosmic Reach of the Savior's Arm

The universality of salvation in John is echoed throughout the New Testament in an array of revealing imagery. There is no other access to the sheepfold except through Jesus "the door" (John 10:1, 7). Jesus is the Lamb of God slain from the foundation of the world (Revelation 13:8), whose death takes away the sins of the world (John 1:29; Revelation 5:12). A crowd without number from every nation and tribe and people and tongue stands "before the Lamb" singing, "Salvation belongs to our God who is seated on the throne, and to the Lamb" (Revelation 7:9-10). This passage indicates that in the liturgy and practice of the early church the resurrected and enthroned Jesus Christ was, like God, the object of prayer and worship. But he was not worshiped as a second, or second-order, God. In a manner that would not be defined until the Council of Nicea in A.D. 325, the early church understood Jesus to be of the same essence of God, and of the same saving authority in the *kosmos*.[11] The resurrected Jesus declares that the one who conquers, that is, the one who stands faithfully in Christ, will share the throne of God with him in eternal glory (Revelation 3:21). Revelation 5 depicts Jesus in three diverse metaphors as the lion of Judah, the root of David, and the slain lamb. The lamb in the last image is alone worthy to open the Book of Life, and is acknowledged by "every creature in heaven and on earth and under the earth" (5:13). Jesus is the Rider of the White Horse who, as "King of Kings and Lord of Lords," smites the nations and rules them with an iron scepter, like the divinely installed king of Psalm 2 (Revelation 19:14-16). In Corinthians Paul reminds Gentile believers that they are no longer yoked to many gods, but like a chaste virgin to one man, Christ (2 Corinthians 11:2). Similarly, in the allegory of Abraham's two sons in Galatians, Paul stresses that the purpose of God does not result in many covenants and heirs, but in the one free heir, Jesus Christ (Galatians 4:21-31). Again in Galatians, Paul speaks of Jesus Christ as the clothing of salvation for all people: "You are all sons of God through faith in Jesus Christ, for all of

---

11. On New Testament texts in which Jesus Christ is either prayed to or worshipped, see Harris, *Three Crucial Questions about Jesus*, 72-76.

you who were baptized into Christ have been clothed with Christ. There is neither Jew nor Greek, slave nor free, male nor female, for you are all one in Christ Jesus" (Galatians 3:26-28).

This collage of images expresses the universal scope and uncompromising character of redemption in Jesus Christ. These images are accompanied by a great number of texts in the New Testament that define and interpret their meaning. Paul reminds readers that the new creation in Jesus Christ is a personal and individual experience of a larger reality of God's reconciliation of the world to himself through Christ. "All this is from God, who reconciled us to himself through Christ, and has given us the ministry of reconciliation" (2 Corinthians 5:18-20). John's Gospel assures readers that all who received Jesus Christ as God's Word were given power "to become children of God" (John 1:12). This announcement comes not as a final conclusion, but as a presupposition of the plan of salvation in the prologue to John's Gospel. In properly speaking of Jesus' role as savior, the New Testament repeatedly resorts to cosmic imagery. The whole world labors under the power of the evil one, but the Son of God has come to reveal light and truth within darkness (1 John 5:19-20). Faith that Jesus is the Son of God "is the victory that conquers the world" (1 John 5:4-5).

The salvation brought by Jesus Christ is not limited to the world as a place of human habitation, or even the sum total of human experience. The salvation of Jesus extends to the *kosmos*, both the physical universe that can be known by science, and the unseen world that extends beyond the empirical universe. At the end of Romans 8 Paul is transported on a current of ecstasy, confident that God's love in Jesus Christ surpasses everything that can be known: "For I am convinced that neither death, nor life, neither angels, nor rulers, nor things present, nor things to come, nor powers, nor height, nor depth, nor anything else in all creation, will be able to separate us from the love of God in Christ Jesus our Lord" (8:37-39). The world over which Jesus Christ rules includes all spiritual realities as well. "We know," wrote the apostle Paul, "that 'no idol in the world really exists,' and that 'there is no God but one.' Indeed, even though there may be so-called gods in heaven or on earth — as in fact there are many gods and many lords — yet for us there is one God, the

Father, from whom are all things and for whom we exist, and one Lord, Jesus Christ, through whom are all things and through whom we exist" (1 Corinthians 8:4-6).[12] Finally, in addition to supremacy over spatial realities, and seen and unseen powers, Jesus' authority extends over time itself. At the end of time Jesus Christ will destroy "every ruler and every authority and power"; he will subdue every enemy and vanquish death itself; and everything except for God will be subjected to God, after which Jesus Christ will relinquish the kingdom to God the Father (1 Corinthians 15:23-28).

The Grand Surprise

This chapter has produced a wealth of imagery and information about Jesus as savior, but at first glance it may look like the disparate dabs and spots of a pointillist painting. Only when we step back does the mass cease to be dabs of paint and become a cohesive picture of a specific subject. The pattern that emerges is one we have already noted: the early church and New Testament authors inevitably found themselves speaking of Jesus with the same words, symbols, images, statements, and texts by which their Jewish forebears spoke of God. The diverse witness to Jesus in the New Testament is not, therefore, a disparate and disconnected witness after all. It is governed by a single economy, the same saving economy, in fact, that governs its understanding of God. The saving activity of Jesus Christ is the expression of the Saving One who, through the prophet Isaiah, declared, "I, I am the LORD, and besides me there is no savior" (43:11).

12. N. T. Wright notes the extraordinary effect of Paul's placement of Jesus as Lord in a passage in which we should expect Yahweh as Lord. "Paul has placed Jesus within an explicit statement of the doctrine that Israel's God is the one and only God, the creator of the world. The Shema was already, at this stage of Judaism, in widespread use as the Jewish daily prayer. Paul has redefined it christologically, producing what we can only call a sort of christological monotheism" ("Monotheism, Christology and Ethics: 1 Corinthians 8," in *The Climax of the Covenant: Christ and the Law in Pauline Theology* (Edinburgh: T&T Clark, 1991), 129 (emphasis in original).

Nevertheless, in trying to say it all, we have perhaps left unsaid the most important thing of all. It is true that the New Testament stands in wonderment at the achievement of Jesus Christ. The volume and variety of images and metaphors and formulations that we have surveyed in this chapter is sufficient testimony to that fact. Nevertheless, it was not simply Jesus' divine attributes that caused the early church to fall to its knees at his name. The first Christians were Jews, and they were already in the habit of recounting Yahweh's universal glory, and worshiping accordingly (see, for example, Psalm 148). That they should recognize in Jesus similar glory, and worship him accordingly, was, to be sure, astounding. But in so doing they were not doing something inherently different from what they had done before. They were rather extending to Jesus something they already had done with respect to God.

What *was* unique in the New Testament drama of salvation was not that Jesus was God, but that in Jesus of Nazareth, God had become a human being. It was the *humbleness* of God — God's ability to stoop to the ground, literally, and not the exaltation of God, that was and is the crowning glory of the Christian gospel. That God should superintend infinity — whether in interstellar space or in the complexity of DNA — we expect. We marvel that this is the case, but this, after all, belongs to the definition of "God." But that God should become small and take on the form of a created being — and not even the greatest of them — we do not expect. Becoming a human being does *not* belong to the definition of God. No other religion besides Christianity has ever considered becoming human essential to its confession of God. But it is essential in the New Testament and Christianity. In Christianity, God is identified as the God of *the human one*, "the God and Father of our Lord Jesus Christ" (2 Corinthians 1:3; Ephesians 1:3; 1 Peter 1:3). We cannot fathom why, but there is a "gravitational pull" of God toward humanity. And when God becomes a human being, that humanity is accentuated. Thus the divine characteristics of Jesus are often muted in order to give full weight to his human solidarity.

This helps answer the question with which we began this chapter, namely, why the New Testament does not say "Jesus is God" as clearly or as often as we suppose it should: why, if Jesus is God, he is so *incognito*?

The answer seems to be that his divinity is simply assumed, whereas his humanity is being demonstrated. An illustration here may help. Suppose that someone is auditioning for a part, say the role of Carmen in Bizet's opera. Suppose, further, that the woman who tries out for the part is a recognized vocalist, but not a recognized actress. In order to land the role, she will need to prove her acting abilities, not her singing abilities. The latter are assumed, but the former need to be demonstrated. She may in fact sing very little in the audition, if at all. But it would be a mistake to deduce from this that she cannot sing. What is assumed, in other words, will normally occupy only a fraction of the space of what needs to be demonstrated.

Something similar is at work in the New Testament's presentation of Jesus. As we saw in the last chapter, Jesus' presumption to divine authority is the *assumption* that makes the New Testament record understandable. The Incarnation means that henceforth knowledge of God is communicated through a human being, "from a human perspective," literally. We know and love God not by denying or escaping humanity, but by receiving God's human appearance in Jesus Christ. The divine classroom is not in heaven but on earth. The Gospel of John picked up a faint foreshadowing of the human enfleshment of God, the Incarnation, and described how a human became the window of God: "The Word became flesh and lived among us" (John 1:14). The Greek word for "lived" in this passage is, literally, "tent," the same word the Old Testament used of the tent of meeting in the wilderness. In Jesus, God "pitches a tent among us." That is the great surprise of the gospel. It is also the great scandal. God becomes low and small; God chooses in Jesus Christ to be rejected and to suffer and die. It is not in heavenly splendor, but in one like us that we see the saving heart of God.[13]

13. This idea is paraphrased from Eduard Schweizer, *Das Evangelium nach Markus* (Göttingen: Vandenhoeck & Ruprecht, 1968), 98.

CHAPTER SEVEN

Can the Gospel Compete
in a Pluralistic World?

We are being told today that the church is facing a radically new situation that it has not faced before, and that it consequently needs a radically new formulation of the gospel. The impetus behind this admonition is the idea that we are now living in a "global village" — a multiethnic, multicultural, multifaith world in which it seems simply untenable and perhaps even immoral to believe in one absolute truth against which everything else is to be measured and judged. This admonition was frequently heard in America in the immediate aftermath of the terrorist attacks of September 11, 2001.

Of course, the hidden assumption in this admonition is that the gospel arose in the insular world of Judaism in an earlier age of intellectual naïveté, and what was suitable in a simpler age is no longer so in a complex, pluralistic age such as ours. But to believe this is to assume that the complexity and interdependence of the modern world are unique in history. The world of the New Testament, by contrast, together with its industries and technologies, is imagined to be a more or less uniform world order under one religion, one military standard, one currency, one Caesar, and indeed one city, Rome. It seems mythically simple in comparison with the modern world.

This popular idea provides a good point of departure for the issue I wish to address in this chapter. Did the gospel, in fact, arise in a simpler and more naïve world than ours? If it did, then the critics may be right in doubting its significance for our day. But if it did not — as I believe to be the case — then we have much to learn from those who first proclaimed the gospel.

The Gospel in a Disintegrating World

Contrary to common assumption, earliest Christianity was not a bucolic movement "beside the Syrian sea," to quote the American poet and hymnist John Greenleaf Whittier.[1] It was, in fact, an urban one. Three New Testament images are useful in understanding the interplay of the emerging gospel with the world. One is Jesus sitting on the Mount of Olives opposite the temple in Jerusalem; another is the apostle Paul debating with Greek philosophers beneath the Acropolis in Athens; a third is the same apostle appealing to Caesar in Rome. All three images are historical. All three show a gospel not holed up in the hinterlands but vigorously engaging the power centers of the Jewish, Greek, and Roman worlds.

What kind of worlds were they? They were certainly not monochromatic. Judaism, the womb from which the gospel was born, was itself a miscellany of religious parties and rivalries, including Pharisees, Sadducees, Herodians, Essenes, Zealots and Sicarii. Each of these groups was distinguished by its unique political and religious beliefs. Over and among them was the Roman occupation, ominously present in soldiers and tax collectors, with its perennially tenuous relationship with the Jewish populace. Its main contact with the Jewish people was through a coalition government, the Sanhedrin, which consisted of the families of the chief priests, the elders of the nation (both Sadducees and Pharisees), and scribal consultants. The vast majority of the populace, however, were the poor, the "people of the land," who felt only limited allegiance to the above parties and sects. They were tenant workers for foreign landowners, nominal Jews attempting in various ways and degrees to satisfy requirements of rival religious factions, and subjects of the foreign occupation.

1. "Dear Lord and Father of Mankind."

Yet Palestine would have seemed positively cozy compared to complex urban centers like Antioch in Syria and Alexandria in Egypt, both of which had sizeable Jewish populations. Religion in these cities was a collage of mystery cults, personality cults, vestigial forms of classical Greek philosophy, polytheism, imperial cults, and nascent forms of Gnosticism and Neo-Platonism. The classical Greek and Roman emphasis on reason and social order had fractured into a blurry patchwork of camps, sects, and parties, leaving individuals personally isolated, privatized, and anxious.[2] The first century was neither a safe nor a sane world to navigate.

Among this welter of powers and principalities the first Christians proclaimed the gospel, and in so doing they defined its relationship to them. Lesslie Newbigin rightly says,

> The world into which the first Christians carried the gospel was a religiously plural world and — as the letters of Paul show — in that world of many lords and many gods, Christians had to work out what it means that in fact Jesus alone is Lord. The first three centuries of church history were a time of intense life-and-death struggle against the seductive power of syncretism.[3]

They defined its relationship, in fact, in a way that echoes modern language theory. One of the conclusions of modern linguistics is that the value of a claim is strengthened when its opposite can be denied. In fact, to assert something whose opposite cannot be denied is to say something without meaning. A claim to truth is substantiated only when a competing claim can be refuted. The statement, "Beets are red," would be essentially meaningless if red were the color of all vegetables. It is a meaningful statement, however, because it differentiates beets from orange carrots and green spinach. Truth, in other words, is specific; it does not include all possibilities, but necessarily excludes opposite assertions. The first Christians demonstrated the truth of this axiom long be-

---

2. See Eduard Schweizer, "Das hellenistische Weltbild als Produkt der Weltangst," in *Neotestamentica: Deutsche und englische Aufsätze 1951-1963* (Zürich: Zwingli Verlag, 1963), 15-28.

3. *The Gospel in a Pluralist Society* (Grand Rapids: Eerdmans, 1992), 157.

fore modern language theory. Not only in later creeds and confessions, but in the New Testament itself, the gospel is proclaimed as both an affirmation and denial. That is to say, Jesus is affirmed for who he is, and his identity is then defined in terms of its relationship to competing cultural truth claims. The three most powerful truth claims in his day were the Jewish Torah, Roman emperor worship, and Hellenistic mystery religions. The supremacy of the gospel was declared to all three.

Not by Law

The first Christians defined Jesus as savior over against Torah, which Jews held to be the once-for-all exclusive self-revelation of God. The Hebrew word *torah* derives from a verb describing the path of an arrow in flight. It is usually translated "law," but it more accurately means "teaching" or "instruction" in pursuit of a true objective. The authoritative nature of Torah was believed to derive from its divine origin. Indeed, the Babylonian Talmud, the comprehensive summation of Jewish law, warns that if the divine origin of even one verse is disputed, the whole Word of God is despised.[4] Torah was believed to be one of seven things created by God before the creation of the world.[5] To add or delete a letter in copying it is said to be the spiritual equivalent of destroying a world.[6] The sanctity of Torah resulted in its unsurpassed worthiness as an object of study: "Dearer to me is a day when you sit and study the Torah than the thousand burnt offerings which thy son Solomon will one day offer me on the altar," said God to David, according to the Talmud.[7] Torah held the pole position in Jewish life. It possessed the power to order and transform the whole of Jewish life, to bring it into conformity with God's revealed will, and to separate Jews from the rest of the world.[8]

4. *b. Sanh.* 99a.
5. *b. Pes.* 54a.
6. *b. Sot.* 20a.
7. *b. Shab.* 30a.
8. On the role of Torah in Judaism, see *Theological Dictionary of the New Testament,* s.v. *nomos;* E. Schürer, *The History of the Jewish People in the Age of Jesus Christ,* rev. and ed.

In many ways, Jesus affirmed Torah. He wore clothing prescribed by Torah (Matthew 9:20; 14:36), he observed Sabbath and attended synagogue (Mark 1:21), and by his own admission he understood his mission as one to fulfill Torah, not overthrow it (Matthew 5:17-19). Jesus was an observant Jew.

He was not defined by the rabbinic guild, however. He rejected the oral interpretation of the rabbis, "the tradition of the elders" (Mark 7:1-23; 10:1-12), as a distortion of the intent of Torah. Nor did he grant to Torah a decisive role as mediator between humanity and God, or as a dividing line between clean (Jews) and unclean humanity (Gentiles). All scholars agree that Jesus regularly associated with people who were outside the circle of ritual purity in Judaism, actually ascribing to them a righteousness that superseded that of Torah: "Truly I tell you, the tax collectors and the prostitutes are going into the kingdom of God ahead of you," he announced to the Jewish authorities (Matthew 21:31; elsewhere Mark 2:13-17; Luke 15; 18:14).

The Gospel writers indicate that in Jesus a new era was at hand that relegated Torah to secondary status. We saw in Chapter 5 how Jesus' self-understanding resulted in an authority *(exousia)* that surpassed that of Moses, the lawgiver. "The law and the prophets were in effect until John came; since then the good news of the kingdom of God is proclaimed, and everyone tries to enter it by force" (Luke 16:16//Matthew 11:13). We also saw in Chapter 5, when we looked at his conversation with the rich man (Mark 10:17-31), that Jesus understood his own person, not Torah, to be the means of eternal life:

> What determines one's relation to God is no longer the Law and one's relation to it. This decisive position is now occupied by the Word of Jesus, indeed, by Jesus Himself. One finds one's relation to God in the relation to Jesus, to the lordship of God which has invaded the world in [Jesus].[9]

G. Vermes, F. Millar, M. Black (Edinburgh: T&T Clark, 1979), 2.464-87; E. P. Sanders, *Judaism: Practice and Belief 3 BCE–66 CE* (Philadelphia: Trinity Press International, 1992), 190-240.

9. *Theological Dictionary of the New Testament*, s.v. *nomos*.

This understanding was given fuller expression by the apostle Paul, a Jewish Pharisee converted to the Way by a vision of the resurrected Christ (Acts 9:1-21). Like Jesus, Paul also acknowledged the importance of Torah as a revelation of God's will (Romans 7:14). In fact, not to submit to Torah was for Jews to show hostility to God (Romans 8:7). Nevertheless, the gospel was no mere counterpart or epilogue to Torah. Throughout his letters Paul asserts that Jesus Christ fulfills Torah and relegates it to a secondary role. Torah was not sufficient for salvation. It was neither able to forgive sins, nor to make one right with God (Acts 13:38). "We know that a person is justified not by the works of the law but through faith in Jesus Christ" (Galatians 2:16). "But now apart from law, the righteousness of God has been disclosed, and is attested by the law and the prophets, the righteousness of God through faith in Jesus Christ for all who believe" (Romans 3:21). "For we hold that a person is justified by faith apart from works prescribed by the law" (Romans 3:28).[10] Paul declared a salvation through faith in Jesus Christ, independent of Torah.

For Paul, the significance of the cross was its universality: nothing, Torah included, could rival it as a saving possibility, "for if justification comes through the law, then Christ died for nothing" (Galatians 2:21; also Romans 7:1ff.; 8:1ff.). With the advent of Christ, and especially in light of the cross of Christ, the measure of one's relationship with God or other human beings could no longer be Torah. Neither Jew nor Gentile could be justified on the basis of law or human merit, for all had sinned (Romans 3:23) and all must rely on faith in Christ alone for salvation (Romans 3:29-30). Henceforth in Christ "there is no longer Jew or Greek, there is no longer slave or free, there is no longer male and female; for all of you are one in Christ Jesus" (Galatians 3:28). The law, according to Paul, was like a Greek slave who went from house to house to take young boys to their schoolmaster (Galatians 3:24). Today we would say that the law was like a school bus. The bus takes children to school, but it is at school, not on the bus, where their education takes place. So Torah led the Jewish people to Christ, but in the end it could not be considered a substitute for him.

10. Further, see Romans 4:5; 9:30–10:4; Galatians 3:2; 3:24; Ephesians 2:8-9; Philippians 3:9.

We noted earlier that the world in which the gospel was first proclaimed was more complex than is often thought. It was also more hazardous, for in locating salvation in Jesus rather than in Torah the first Christians risked excommunication from the Jewish community. The statement of Jesus recorded in Luke's litany of blessings and woes, "Blessed are you when people hate you, and when they exclude you, revile you, and defame you" (Luke 6:22) probably refers to expulsion from the synagogue, a looming peril whenever Jewish followers of Jesus confessed their allegiance to him. Likewise, three caustic references in the Gospel of John speak of believers in Jesus suffering "expulsion from the synagogue" (John 9:22; 12:42; 16:2). The Greek word John uses, *aposynagogos,* is unknown in Greek literature outside the New Testament. It appears to have been coined with special reference to the fate of early Jewish Christians who confessed Jesus.

First-century Judaism practiced discipline in varying degrees. The lightest penalty was normally a thirty-day suspension from the congregation; it could be applied for such diverse infractions as pronouncing the divine name, treating teachers of Torah disrespectfully, or spurning certain decrees of Torah. A severer sixty-day penalty entailed unlimited exclusion from the synagogue, including economic, educational, and social exclusion. Josephus testifies to the wretched conditions of those convicted of crimes warranting this penalty; cut off from their communities, many could even starve to death.[11] The purpose of these two forms of discipline was chastisement and the eventual restoration of wrongdoers to fellowship.

John's *aposynagogos* refers to a curse or ban, however, rather than to a disciplinary measure. "Whoever goes round defaming the Many," according to the Dead Sea Scrolls, "shall be expelled from their midst and will never return. And whoever complains against the foundation of the Community shall be expelled and will not return."[12] Severer still is the Talmud:

---

11. "Those who are convicted of serious crimes [the Essenes] expel from the order; and the ejected individual often comes to a most miserable end. For, being banned by their oaths and usages, he is not at liberty to partake of other men's food, and so falls to eating grass and wastes away and dies of starvation" (*Wars of the Jews* 2.143).

12. 1QS 7:16-17.

Heretics and apostates and traitors and free-spirits and rejecters of Torah and those who leave the ways of the community and those who deny the resurrection of the dead, and whoever sins and induces others to sin. . . . Hell is bolted behind them and they will be eternally punished in it for all generations.[13]

The Talmud was not completed until four centuries after the New Testament, but already by A.D. 90 the cursing of Nazarenes (that is, Christians) had become a regular part of synagogue worship and prayer.[14] A.D. 90 is close to the probable date when the Gospel of John was composed. Exclusion from one's people — especially a people as close-knit as the Jewish people — was then as now a high price to pay for one's commitments. Early Jewish Christians certainly did not want to part ways from Judaism. We may imagine that many of them were unwilling to pay the price; those who did can only have done so on the most resolute convictions. Their willingness to sever relationships with the communities in which they were born and raised testifies to their steadfast adherence to Jesus, not Torah, as their eternal hope.[15]

Not by Caesar

When the gospel overflowed the banks of Judaism and began to trickle into the Roman world it encountered another authority. Beginning with Julius (100-44 B.C.) and Augustus Caesar (63 B.C.–A.D. 14), the idea of divinized Roman rulers blossomed into an imperial cult. In its early phase, the cult was largely one of emperor veneration. But beginning with Nero

---

13. *Sanh.* 13.5. Quoted from H. L. Strack and P. Billerbeck, *Kommentar zum Neuen Testament aus Talmud und Midrasch,* 6 vols. (Munich, 1922-1961), 3.230.

14. Justin, *Dialogue with Trypho* 16; Epiphanius, *Panarion* 29.9.

15. On excommunication in first-century Judaism, see Strack and Billerbeck, *Kommentar,* 293-333; *Theological Dictionary of the New Testament,* s.v. *aposynagogos;* Schürer, *The History of the Jewish People;* and K. L. Carroll, "The Fourth Gospel and the Exclusion of Christians from the Synagogues," *Bulletin of the John Rylands Library* 40 (1957/58): 19-32.

(emperor A.D. 54-68), and certainly by the time of Domitian (emperor A.D. 81-96), the cult had blossomed into full-fledged emperor worship.

Julius Caesar, the first emperor following the collapse of the Roman Republic, was also the first to be "called a god because of his deeds"; the title was given to him because of his successful subjugation of Britain.[16] Before becoming dictator, Caesar sought and procured the honor of Pontifex Maximus, the highest religious office of the Roman state. His desire for the office indicates his intention of consolidating total power — religious, political, and military — in his person. In the spring of 45 B.C., a year before his assassination, Caesar took the titles of *imperator* and *liberator*, had a temple built in his honor, and at festivals wore the laurel crown of the god Jupiter (which conveniently disguised his baldness). A statue of himself bearing the inscription, "To the undefeated god," was placed in the temple of Quirinus and borne in procession during the four-yearly games.[17] A public monument unearthed in Ephesus hailing Caesar as "the manifest God of Mars and Venus" indicates that his accolades were not limited to Rome.[18]

Caesar was succeeded by his nephew Octavian, who adopted the name Augustus, "majestic" or "holy one." According to legend, Augustus was the son of Apollo, who impregnated Caesar's mother by means of a divine serpent.[19] A half-century before the birth of Jesus, the Roman poet Virgil gave mythical expression to Augustus as the divine child of Jupiter who, as God, would bring peace to the world, govern it with justice and power, vanquish evil, and usher in a golden age.[20] The eastern parts of the Empire, in particular, saw in Augustus the fulfillment of this sublime prophecy. Inscriptions preserved from a number of eastern cities laud him as "God," "son of God," "noble Benefactor," and (like nearly all emperors in the first century A.D.) "Savior of the World."

16. Diodorus of Sicily, 5.21.2.

17. For an overview of Julius Caesar and the emperor cult, see C. Meier, *Caesar*, trans. D. McLintock (London: Fontana Press, 1996), 458-74.

18. Cited from E. Lohmeyer, *Christuskult und Kaiserkult* (Tübingen: Mohr/Siebeck, 1919), 9.

19. Suetonius, *Lives of the Caesars* 2.94.4.

20. *Fourth Eclogue.*

The frontier between heaven and earth was seen as more fluid then than now, but these titles still seem to have been understood, for the most part, as grandiose acclaim for economic and political accomplishments.[21] It was the custom in the Greco-Roman world, in fact, to honor extraordinary individuals with divine or semi-divine names. The successors of Augustus, Tiberius (emperor 14-37) and Claudius (emperor 41-54), as a rule declined divine titles or relegated them to flattery.[22] The only emperor before Nero who put great stock in them was Caligula (emperor 37-41), whose name means "Little Boots" (which he acquired from the boots he wore as a boy in the military camp of Germanicus). There was nothing diminutive about Caligula's self-image, however. He attempted to erect a statue of himself to be worshipped in the one place that had always been exempt from the emperor cult — the temple in Jerusalem.[23] To the immense relief of the Jewish people, however, his assassination four years into his reign put an end to his megalomania. With the brief and abortive exception of Caligula, the flamboyant titles of the early emperors, although meant to be taken seriously, were generally understood as honorific rather than ontological, and they were not mandated of the population.

This changed when Nero became emperor (54-68). The eastern provinces of the Empire had long entertained the cult of the divine person — those extraordinary poets, philosophers, miracle workers, heroes, warriors, and rulers who were believed to have been promoted to the rank of

21. See, for example, the inscription from Halicarnassus that is preserved in the British Museum: "The eternal and immortal nature of all things graciously granted the wonderfully good Caesar August to perform good deeds in abundance to men in order that they might enjoy prosperity of life. He is the father of his divine homeland Rome, inherited from his father Zeus, and a savior of the common folk. His foresight not only fulfilled the entreaties of all people, but surpassed them, making peace for land and sea, while cities bloom with order, harmony, and good seasons; the productivity of all things is good and at its prime, there are fond hopes for the future and good will during the present which fills all men, so that they ought to bear pleasing sacrifices and hymns. . . ." Cited from H. Klienknecht, *Pantheion: Religiöse Texte des Griechentums* (Tübingen: Mohr, 1959), 40.

22. Tacitus, *Annals* 4.37-38.

23. Josephus, *War of the Jews* 2.184-203.

deity. Nero drank deeply of this heady wine. He was the first emperor to be called a god on Roman coinage ("the new Helios"), and the first since Julius Caesar to allow a statue of himself to be erected in the temple of Mars, thereby associating himself with an existing Roman god.[24] In 67, the year before he committed suicide, Nero was called "lord of the whole world" in Boeotia,[25] and "master" and "god" by the king of Armenia.[26] We do not know for certain that Nero required his subjects to worship him, but it is possible that he did (at least in Rome), for in Revelation 13:18, the number of the monster (666) has the same numerical equivalent as the Greek spelling of his name *Neron Kaisar* (when transliterated into Hebrew script). This may suggest that Nero exacted worship of himself in the 60s of the first century. Nero's religious greed may also have had something to do with the Jewish revolt in Palestine in A.D. 66, at the height of his religious megalomania. At any rate, with Nero the emperor cult shifted from an official formality to an intensely personal identification. The quintessential totalitarian ruler, Nero saw the ideals of the state embodied in himself, and the state as an absolute extension of himself.

The first emperor to mandate worship of himself throughout the Empire was Domitian (emperor 81-98), who issued letters referring to himself as "Master and God."[27] Severe punishments were meted out for those who declined. The book of Revelation was composed during the reign of Domitian and describes such punishments, including death (Revelation 6:9; 13:15).[28] Following Domitian, all Roman emperors promoted the emperor cult in earnest. Divine nomenclature reached its climax with Hadrian (emperor 117-138), under whom the Roman Empire reached its greatest geographical extent.

---

24. Tacitus, *Annals* 13.8.1.

25. Cited in A. Deissmann, *Light from the Ancient East*, trans. L. R. M. Strachan (Grand Rapids: Baker Book House, 1978), 354.

26. Dio Cassius, *Roman History* 63.14.

27. Suetonius, *Lives of the Caesars*, 8.13.2.

28. According to Revelation 17:9-11, the seven kings preceding "the beast" would be (1) Augustus, (2) Tiberius, (3) Caligula, (4) Claudius, (5) Nero (omitting the brief reigns of Otho, Galba, Vitellius), (6) Vespasian, and (7) Titus, who was succeeded by (8) Domitian.

Jews were fortunately excluded from observing Roman religion and emperor worship because their adamant loyalty to Torah and monotheism was well known. Christians, who were counted as Jews, initially benefited from this exemption. But when church and synagogue parted ways near the end of the first century, Christians forfeited their immunity. From then on they were treated like any non-Jews who failed to confess Caesar as Lord. The consequences could be serious. In a famous letter to the Emperor Trajan in 112, Pliny the Younger wrote that his policy was to give Christians three chances to renounce their faith, but "if they persist I sentence them to death."[29] The martyrdom of Polycarp, bishop of Symrna, under Hadrian's successor Antoninus Pius (emperor 138-161), was a sober reminder well into the second century that Christians who refused to hail the emperor as "Lord Caesar" were courting death. In Polycarp's case, it was death by burning at the stake.[30]

When the emperor cult metastasized into full-fledged worship in Nero's day, Christianity was making its entry into the Roman world. Whether that was a coincidence or was due in part to the mission outreach of the gospel is difficult to say. There is no doubt, however, that the emperor cult posed a serious threat to Christians.[31] Essential to the cult was the claim of universal authority, and this collided with the authority of Jesus as *Lord*. With very few exceptions, every Caesar from Julius onward called himself "Savior of the World," by which the ancients understood themselves to share one religion as they shared one kingdom under one emperor, who was considered one lord and savior of all:

29. See H. C. Kee, *The New Testament in Context: Sources and Documents* (Englewood Cliffs: Prentice-Hall, 1984), 44-45.

30. *Martyrdom of Polycarp* 8:2.

31. *Theological Dictionary of the New Testament*, s.v. *sōtēr*, views the emperor cult as a rather harmless expression of political formality or sycophancy. That is an understatement of its potential peril to early Christianity. See the rebuttals in O. Cullmann, *The Christology of the New Testament*, trans. S. Guthrie and C. Hall (Philadelphia: Westminster Press, 1963), 195-99; and especially E. Lohmeyer, *Christuskult und Kaiserkult*, 2-5, who rightly argues that despite its flattery and obsequiousness, Roman imperial worship embodied an unmistakable religious ardor which, among other things, expressed itself in fanatical persecution of those who refused to submit to it.

The Caesar-cult encompassed the totality of the Roman Empire. Since the empire was seen as the image of the cosmos or world-order, it was therefore believed to be universal and eternal. As the ruler of the world, Caesar was at the same time lord of the world. This universal state-religion was grounded in the one central thought that the emperor was in some way the incarnation of deity, and that he was the visible, earthly manifestation of the revealed God.[32]

Christians did not have the wind at their backs when they proclaimed the gospel in the Roman Empire. Nor was the ideological climate simply neutral or non-aligned. Depending how local authorities chose to enforce emperor worship, martyrdom was always a very real possibility. The writers of the New Testament seem intent on not aggravating this grim reality. The fledgling Christian movement was a mouse before an imperial cat; it had nothing to gain by provoking a confrontation with Rome. The New Testament does not indulge in outright contempt for the emperor cult, flamboyant and decadent though it was.[33] Nevertheless, there are unmistakable warnings in the New Testament against confusing Caesar and Christ.

Take, for example, Paul's statement to the Corinthians in the mid-fifties of the first century: "Indeed, even though there may be so-called gods in heaven or on earth — as in fact there are many gods and many lords — yet for us there is one God, the Father, from whom are all things and for whom we exist, and one Lord, Jesus Christ, through whom are all things and through whom we exist" (1 Corinthians 8:5-6). The reference to "many gods and many lords" surely would have called to mind the Caesar cult. Note in this passage how the description of Jesus is consciously paral-

---

32. Lohmeyer, *Christuskult und Kaiserkult*, 12-20. The quotation is from 17-18 (my translation).

33. The only example of religious contempt in the New Testament is in instances of blasphemy (Acts 8:9-24; 13:6-11). Otherwise, the following statement of Origen seems to have spoken for most Christians in the early church: "While we do nothing that is contrary to the law and word of God, we are not so mad as to stir up against us the wrath of kings and princes, which will bring upon us sufferings and tortures, or even death" (*Against Celsus* 8.65).

lel (and not subordinate) to that of God the Father. It is "Jesus Christ, through whom are all things and through whom we exist." That is to say, believers were created by Jesus Christ and they belong to Jesus Christ, not to Caesar. All power in heaven and on earth has been given to Christ, besides whom there are no other lords and gods. The Caesar-cult, like the powers and authorities in heavenly places (1 Corinthians 15:24; Ephesians 1:21; Colossians 1:13, 16; 2:10, 15), has been subjected to Christ.[34]

Some of the allusions to the Caesar cult in the New Testament may escape our notice. For instance, the title "Lord and Savior" in 2 Peter (1:1-2, 11; 2:20; 3:2, 18) carried unmistakable political freight, as it was a default term for Caesar in the emperor cult of the first and second centuries. Five repetitions of these titles in a letter of three short chapters firmly reminded readers that Jesus, not Caesar, was Lord and Savior. The supremacy of Christ to Caesar is also established by Luke's infancy narrative, in which an angel of God, supported by a glorious heavenly chorus, declared the child born in Bethlehem as Savior, Messiah, and Lord in the City of David (Luke 2:9-11). Savior, Messiah, Lord, and Davidic Jerusalem were four pillars of salvation in Israel. Here, however, the context is Roman, not Jewish; and that context is important in understanding Luke's birthday celebration. The birth of Augustus, it will be remembered, aroused hopes for peace and good will on earth; and at the birth of Jesus, Augustus presumed to register and control "all the world" (2:1). The angelic host, however, ascribes the authority presumed by Augustus to Jesus — indeed, the *infant* Jesus. In self-adulation Augustus presented himself as "good news," but heaven declares a baby lying in a feed trough as truly "good news of great joy for all the people" (2:10).

Later, in Acts 2, Luke lists the languages of the various peoples and nations that were spoken at Pentecost. Most of those peoples and nations were Caesar's subjects. The first name, however, Parthia, was a region that had successfully resisted Roman subjugation. Parthia might successfully resist Caesar's influence, but it could not resist the influence

---

34. See Cullmann, *The Christology of the New Testament*, 197. On the "many gods and many lords" of 1 Corinthians 8:5, Origen declares, "It is the Son alone who leads us to God, the creator of the universe" (*Against Celsus* 8.4)

of the Holy Spirit at Pentecost. Jesus, not Caesar, Luke suggests, is the true ruler of the world.[35] And in Matthew's infancy narrative, the *magoi*, magicians or wise men from the east, inevitably diminished the luster of the emperor cult (2:1-12). For once, all roads did not lead to Rome. At the birth of Jesus, savants from the East (which was the home court of the Caesar cult) followed a portentous star to Judea instead of Rome.

It would be easy to miss the above allusions to the Caesar cult. But there are others that cannot be missed. To the question in the temple about paying taxes to Caesar, Jesus acknowledged Caesar's temporal authority, but distinctly subordinated it to God's authority. If the image of Caesar appeared on a coin, then the coin belonged to Caesar; but if the image of God is found in humanity, then humanity belongs to God. In that equation, Caesar cannot be lord and ruler of all.

In a few instances, the contrast between Christ and Caesar is undeniably confrontational. In the pagan world, the most frequently employed title for divinized humans, including Caesar, was the Greek word *euergetēs*, "benefactor." This word occurs only once in the New Testament, where it is abruptly dismissed.

> A dispute also arose among [the disciples] as to which one of them was to be regarded as the greatest. But [Jesus] said to them, "The kings of the Gentiles lord it over them and those in authority over them are called benefactors. But not so with you; rather the greatest among you must become like the younger, and the leader like one who serves." (Luke 22:24-26)[36]

The reference to Gentile lords as "benefactors" is an unmistakable reference to the Caesar cult. The benefactors who so impressed the ancient

---

35. Gary Gilbert, "The List of Nations in Acts 2: Roman Propaganda and the Lukan Response," *Journal of Biblical Literature* 121/3 (2002): 497-529.

36. This verse forms the backbone of R. J. Cassidy's discussion of the New Testament response to the emperor cult. See *Christians and Roman Rule in the New Testament*, Companions to the New Testament (New York: Herder and Herder/Crossroad Publishing Company, 2001), 19-36. For an examination of divine person and Caesar cult titles and their use in the New Testament, see J. R. Edwards, *The Gospel According to Mark*, Pillar New Testament Commentary (Grand Rapids: Eerdmans, 2002), 106.

world failed to make the same impression on early Christianity, however. In recording this saying, Luke reminded Theophilus, the Roman official to whom he dedicated his Gospel (Luke 2:3), that the posture of Christ is antithetical to Roman imperial "benefactors."

In the Pastoral Letters (1 and 2 Timothy and Titus) the word "savior," a catchword in the Caesar cult, occurs with disproportionate frequency. God, for instance, is called savior unusually often (1 Timothy 1:1; 2:3; 4:10; Titus 1:3; 2:10; 3:4). This is sometimes seen as an argument against the Pauline authorship of the Pastorals, since in the indisputable Pauline letters God is not usually called savior. This argument is robbed of some of its force, however, if the backdrop of the emperor cult is considered. If the Pastorals stem from Paul, they must have been written in the 60s — when Nero was madly promoting himself as god. It is not difficult to understand why Paul, like any other Christian author, would emphasize *God* as the true savior, not Caesar.

Even more instructive are the titles used of Jesus in the Pastorals, who is brought into the closest possible relationship with God (1 Timothy 6:15; 2 Timothy 1:9-10; 4:1; Titus 2:11; 3:4; see also Jude 4). Jesus is called the *manifestation* of God, the *savior*, the *redeemer*, the *epiphany* of *glory*, *salvation*, and *hope*. Each of these terms belonged to the official vocabulary of the emperor cult. The author of the Pastorals wants to assure the church that the creedal formulations of the Caesar cult belong, in truth, to Jesus, "the blessed and only Sovereign, the King of kings and Lord of lords" (1 Timothy 6:15).

Finally let us look at the Revelation, where the most antagonistic allusions to the emperor cult in the New Testament are found. The Revelation was probably written during the fierce and bloody persecution of the infant church in Asia Minor under the Emperor Domitian (81-98). The veneer of the Empire had been stripped of its civil virtue and its idolatrous nature was inescapable to those who considered themselves Christians. The church was battling for its life (Revelation 17:14). The author of the Revelation saw the struggle in cataclysmic proportions and portrayed it accordingly. The Empire was the accuser of the brothers and sisters (12:10), the devil who had descended in great wrath (12:12) and sits on the throne of Satan (2:13). The emperor was depicted as a brazen whore who fornicated with the nations on the Seven Hills of Rome (chapter 17). Caesar was not one but two blasphemous beasts (chapter 13); no, a cosmic dragon lurking to devour the newborn child (that is, the gospel) of a celestial woman (the church; 12:1-7). The terrifying imagery betrays the vulnerability that the fledgling church felt before imperial might gone mad.[37]

The Revelation depicts the early Christians as helpless, but not hopeless. The schemes of Caesar, terrible though they were, were no match for the sovereignty of God that extends over all creation, in heaven, on earth, and in the sea (Revelation 5:13). It is sheer folly for Caesar to aspire to do what only God can do. And not simply God, but God working through the Son. Contrary to all human powers and expectations, the victory over the beast — that is, over Caesar — has already been won by the blood of the Lamb and the witness of the martyrs (10:11). This victory is a prolepsis of the final advent of the Rider on the White Horse, who is "the King of kings and the Lord of lords" (19:11-16). The Rider is Jesus Christ, the Son of God — crucified, resurrected, enthroned, and returned in final glory and judgment. It is he, not Caesar, who is the first and last (22:12), who makes all things new (21:5), and to whom the church prays, "Come, *Lord Jesus!*" (22:20).

Not by Mystery Religions

A third force with which early Christianity had to contend was the forest of mystery cults that dotted the eastern half of the Mediterranean, primarily in Greece, Asia Minor, Persia, and Egypt. By the first century A.D. the once-dominant philosophical systems of Greece, especially as represented by Plato and Aristotle, were suffering a bear market. The confidence that greets us in a character like Socrates was beating a retreat, leaving a wake of apprehension and angst that was filled, in part, by a

---

37. Revelation 13 is actually a remythologizing of the Emperor cult. No longer a peaceful benefactor, the Emperor (Domitian) is depicted as a monster, Behemoth and Leviathan. See S. J. Friesen, "Myth and Symbolic Resistance in Revelation 13," *Journal of Biblical Literature* 123/2 (2004): 281-313.

spate of mystery cults not based in philosophy or reason. The Greek word *mysterion* derives from a verb meaning "to close," and this is the first clue to the puzzle of the cults: their adherents maintained sealed lips, taking pledges not to divulge the mysteries to outsiders. For if the secrets of the cults were divulged, it was believed, they were rendered as impotent as Samson shorn of his hair.

Our incomplete knowledge of the cults is due in large part to those vows of secrecy. Some of the cults are almost wholly lost apart from their names, such as the Oracles of Clarian or Amphiaraus, the Mysteries of Aphrodite, Attis, Corybantes, Cabeiri, Zeus Sebazius, and Ge Themis. Others are better known: Mithra, Isis and Osiris, Cybele (or Magna Mater), Dionysos or Bacchos, Eleusis, and the Andanian Mysteries. Given the secrecy surrounding the fundamental beliefs of the cults, the exotic names themselves may have beckoned the inquisitive into their enigmas.

Common to most of the cults was awe of the power of fertility and the cycles of death and rebirth in nature. Some, like Eleusis, the most famous of the cults, were corn cults that originated near Athens as early as the seventh century B.C. In one of its rituals a single head of grain was held aloft in silence, symbolizing the archetypes of fertility, dying, and rising as depicted in the myth of Demeter, goddess of corn, who ventured to the underworld in search of her abducted daughter Kore (also called Persephone). Another Greek cult, also celebrating the power of fertility, was "raving Dionysos," as the second-century church father Clement of Alexandria referred to it. The cult of Dionysos reveled in virility and vented itself in sexual ecstasies and drunkenness, as symbolized by phallus and goblet. The crowning ceremony of Dionysos was "a sacred frenzy by a feast of raw flesh."[38] From eastern Turkey arose Magna Mater or Cybele, the Great Mother, renowned for the *taurobolium*, the drenching of an initiate in the warm blood of a ritually slaughtered bull, symbolizing eternal rebirth. The Egyptian cult of Isis and Osiris had established itself throughout the Greco-Roman world by the first century. It, too, reenacted the theme of dying and rising, as represented by the myth of Isis, wife and sister of Osiris (also called Serapis), whose

---

38. Clement of Alexandria, *Exhortation to the Greeks* 2.

slain and dismembered body was subsequently recovered by Isis. From Persia came the cult of Mithra, whose initiates proceeded through as many as seven stages of initiation. The culminating stage was the *tauroctony,* the mythical depiction of Mithra slaying a bull, whose blood invigorated or saved adherents. This cult, we know, was heavily patronized by soldiers, sailors, and officials.

The emperor cult, as we have seen, enshrined the virtues of the *polis,* the state, in outward expressions of public allegiance. Mystery cults, by contrast, stressed individual choices to affiliate with voluntary societies for the purposes of social well-being and the soul's future destiny. The emperor cult was political religion; mystery cults were private religion. Most of the cults practiced elaborate and sometimes bloody initiation rites, as well as sacred meals and ceremonies imitating death and rebirth experiences. The purpose of these rituals was to induct adherents into a shared experience and produce a frame of mind that was emotionally gripping. The accent fell on experience. With the exception of Eleusis, Clement of Alexandria castigated all the Mysteries for channeling that experience through eroticism. Most of the cults did not presume to impart special knowledge or teach things adherents did not know before. The cults, rather, were dramas — sacred dramas — that were meant to be experienced.

The mystery cults did not challenge early Christianity to the same degree that Torah and the Caesar cult did.[39] We have already noted the high degree of improbability that early Christians, who were Jewish monotheists, would have patterned their religious practices after pagan polytheism and mythology that they disdained. In the post-Constantinian era of the fourth century, the church began to absorb certain pagan practices, including the tonsure of priests, certain funeral rites, and the use of lighted

---

39. The question of the relationship of Christianity to the Mysteries, especially with regard to the Christian practices of baptism and the Lord's Supper, has loomed prominently in the history of religious debate in the nineteenth and twentieth centuries. The trend has changed from early scholars like Richard Reitzenstein and Wilhelm Bousset, who believed that the Mysteries played formative roles in early Christianity, to modern scholars who are decidedly less convinced of direct influence. This latter position (for reasons partly discussed below) is doubtless correct.

tapers. The cult of Mary, Jesus' mother, also seems to have grown after the acceptance of Christianity under Constantine. Pre-Constantinian Christianity, however, was a tiny minority within Greco-Roman culture. It maintained its identity by resisting religious syncretism, not by adapting to it, as evidenced by Justin Martyr's second-century description of the Mysteries as mockeries and demonic imitations of Christianity.[40]

One reason the cults did not greatly rival or influence Christianity is because there was no systematic whole to them, no underlying pattern of theology — at least until they were annexed by Neo-Platonism in the third century (and that is beyond our time frame of interest). The cycles of death and rebirth that characterized the cults are for the most part the same themes and patterns that are common to mythology the world over. The collapse of the Greek philosophical systems and the rise of imperial political theology left a craving for belonging and community in late antiquity. The cults addressed existential concerns such as these. Their adherents sought experience and customs that fostered a sense of belonging, and the divine sanction for that belonging. The Mysteries appealed to those cravings not with knowledge or revelation, but with universal archetypes and symbols that could be enacted in cult rituals.

The Mysteries do not appear to have made significant inroads into Palestine where Christianity was born. Archaeology, at any rate, has failed to uncover traces of them there. The load-bearing terminology of the Mysteries is also by and large absent from the New Testament.[41] Nevertheless, when the apostle Paul or other early Christian missionaries traveled to Phrygia or Macedonia they certainly preached to people who were steeped in their terminology and perhaps also in their practices. "Among the mature we do speak wisdom, though it is not a wisdom of this age or of the rulers of this age, who are doomed to perish. But we speak God's wisdom, secret and hidden, which God decreed before the ages for our glory,"

40. *First Apology* 66.4; *Dialogue with Trypho* 70.1.

41. Bruce M. Metzger, *Historical and Literary Studies: Pagan, Jewish, and Christian* (Grand Rapids: Eerdmans, 1968), 12, lists seventeen catchwords among the Mysteries that do not appear in the New Testament. Similarly, Arthur Darby Nock, *Early Gentile Christianity and Its Hellenistic Background* (New York: Harper Torchbooks, 1964), 29-31.

wrote Paul to the Corinthians (1 Corinthians 2:6-7). The words for "mature" (Greek *teleios*) and "wisdom, secret and hidden" (Greek *mystērion*) were catchwords among the Mysteries. The apostle seems to have used technical terms of the Mysteries in this instance to argue that the ideals of maturity and wisdom are not fulfilled in the Mysteries but in the gospel. Again, when Paul spoke of "entering into" the worship of angels in Colossians 2:18, the Greek word he used may refer to entering the shrine of a mystery cult. Yet again, the statement that Christians are "eyewitnesses of [Christ's] majesty" in 2 Peter 1:16 may have been intended to contrast the vision of Jesus' transfiguration with pagan visions.

We noted above that Mystery adherents were silent about their secret beliefs and rituals. The New Testament is nearly as silent about the Mysteries. This is due to the fact that Christianity and the Mysteries moved in different orbits. Christianity was a story about a historical figure, whereas the Mysteries were mythological.[42] The Mysteries sometimes recalled stories of dying deities, but those deaths were deaths by compulsion, not by choice; and sometimes in bitterness and despair, not in self-giving love as in the case of Jesus. The deities of the Mysteries were "nebulous figures of an imaginary past,"[43] but the Christian gospel was about Jesus of Nazareth, who "was crucified under Pontius Pilate" and, on the testimony of many named witnesses, resurrected on the third day.

The Mysteries avoided publicity and proclamation in favor of ineffability, whereas the gospel was not the gospel unless it was publicly proclaimed. In the mystery cults, revelation occurred in the inner sanctum; in Christianity it was announced in the marketplace. In today's terms, we might think of Christianity as developing a Web site and the Mysteries maintaining unlisted telephone numbers. The Greek word for "proclamation," *keryssein*, occurs nearly seventy times in the New Testament with reference to the story of Jesus. It is the same word used of the prophetic proclamation in the Greek translation of the Old Testament, where, as in the New Testament, it means the proclamation of an act of

---

42. See, for example, Origen's insistence to the pagan critic Celsus that in Jesus, God appeared in a true human being, not in a mythological type (*Against Celsus* 3.23-25).

43. Metzger, *Historical and Literary Studies*, 13.

God. God's saving outreach to the world occurs above all in the cross of Christ, but that saving outreach is *re-presented* in the proclamation of the gospel. The saving historical death of Christ is made present whenever the gospel is proclaimed in his name. Through proclamation of the gospel, Christ is made present to save. Christianity "does not preach the myth of a dying and rising god, nor a timeless idea, but a once-for-all, factual event, the life of Jesus."[44] The story of Jesus is "the power of God and the wisdom of God" (1 Corinthians 1:24).

The divide between the Mysteries and Christianity widens when we consider the type of allegiance each required. The Mysteries attracted adherents, whereas Christianity produced converts. There is an important difference between adhesion and conversion. Adhesion is a choice on the part of an individual to hold to one or more groups; conversion is the transformation of one's entire being by the greater life promised in a particular belief system. The Mysteries celebrated cyclical, recurring patterns of renewal in which their adherents participated. The purpose of the participation was to produce a quality of experience, a "high," as we would say. But one cannot convert to a high. The gospel, of course, is also an experience, but an experience of grace, which is a different kind of experience. Mystery adherents did not need to give up anything to gain a mystic high. Indeed, they often joined not one but several Mysteries if their means and leisure allowed, and without any signs of disapproval from the various cults. Doing so seems to have been viewed rather like we view diversifying investments today: it was safe course of action. Christianity, however, demanded a turning away from the old to the new, as contained in the story and dogma of the gospel. Mysteries promised an emotional experience *in* life; Christianity, which appealed to the will and mind, promised a new *life*.

These different purposes resulted in different ceremonies and communities. The ceremonies of the Mysteries conveyed their benefits naturally and automatically, assuming initiates and officiants followed the rules. Christian sacraments, to the contrary, were not benefits, but gifts to the unworthy by the grace of Jesus Christ. The Christian communities

44. *Theological Dictionary of the New Testament*, s.v. *kērysso*.

were very different from the Mystery gatherings. The Mysteries were a means of individual access to the spiritual world. A mystery cult was like an electrical outlet on a wall that provided access to a source of power. Plugging into the outlet was an individual matter. Mysteries did not need nor did they form communities, as did Jews and Christians in synagogues and churches. The concept of the *ecclesia,* the people of God called out and set apart in the church, had no equivalent in the Mysteries. To participate in a Mystery one went to a particular place, or perhaps to one of several places where the Mystery was celebrated. But neither synagogue nor church was determined by place. To participate in the church, one joined a people. In the early centuries of Christianity, that people became a substitute society, providing for education, fellowship, and support. The church, in fact, was a community in which believers experienced the firstfruits of eternal fellowship with one another and God. It was a self-reproducing community that moved the gospel in mission across the ancient world. Its organization and hierarchy became the vessel that promoted and made permanent the gospel story upon which it was founded.[45]

Finally, the Mysteries and the gospel appealed to different audiences. Adherents to mystery cults certainly experienced the camaraderie of other adherents, and in this respect they succeeded in breaking down some social barriers. Nevertheless, adherents were almost exclusively males; indeed, males who possessed the leisure and wealth required to participate in them. The purchase of a bull to be slain at a *taurobolium,* for example, cannot have been within the financial means of many ancients. Christianity, on the contrary, was profoundly universal. It proclaimed the same promise to Jew and Gentile, male and female, slave and free. At the conclusion of his *Exhortation to the Greeks,* Clement of Alexandria marveled at the universal inclusiveness of the gospel. *Whoever* wants to revel in the true Mystery, says Clement, need simply join in a hymn to "this Jesus [who,] being eternal, one great high priest of one God who is

45. On Christianity and the Mysteries, see Arthur Darby Nock, *Conversion: The Old and the New in Religion from Alexander the Great to Augustine of Hippo* (London: Oxford University Press, 1933), and *Early Gentile Christianity and Its Hellenistic Background;* Metzger, *Historical and Literary Studies,* 1-24; Walter Burkert, *Ancient Mystery Cults* (Cambridge, Mass.: Harvard University Press, 1987).

also Father, prays for humanity and encourages humanity: 'Give ear, you myriad peoples,' or rather, so many of humanity as are governed by reason, both barbarians and Greeks; the whole human race I call, I who was their Creator by the Father's will. Come to me, that you may find your place under one God and the one Word of God.'"

Of the three challenges to early Christianity discussed in this chapter, the mystery cults are likely to strike the closest resonance with our day. The present-day swell of interest in spirituality is, like the ancient Mysteries, eclectic and non-rational; it is private, individualistic, and non-established; and it is directed toward access to powers of self-fulfillment and self-enhancement. The chief difference between mystery cults (then and now) and Christianity, however, remains that Mysteries were (and are) mythological, whereas Christianity is historical, a well-documented record of a divine intrusion into history. The gospel is a factual story of a real person who lived and died to make God's redemptive love available to the world. Those who surrender to that purposeful love find their lives transformed to the image of Christ. They discover a new and identifiable community of people, the church. Their lives are given eternal significance. The Mysteries, both then and now, are expressions of human longings; the gospel was, is, and ever will be a demonstration of *God's* longing to redeem people from self-absorption and usher them into a divine life of freedom and joy in Christ.

The Past as Prologue

I have risked erring on the side of detail in this chapter in order to dispel the illusion that the first Christians lived in a simple world unlike ours. The truth is that they witnessed to the gospel in the face of conflicting claims of salvation, including Torah loyalty, the Caesar cult, and esoteric mystery cults. Not unlike today, the first Christians faced rival belief systems in morality, in civil religion, and in spiritual experience. Christianity did not reject Torah because it opposed morality. It did not reject the emperor cult because it was anti-Roman, or the Mysteries because it opposed spiritual experience. In varying degrees, all three were things

Christianity affirmed. The lists of moral behaviors in the New Testament (Romans 12:9-21, for example), the calls to obey rulers (Romans 13:1-7; 1 Peter 2:13-17), and the descriptions of spiritual experience (as in 1 Corinthians 2:6-16) are evidence of this.

The problem was simply one of final allegiance. When morality, obedience to rulers, and spiritual experience were promoted as absolute values, Christians could no longer render absolute allegiance to them. The early church needed to define the relationship of the gospel to such values because the higher the good, the more important the need to define its relationship to the final good in Christ. The apostle Paul answered the question when he wrote, "For us there is one God, the Father, from whom are all things and for whom we exist, and one Lord Jesus Christ, through whom are all things and through whom we exist" (1 Corinthians 8:6). In answering the question of ultimate allegiance with "Jesus is Lord," early Christians declared Jesus Christ as the full and final revelation of God, the savior and judge of the world.

Morality was good because it was commanded by God. But Torah and morality were not God, and when they presumed a place in the divine hierarchy above God they were misplaced. Likewise, civil obedience was commanded by God, but obedience to rulers could not be rendered above obedience to God (Acts 4:19-20). Finally, when Jesus says that one does not live by "bread alone" (Matthew 4:4), or when Paul enjoins his readers to train themselves in godliness (1 Timothy 4:7), people were encouraged to understand their lives in terms of potential for spiritual meaning and relationships. But when spiritual experience replaced God, or was directed to something other than the God revealed in Jesus Christ, then people had "exchanged the truth about God for a lie and worshiped and served the creature rather than the Creator, who is blessed forever!" (Romans 1:25). Richard Cassidy's description of the early church's posture vis-à-vis the emperor cult summarizes its posture to Torah and the mysteries as well:

> In the event of a conflict between the things that God desires and the things that the political authorities insist upon, Christians were called to make manifest that their primary allegiance was to God. It was not

that the apostles were anti-Roman. It was simply that their fundamental allegiance always belonged to Jesus.[46]

The attraction of morality, civil obedience, and spiritual experience was as strong in the first century as it is now. It is tempting to ground religion in steps that can be measured and controlled. Fixed rules offer security and assurance; they tell us what to do and when we have done them. Rules and rewards are gratifying. The commandment of Jesus to "Go and do likewise" (Luke 10:37) is harder to follow because it demands more than following the Master's hand or obeying his voice. It requires that we know his heart. The veneration of emperors and empire in the early centuries, like unquestioning nationalism today, for instance, is safe and reassuring. More difficult, as Paul enjoins in Romans 13, is to ensure that political, economic, and social forces are servants of God rather than gods themselves.

Whenever something in the divine hierarchy, whether morality, politics, or spirituality, rivals the Lordship of Christ, then idolatry stands at the door. "You cannot drink the cup of the Lord and the cup of demons. You cannot partake of the table of the Lord and the table of demons. Or are we provoking the Lord to jealousy? Are we stronger than he?" (1 Corinthians 10:21-22). When God is supremely honored, then all things take their rightful place in relation to him. In their rightful place they can be properly enjoyed, for "God created [them] to be received with thanksgiving by those who believe and know the truth. For everything created by God is good, and nothing is to be rejected if it is received with thanksgiving; for it is sanctified by God's word and by prayer" (1 Timothy 4:3-4). To everything — to morality, obedience to rulers, and spiritual experience — its proper place. But to the name of Jesus,

> that is above every name, . . .
> every knee should bend,
> in heaven and on earth and under the earth,
> and every tongue should confess
> that Jesus Christ is Lord,
> to the glory of God the Father.   (Philippians 2:9-11)

46. Cassidy, *Christians and Roman Rule*, 129.

CHAPTER EIGHT

Is a Savior from Sin Meaningful in a Day of Moral Relativism?

The least attractive aspect of Christianity to many seekers is probably its doctrine of sin. People want religion to be something that affirms them and makes them feel good. There are enough problems in life without being made to feel we are bad. And besides, the notion does not ring true. Most of us feel that a grim doctrine of sin may describe a notorious remnant in the world — the Adolf Hitlers and Osama bin Ladens and so forth — but how could it describe us? I spent two years in the late 1960s working with street kids in West Harlem in New York City. They were a rough bunch, by and large, and they did many bad things. They stoutly resisted the idea that they were sinners, however. Some of them would punch you out if necessary to convince you that they were as good as the next guy.

Christianity, however, makes the serious indictment that we are without excuse, whoever we are, "for in passing judgment on another you condemn yourself, because you, the judge, are doing the very same things" (Romans 2:1). The plain sense of this indictment seems to us preposterous. We read and hear of terrible things that people do all the time. We also rebel against the insinuation that we have either done or could do such things. We are hopefully right on the first account, but that may not be entirely to our credit. Most of us have not been given the opportunity of doing the things we abhor in others. Yet we are entirely capable of hatching grim plots mentally against our enemies. What we would do if we had the power and opportunity to do them remains an open question.

I was forced to admit this sober truth in my own life not too long ago. Like many people, I was shocked by the tragedy on Mount Everest in May 1996 in which a dozen mountaineers perished. For me, one of the most disturbing aspects of the catastrophe was a little-known sideshow to it. Two Japanese climbers, in making their summit bid, bypassed three injured, starving, and freezing climbers. These two had sufficient provisions with them to aid the stranded trio, but they did not want to jeopardize their ascent by stopping to assist them. As a result, all three climbers died. When asked why they did not help them, they said, "Above 8,000 meters [26,000 feet] is not a place where people can afford morality."[1]

The attitude and action of the Japanese climbers invites our indignation. It certainly did mine. A few years later, however, I was hiking up Mount Sinai while leading a college study tour to the Middle East. Mount Sinai is a tame 7,500 feet compared to Everest's 29,000. We were ascending Mount Sinai in darkness in order to be on the summit at sunrise. As we neared the top two Bedouins were carrying a man down. He was unconscious, and his sporadic, rattling breath indicated he was suffering from pulmonary edema, a mountaineering malady caused by ascending too rapidly. Climbers struck with pulmonary edema must be taken rapidly down to lower altitudes if they are to survive. For a moment I considered halting my ascent and assisting with the rescue. But I wanted to see the sunrise on the summit with my students, so I gave one of the Bedouins my flashlight to use and continued upward. They seemed to be doing all right by themselves.

On the way down, not far from where the Bedouins had passed us, I saw a figure covered with a blanket lying on the ground. It was the climber with pulmonary edema. He had died. The sight of his body smote my conscience. I was condemned by my own judgments of the Japanese climbers. Whether my action would have saved the man's life or not seems beside the point. My judgments and subsequent inaction show how I qualify for the Christian doctrine of sin.

1. Jon Krakauer, *Into Thin Air* (New York: Villard Press, 1997), 240-41.

The Theory of Moral Relativism

This chapter is about sin. More specifically, this chapter is about the affects of pluralism and moral relativism on our understanding of sin. Let me clarify that I am not referring to pluralism as a social virtue guaranteeing the rights of society to those who consent to live responsibly within those rights. I take it for granted that this kind of practical pluralism cannot be compromised without compromising the foundations of a democratic society. The pluralism I have in mind is not practical pluralism, but rather an ideological pluralism that is an outgrowth of the individualism of our culture. Individualism asserts that individuals are the sole arbiters of their existence, and that they should be able to do whatever they please. Ideological pluralism is the other side of the coin of individualism. It demands that we grant to others the same right we expect them to grant to us: the right to self-expression, regardless of its social or moral consequences. In ideological pluralism, objective virtues are replaced by subjective opinions. When virtues are replaced by subjective judgments, then statements about virtue become like color preferences. One opinion of right or wrong, virtue or vice, beauty or ugliness is as valid as another.

I first became aware of the degree to which this kind of thinking has permeated our culture when I taught ethics to college students. On questions of sexual behavior, abortion, corporate ethics, truth-telling, end-of-life issues, and so forth, I discovered that my students regularly believed — or thought they believed — that there were no objective right or wrong answers. They invariably said such matters should be decided by individual conscience. I suspected that their opinions were more than the iconoclasm typical of college students. Most of them were freshmen or sophomores, and still fairly close to the thinking of their home and high school environments. Most of them also came from some affiliation with mainline churches. I did not know them all to the same extent, but they seemed to mirror contemporary North American culture rather than be insurgents against it.

Following an examination on relativism, one of my colleagues stacked the tests on his desk and, without having read them, gave the first an A, the second a B, the third a C, and so on. Each paper randomly received the grade of A, B, C, D, or F, regardless of merit. When the tests were returned, student reactions ranged from amazement to outrage. Students who received higher grades than expected beamed; those who got lower grades erupted in protest. Those protests, as you probably suspect, proved my colleague's point: a student who professes moral relativism has a difficult time arguing a case on the basis of an independent standard of merit.

The Deflation of Sin

I believe that the prevailing climate of moral relativism has gutted our understanding of and language about sin. True, people resist the label "sinner," but sin is simply no longer very offensive to many people in and of itself. One reason for this is that we have difficulty ascribing the same degree of seriousness to unseen things that we do to seen realities. According to Christian Scripture and creed, sin is a willful infraction of God's holy and righteous will. This very definition illustrates our problem, for God is unseen, and most sins against God are unseen. In our materialistic age, non-material things (like God and sin) seem to us less real than material ones. When we stop to think of it, of course, there are any number of things that we cannot detect with our five sense that we take quite seriously. These powerful unseen realities can actually be a clue to the reality of sin. Most of us take with absolute seriousness the existence of things like X-rays and radio waves and the law of gravity. We believe in such things not because our five senses tell us to, but because of the effects of the things themselves — like pictures of our bones, and radio programs, and falling bodies. Sin is like that. It is not something we can detect with our senses, but we can see its effects. Traditional Christianity thinks of the reality of sin in a similar way that modern people think of the reality of an X-ray.

But immateriality is not the only reason we have difficulty taking sin seriously. We also devalue sin because of our commitment to permissiveness. We value self-gratification, and the concept of sin — indeed, of

145

objective right and wrong in general — jeopardizes that value. We want to be able to do what we want to do without being judged. There are times, of course, when the reality we repress bites our hand. Sin appears in a very different light depending on whether I am a perpetrator or a victim. When I cheat somebody I can find lots of ways to rationalize it: "It may have been a shabby thing to do, but I needed the money more than she did. She should get over it." When I am cheated, however, sin becomes a hard reality. It is not for me to get over it; it is for the offender to make restitution. Sin suddenly becomes more than an opinion. It is a fact that needs to be rectified.

When we are honest, I think most of us know that sin is something real and grave. But I also think that most of the time we *choose* to believe otherwise. Sin may be as fatal as prolonged exposure to X-rays, but people do not show the same degree of caution in protecting themselves from it. Sin is nowadays thought of as bad form, not as something fatal. We have all but dropped the word. Sins are now called "shortcomings," "lapses," "mistakes," "slips," and "screw-ups." What until recently was known as "scientific fraud" — plagiarizing or falsifying of scientific evidence — is now "scientific misconduct." Similarly, a news reporter described a man who embezzled $60 million as guilty of "improprieties."

This change in vocabulary reflects a change in values. If sin is an infraction against God, then it needs to be confessed before God and forgiven by God. An action of God is necessary to rectify it. But a lapse or mistake needs no outside intervention, and certainly no divine intervention. It needs only to be corrected by the offender. Sin demands a savior; a screw up demands only a new leaf, a new attitude, a better intention. One demands God, and whatever provision God requires for the remission of sin; the other needs only help, and perhaps only self-help.

What is true with respect to sin is even truer with respect to the concept of hell. In public life, references to hell stigmatize one as an intellectual troglodyte. Hell has become not simply something archaic; it has become an embarrassment. (As a reader you may be feeling this embarrassment at this moment.) The only time I can recall hearing hell used publicly in both a real and approved sense is when the families of several women killed by a serial killer told the killer they hoped "he would rot in hell for eternity." I followed the case closely and I could not detect any metaphorical sense in their use of "hell."

Hell seems to have been virtually purged from the vocabulary of the Christian faith, except as a metaphor of evil. I have attended church for fifty years and have never heard a sermon on hell, or an entire sermon on sin. I am not complaining about this, and I am not here appealing for more sermons on hell. Belief in hell and the devil do not belong to the *diapheronta* of the Christian faith — the essentials that have saving significance — and they need not be the subject of a great many sermons.

It is not the absence of sermons on sin, hell, and the devil that concerns me. It is the loss of an understanding of a real infraction against God and a real separation from God that concerns me. We have spoken of sin as something that really separates one from God. It is only logical, as Christian theology historically agrees, that the same reality that separates one from God will, unless repented of, separate one eternally from God. That state of separation is hell.

In *The Divine Comedy,* the Italian poet Dante was right to assert that hell is the final and irrevocable choice of something that is not God over God. Hell is not a place to which God consigns people, but an existence people choose in contrast to God's will for them. God does not will people to make this choice, but God permits them to do so because of the divine commitment to human freedom. The modern world assumes that with the passage of time the gravity of a wrong is diminished and is thus eventually irrelevant: "time heals all wounds," we sometimes hear people say. The Christian tradition does not agree. Human choices have eternal consequences. The passage of time is as irrelevant to those consequences as is distance to the points of the compass.

Martin Luther, the reformer, contended that without a real and transcendent dimension of evil, a real and transcendent savior was unnecessary and meaningless. Luther located that transcendent dimension of evil in the devil. Luther's devil was not a Halloween figure with horns and a pitchfork, but rather a personification of evil itself. I am not advancing a particular doctrine about the devil in this book; readers must come to their own judgment on that matter. I am instead directing our attention to the force of Luther's logic, that if the reality of evil is denied, then the reality of God becomes unnecessary. Without a transcendent dimension of evil, there is no need for a transcendent redemption. Without a transcendent redemption, whatever needs to be done for humanity can (and must) be done by humanity. Christianity then becomes an inner frame of mind synonymous with "conscience." If sin and hell are merely metaphors, perhaps God, heaven, and salvation are metaphors too.[2]

A Tectonic Shift in Theology

I should like to argue that in much modern theology this is precisely what has happened. A metaphorical understanding of sin has resulted in a metaphorical concept of salvation. A distinctive feature of much modern theology is a paradigm shift away from a theology of redemption to a theology of creation and to nature itself. The center of gravity is no longer in what God has done through Jesus Christ, but in what God has done in creation, apart from Jesus Christ. The new theology argues that what *is*, is essentially good and right. There is less emphasis today on being transformed according to the image of Jesus Christ. There is a growing assumption, even a declaration, that God affirms us as we are without any need for change. The new theology encourages an acceptance, both of self and others, as we are. The proclamation of the saving grace of the gospel has historically been expressed in transitive verbs — believe, turn, repent, follow. These verbs express the need to move, to change, to convert. The new theology is clothed in intransitive verbs of affirmation: am, becoming, being. The focus has shifted from transcendence to immanence, from a Trinitarian theology rooted in Scripture and creed to a unitary theology of creation that has strong affinities with Deism and universalism. Our gaze is redirected from Mount Zion and from Mount Calvary to nature, to ourselves, to the "god within."

This new theology identifies God closely with creation and with ourselves. Taken to its ultimate conclusion, this God becomes a personi-

2. See Heiko Oberman, *Luther: Man between God and the Devil,* trans. E. Walliser-Schwarzbart (New York: Doubleday, 1989), 155.

fication of the *élan vital,* the life force of the world. This God is immediate, accessible, compatible, and inherent, and because of these qualities, very appealing to modern sensibilities. There is no distance between this God and humanity, except the distance of ignorance or insensibility. There is no need for a mediator between this God and humanity, except perhaps the mediation of heightened awareness or deeper understanding. This God is found not in journeys outward but in the created order and in the introspective journey inward.

Allow me to show how the above ideas are illustrated by Episcopal Bishop John Spong in his book *A New Christianity for a New World: Why Traditional Faith Is Dying and How a New Faith Is Being Born.* Spong believes that the traditional view of God — as a supernatural being who exists outside the world but is nevertheless active in it — is on its deathbed. He believes theism arose by an evolutionary process of personalizing human self-consciousness, thereby transforming the personalized human psyche into "a parental God in the sky."[3] This God is a crutch, "a human coping device, created by traumatized self-conscious creatures to enable them to deal with the anxiety of self-awareness."[4] (Readers familiar with post-Enlightenment attempts to explain the existence of religions along atheistic lines will recognize in these ideas the theories of James Frazer, Ludwig Feuerbach, and Carl Jung, although Spong does not cite them.[5]) The kind of Christianity represented in the Apostles' Creed or the New Testament is a critically ill patient, in Spong's assessment. Spong believes he has a life-support system that can save the patient. He discards the Christian creeds, doctrines, traditions, and even the idea of God as a personal being. In place of the old gasping theism, he substitutes a god

3. *A New Christianity for a New World* (San Francisco: HarperSanFrancisco, 2001), 74.
4. *A New Christianity,* 49.
5. All three models explain the development of religion along evolutionary lines. Frazer interpreted the history of humanity along a continuum of magic — religion — science, i.e., that religion developed from magical practices and would yield to modern science. Feuerbach postulated that God was simply a psychological projection of humanity (hence, Spong's "traumatized self-consciousness" that contrives a "parental God in the sky"). Jung explained human personality as an emergence from the "shadows" of theistic repressions and fears to responsible adulthood.

that he discovers within the cycle of life. "My life reveals the divine life. I love with divine love. . . . 'My Me is God.'"[6]

There we see the tectonic shift from transcendence to nature that we noted above. God is not differentiated from the world, but nearly identical to it. One further step is required in rehabilitating God, however, and that is to dismantle the Christian doctrine of sin. The death of Christ on the cross for the forgiveness of sin is regarded as a particularly primitive and repulsive doctrine, a veritable form of divine child abuse. And rightly so if sin is merely a misdemeanor to be corrected. Spong believes the universe as a whole is part of an expanding and evolving enterprise, not a fallen one. Sin is not something that exists in the world like an X-ray exists. It is simply a byproduct of misdirected "inner needs."[7]

Sin, on this understanding, is like the self-centeredness of children, or puberty: it is a natural part of our being that we need to grow through. Here is the particular program Spong advocates:

> That radically new Christian vocation is begun, I believe, when theism dies and God, as a being external to life, disappears from our consciousness and our vocabulary. . . . But the reformation will not be complete until the Devil, the satanic figure, also dies as something external to life and thus also disappears from our consciousness and our vocabulary. That is the revolution that is needed to complete the picture. Human life is not perfectible: evil cannot be removed from our being because it is part of our being.[8]

In doing away with sin, Spong admits to having done away with the Christian God. Luther was right: where sin becomes a metaphor, then God becomes a metaphor. If sin is simply misdirected inner needs in the struggle for survival, then it is something *created* by God, as Spong maintains. If that were true, I am sure we all would agree that the sacrifice of God's Son on a horrible cross would be a senseless outrage.

More than twenty years ago Joseph Campbell, the great mytholo-

6. *A New Christianity,* 76.
7. *A New Christianity,* 162.
8. *A New Christianity,* 167.

gist, told me that the Western world is entering into "a new paganism." We see the contours of a new paganism in the above makeover of Christianity. Spong does to the life-cycle of nature what he criticized theism for doing to human self-consciousness: he personifies it as a god. Christianity has ceased being a historical revelation of God. It is now a mythology in which the twilight of the gods becomes the starting point for the deification of nature. All life — humanity included — is part of an evolving, materialistic process. There is no external intrusion of sin, and no external God who creates and redeems. The doctrine of the atonement is not only an outrage, it is an impossibility.

The doctrine of atonement obviously hangs on the doctrine of sin. A physician who removes a leg because of a splinter is a monster. A physician who removes a leg because of cancer or gangrene, on the other hand, is a hero who saves his or her patient's life. It all depends on the nature and seriousness of the problem. Spong and others see sin as a splinter; the New Testament sees it as a cancer that is fatal if left untreated. And that accounts for the sacrifice of Jesus Christ on a cross of cruelty and shame. The cross is indeed an outrage — an outrage of grace. If this is the kind of world in which we live — and I believe it is — then the death of God's Son for the sins of the world is the *only* way the world can be reunited with its Maker and Redeemer.

Radical Sin Demands Radical Grace

Turning from the world described above to the world of the New Testament is like emerging from a fog. A world of isolating loneliness and myopia, a world whose ultimate destination is pessimism and fatalism, suddenly becomes bright, vast, sharp, and hopeful. People who begin to read the New Testament discover a world they intuitively recognize, even though they may be total strangers to it. It awakens a longing in them, a homesickness for a place they have never been. A friend of mine who came to faith in Christ after spending a lifetime in a cult put it this way: "I feel like I have come home, like a hole has finally been filled." Another friend, a convert to Christianity from Hinduism, spoke of his conversion process in these words: "Before I became a Christian I was reading the [Bhagavad] Gita; but the New Testament was reading *me*."

The New Testament has a self-authenticating quality about it because it bears witness to a world we instinctively know to be true. It does not reduce sins to misdirected inner needs and improprieties. It does not reduce God to the human conscience or the life force of nature. The gospel is the historical narrative of a real healing for a real wound, a full and sufficient payment for a serious debt. It is not a coincidence that most Christian prayers end with the words "through Jesus Christ our Lord." They do so not only because Jesus is the revealer of God. If he were only the revealer he would be a source of knowledge and enlightenment about God, but not necessarily a source of power from God. Jesus conveys to the world something more than a new and better understanding of God. He brings that which an immanent God, closely identified with the material world of creation, cannot bring. Jesus brings what we cannot find within creation, what we cannot offer ourselves. He brings grace — grace that accepts, forgives, and transforms.

The Jewish sacrificial system, despite its elaborate occupation with sacrifices, could provide only a provisional answer to the problem of sin. The Christian proclamation, on the contrary, declares that the besetting alienation of humanity from God has in the work of Jesus Christ received a conclusive resolution. The most basic formulation is simply, "Christ died for our sins" (1 Corinthians 15:3; Romans 5:8). It is "of first importance," the crucial and pivotal work of salvation. Salvation from sin was the reason why Jesus was sent into the world (1 Timothy 1:15). God made Jesus "Leader and Savior that he might give . . . forgiveness of sins" (Acts 5:31). The Greek word translated "leader," *archēgos,* more accurately means "originator," "founder." God acted in Jesus in a unique and conclusive way with regard to sin. God has not acted that way before or since. The name of Jesus is effective for the forgiveness of sins (1 John 2:12) because God raised him from the dead. The resurrection is the divine confirmation of Jesus' sacrificial death on the cross (Acts 3:26; 1 Corinthians 15:14, 17). The death of Jesus Christ effected a revolutionary transformation of human circumstances. Whereas humanity was formerly dead, it has now been made alive with Christ (Ephesians 2:5-9), indeed "set free from the present evil age" (Galatians 1:4). There is nothing for humanity to do — no promises, payments, or sacrifices — except to "repent and turn to God so that your sins may be wiped out" (Acts 3:19).

The death of Christ was effective for the removal of sin because Christ was a righteous sin-bearer. A "righteous sin-bearer" is, of course, an oxymoron, for sin makes one *unrighteous*. The oxymoron is nevertheless true, because in his sacrificial death on the cross, Jesus Christ exchanged his righteousness for humanity's sinfulness. "For Christ suffered for sins once for all, the righteous for the unrighteous, in order to bring you to God" (1 Peter 3:18). Unlike the Old Testament sacrifices that, despite their repetition, were only provisional, the death of Jesus was final, "once for all." Jesus fulfilled the role of the high priest by making expiation for the sins of all people (Hebrews 2:17). Unlike earthly high priests, whose sacrificial offerings included payment for their own sins (Hebrews 5:1-2; 10:11), Jesus was righteous and needed to offer no sin offering on his own behalf (1 Peter 3:18). Moreover, Jesus was not only the perfect sacrificer; he was also the perfect sacrifice. He was the unblemished "Lamb of God who takes away the sin of the world" (John 1:29). In a plethora of sacrificial imagery, Hebrews attests that the blood of Christ effected eternal redemption: "[Christ] through the eternal Spirit offered himself without blemish to God, purifying our conscience from dead works to worship the living God" (Hebrews 9:11-14).

The most important term in the New Testament with reference to the death of Jesus as a sin offering is the Greek word *hilastērion*, "sacrifice of atonement." The term does not occur often, but it provides the key to understanding the many references to the effectiveness of Jesus' death, and particularly to the shedding of his blood (Hebrews 10:19-20; 12:24; 13:20-21) for the forgiveness of sins. In a passage packed with high-caliber theological terminology, Paul says that "God put forward [Jesus Christ] as a sacrifice of atonement by his blood" (Romans 3:25). *Hilastērion* also occurs twice in 1 John. "If anyone sins, we have an advocate with the Father, Jesus Christ the righteous; and he is the atoning sacrifice for our sins, and not for our sins only but also for the sins of the whole world" (1 John 2:1-2). Again in 1 John 4:9-10, "God sent his only Son into the world so that we might live through him. In this is love, not that we loved God but that he loved us and sent his Son to be the atoning sacrifice for our sins."

In secular Greek literature *hilastērion* was reserved for gifts of consecration or expiation presented to the gods. In the Septuagint, the Greek translation of the Old Testament, *hilastērion* received its definitive stamp as the fixed translation of *kapporet*, the Hebrew word depicting the mercy seat on top of the Ark of the Covenant in the Holy of Holies of the Jerusalem temple (Exodus 25:17-22). The most holy object in the most holy place in Israel was the *hilastērion*. Both sides of the mercy seat were flanked by stylized cherubim, whose outstretched wings covered the abode of the invisible God (Hebrews 9:5). The Ark of the Covenant was the place where the high priest made atonement for all Israel on the Day of Atonement by sprinkling the blood of a young bull on the mercy seat. The mercy seat was not a place where goods or property were expiated. It was a place where *life* was expiated (Exodus 32:30; Deuteronomy 32:43; 2 Samuel 21:3).

Israel did not simply *hope* that God would satisfy sin on the mercy seat. It was assured by the promise and decree of God that human sins were fully cleansed and forgiven there. The New Testament writers saw the Ark of the Covenant as an anticipation or foreshadowing of the final redemption effected by the cross of Christ. This graphic term signifies that the death of Jesus was the eschatological event of expiation proposed by God that fulfilled, transcended, and abrogated all previous forms of atonement in Israel. The *hilastērion*, in other words, is entirely transferred to and fulfilled in Jesus:

> In the place of the *kapporet* concealed in the temple and the ritual of the rite of expiation associated with it, God has put forward Jesus to bring about expiation through "his blood," i.e., by giving his life. *The crucified one has thus become the place where God himself has brought about expiation publicly and for all.* Thus Good Friday has become the great Day of Atonement.[9]

---

9. *Exegetical Dictionary of the New Testament,* s.v. hilastērion (emphasis mine). See also *Theological Dictionary of the New Testament,* s.v. hilastērion.

Grace on Behalf of Others

All New Testament references and allusions to Christ's death — and they are legion — are rooted in the necessity of making an atoning sacrifice for human sin. Already in the infancy narratives of Matthew an angel announces to Joseph that the child engendered by the Holy Spirit in Mary's womb "will save his people from their sins" (Matthew 1:21). In the Gospel of Luke, aged Anna proclaims that in the baby Jesus the hopes of "the redemption of Jerusalem" would be realized (Luke 2:38). The idea that Jesus' life, ministry, and death provided a vicarious covering "on behalf of others" is the dominant template for the New Testament understanding of Jesus.

The template was not invented by the earthly church, but derived from Jesus himself, who occasionally interpreted his actions in the same light. To a fraudulent tax collector Jesus announced, "For the Son of Man came to seek and save the lost" (Luke 19:10). Jesus explained the purpose of his impending death as "a ransom for many" (Matthew 20:28; Mark 10:45). The Greek word for "ransom," *lytron,* which also underlies the imagery of Anna's reference to Jesus as "the redemption *(lytrōsis)* of Jerusalem" (Luke 2:38), is rooted in the same Hebrew verb *kipper,* from which *kipporet,* or "mercy seat," is derived. "Ransom" also connotes "covering over," "atoning for," or "expiating." The Greek word *lytron* referred to epic transactions between humans and gods — the forgiveness of sins, expiation of offenses, and manumission of slaves. At the Last Supper, when Jesus interpreted the outpouring of his blood as a vicarious ransom *on behalf of* "many," he placed his sacrifice in the same orbit of ideas (Matthew 26:26-29; Mark 14:22-25; Luke 22:19-20).[10] He was supremely conscious that in his impending death he was offering a payment to God that could be offered by no one else.

The formula of Jesus laying down his life *for us,* which permeates the New Testament, recalls the shedding of the blood of an innocent animal

---

10. See *Theological Dictionary of the New Testament,* s.v. *lytron; Exegetical Dictionary of the New Testament,* s.v. *lytron;* A. Y. Collins, "The Signification of Mark 10:45 among Gentile Christians," *Harvard Theological Review* 90 (1997): 371-82.

on behalf of Israel. The apostle Paul, especially, relied heavily on the prepositional phrase "on behalf of" to communicate the saving effects of Jesus' death. He associated the death of Christ with the sacrificial imagery of the pleasing odor of a burnt offering: "Christ loved us and gave himself up for us, a fragrant offering and sacrifice to God" (Ephesians 5:2). Elsewhere and often Paul says that "God did not withhold his own Son, but gave him up for all of us" (Romans 8:32). "We are convinced that one has died for all; therefore all have died. And he died for all, so that those who live might live no longer for themselves, but for him who died and was raised for them" (2 Corinthians 5:14-15). God sent his Son to die on behalf of the godless (Romans 5:6-8), to redeem and cleanse them from all lawlessness (Titus 2:14), and to save them in the future (Romans 5:9-10). When Paul wrote to the Corinthians, some twenty-five years after the Last Supper, that "our paschal lamb, Christ, has been sacrificed" (1 Corinthians 5:7), he was transferring the sacrificially rich imagery of the temple cult directly to the life and death of Jesus.

I cannot think of sacrifice without thinking of the following story: After I graduated from seminary, I studied theology for a year at the University of Zürich in Switzerland. While there I had an experience that gave me an insight into the deeper realities of sin and sacrifice in the Bible. Late one night, as my wife Janie and I were driving the twenty kilometers from Zürich to the village where we lived, several deer leaped across the road in front of our car. Before I could hit the brakes, I plowed into one of them. I stopped the car, got out, and walked back to remove the carcass from the road. To my dismay, the animal was not dead, but desperately struggling to get to its feet. I went back to the car and explained the situation to Janie. We agreed that I should take a hunting knife and end the animal's suffering. I went back to the deer, grasped its head, and cut its throat with the knife. I held the animal as its life flowed out. In that dark, lonely moment I had a vivid mental picture of an Israelite patriarch or priest slaying an innocent animal for the remission of sin. If I had to do something this dreadful every time I sinned, I thought to myself, I would take my sin more seriously. In that dark moment, the awe-full mystery of sin and sacrifice dawned on me with a new clarity. Sin is something terrible that demands something terribly costly in return.

Three Effects of God's Grace in Christ

The costly counterpart to sin is divine grace. The forgiving and reconciling word of grace is a word we do not deserve. "Therefore, since we have been justified by faith, we have peace with God through our Lord Jesus Christ, through whom we have obtained access to this grace in which we stand" (Romans 5:1-2). "Set your hope on the grace that is brought to you in the revelation of Jesus Christ" (1 Peter 1:13). Jesus is the conduit of grace, the bridge over which salvation is transmitted to the world. "There is one God; there is also one mediator between God and humankind, Christ Jesus, himself human, who gave himself a ransom for all" (1 Timothy 2:5-6). The grace that is accessible through Jesus is the grace of God. Hence the Pastoral Letters in particular speak of God as savior rather than Christ, but the difference is not a material difference because the source of the salvation and the effecting of the salvation are the result of one and the same divine will. "To the only God our Savior, *through* Jesus Christ our Lord" (Jude 24). "The power of God saved us and called us with a holy calling, not according to our works but according to his own purpose and grace. This grace was given to us in Christ Jesus before the ages began" (2 Timothy 1:9-10).

The New Testament speaks of the grace of God revealed in the sacrificial death of Jesus in three general categories. The first category relates to human *standing* before God. The apostle Paul likes to speak of this standing or status as "righteousness," or "justification." Both terms derive from the same Greek word, *dikaiosyne,* which carries the sense that a status has been attributed to humanity that is not native to it. In 2 Corinthians 5:21 Paul attests that "For our sake [God] made [Christ] to be sin who knew no sin, so that in him we might become the righteousness of God" (also Romans 3:24). This righteousness fully alters human standing before God. Believers stand in a cleansed and purified state before God. "You were washed, you were sanctified, you were justified in the name of the Lord Jesus Christ and in the Spirit of our God" (2 Corinthians 6:11). In a graphic oxymoron, the author of the book of Revelation says that believers "have washed their robes and made them white in the blood of the Lamb" (Revelation 17:14). The status that results alters the orientation of one not simply to God, but to all reality.

The second consequence of grace allows humanity to *experience God*. The grace given to believers as a result of faith in Jesus Christ produces not just a new dimension of life, but new life. In the Gospel of John, Jesus is described as life-giving "bread from heaven" that satisfies the world's hunger and thirst. Whoever does not eat and drink of the Son of Man does not have life (John 6:32-58). Paul uses the imagery of food with reference to believers themselves. Believers are "first fruits" — Exhibit A, we might say — of what God can do in a fallen world to change and restore it (2 Thessalonians 2:13-14). The book of Hebrews depicts Jesus Christ as the fulfillment of the temple cult and emphasizes that redeemed life is sanctified life, cleansed and restored for its rightful purposes with God (Hebrews 10:10-14; 13:12).

Most importantly, the experience of grace is the *experience of life in Christ and for Christ*. It is not better life, but new life. As such, the imagery of birth or rebirth is appropriate to depict it. "By his great mercy," says 1 Peter 1:3-5, "[God] has given us a new birth into a living hope through the resurrection of Jesus Christ from the dead, and into a new inheritance that is imperishable, undefiled, and unfading, kept in heaven for you." "Everyone who believes that Jesus is the Christ has been born of God," says 1 John 5:1. The new life of grace is not lived on one's own but in relationship with the Creator and Redeemer of the world. Paul speaks of the new life in terms of adoption into the life of God as *abba*, the intimate and compassionate Father (Romans 8:15; Galatians 4:4-6), and Christ as elder brother (Romans 8:29).

The new life of grace is inseparably identified with the historical experience of Jesus. The death that Jesus died is in a mystical yet practical way the same death that believers must die. Hence, Paul can say that he died to the law so that he might live to God. "I have been crucified with Christ; and it is no longer I who live, but it is Christ who lives in me. And the life I now live in the flesh I live by faith in the Son of God who loved me and gave himself for me" (Galatians 2:19-20). The life of faith is not a mere furtherance or prolongation of the former life, but a new life in which believers grow into completed personhood. Ephesians 4:13 speaks of this maturity as "the measure of the full stature of Christ." Simply but elegantly stated, the life of grace is a condition of mutual existence with

God: "God abides in those who confess that Jesus is the Son of God, and they abide in God" (1 John 4:15).

Existence in grace has an added dimension, already noted in many of the foregoing references. It is not autonomous life, in which individuals get a second chance with a clean slate. It is, rather, life in relationship and belonging and fellowship with Christ and God. The motivation for this life in communion is not left to the individual, but enabled and empowered by the Spirit of God. Paul declares that even the confession of Jesus as Lord, fundamental to the whole grace-existence, is made possible only by God's Spirit (1 Corinthians 12:3). It is God's Spirit that enables us to be received into and participate in God's family as adopted children (Romans 8:15). The law produces a conditional, even adversarial, relationship in which people fear God (Romans 8:15). And for good reason: the law is a "ministry of death" to those who do not obey it (2 Corinthians 3:7). But the gospel of Jesus Christ is a "ministry of the Spirit" (2 Corinthians 3:8), and the Spirit testifies deep within believers that they are children of God (Romans 8:15). As children, believers are bound by the Spirit to God so that they belong to God (Romans 8:9). In short, what God did *for* humanity in the cross of Jesus Christ, God now does *in* humanity through the Holy Spirit, who applies the work of Christ to believers. The application of that work causes a rebirth, remaking, and renewal of believers "as the first fruits for salvation through sanctification by the Spirit" (2 Thessalonians 2:13).

This introduces the third consequence of grace. In addition to a new status before God and a new existence with God, grace creates a new *destiny.* "The wages of sin is death," said the apostle Paul, "but the free gift of God is eternal life in Christ Jesus our Lord" (Romans 6:23). As the destiny of believers, eternal life is most frequently identified with the defeat of death. In 1 Corinthians 15, the most sustained discussion of the resurrection in the New Testament, Paul concludes that because of the resurrection of Jesus from the dead "we will not all die, but be changed." Exactly when the change will occur remains a "mystery," but the change nevertheless remains assured. "The dead will be raised imperishable and we will be changed. For this perishable body must put on imperishability, and this mortal body must put on immortality. When this perishable body puts on imperishability, and this mortal body puts on immortality, then the saying that is written will be fulfilled, 'Death has been swallowed up in victory'" (1 Corinthians 15:51-54). The New Testament is unanimously agreed that Jesus' resurrection experience is the destiny of all believers. The life Jesus now lives is the life that believers, by his grace, will live — free from death, living eternally with God (Romans 8:1-3; Hebrews 7:25; Jude 21).

Eternal life is not limited to a future state of existence, however. The Holy Spirit is even now projecting future certainties into present earthly realities of believers. Paul assures believers that the Spirit who raised Jesus from the dead is also at work to make their mortal bodies come alive (Romans 8:10-11). To be sure, the resurrection of the dead is primarily a future existence, but it is not an empty hope until then. Even now God's grace is operative, transforming human existence into its final and eschatological contours. Paul assures believers that God's Spirit testifies with our consciences that we are fellow heirs of the glory of Jesus Christ (Romans 8:16-17). The Gospel of John, too, accentuates the already-present-but-not-yet-fulfilled nature of eternal life. "All who see the Son and believe in him may have eternal life; and I will raise them up on the last day."

Allow me to conclude this story of God's rescue of sinful humanity with the story of another rescue, a true story from Switzerland in 1957. In August of that year four climbers — two Italians and two Germans — were climbing the six-thousand-foot near-vertical North Face of the Eiger. After eight punishing days on the face, the party was trapped. The two Germans had headed for the summit alone, and were never heard from again. The Italians, exhausted and dying, were marooned on two narrow ledges a thousand feet below the summit. Although the Swiss Alpine Club forbade both climbing the North Face and rescue attempts on it, a small group of climbers decided to launch a private effort to save the Italians. Climbing the Eiger by easier routes, they lowered a climber named Alfred Hellepart from the summit on a slender steel cable a fraction of an inch thick down the North Face to attempt to rescue Claudio Corti, the higher of the two Italians. In Hellepart's own words:

As I was lowered down the summit ice-field, my comrades on top grew further and further distant, until they disappeared from sight. At this moment I felt an indescribable aloneness. Then for the first time I peered down the abyss of the North Face of the Eiger. The terror of the sight robbed me of breath, and a cry escaped involuntarily from me. The brooding blackness of the Face, falling away in almost endless expanse beneath me, made me look with awful longing to the thin cable disappearing above me in the mist. I was a tiny human being dangling in space between heaven and hell. The sole relief from the terror was the human voice on my Walkie-talkie and my mission to save the climber below.

Hellepart managed to descend to Corti, strapped him on his back, and in the most dramatic rescue in alpine history was winched to the summit and safety.[11]

In 2003 my son Mark and I climbed the Eiger by the precipitous Mittellegi Ridge and stood at the place where Hellepart had peered down the North Face. I know from experience what he felt. The courage Hellepart displayed in rescuing Claudio Corti is an illustration of Christ the sin-bearer, descending to our ledges of sin and carrying us on his back to the summit.

The Divine Comedy

A comedy is a story that begins in sadness and ends in joy. The gospel is the great comedy of the universe because it turns wretched beginnings

---

11. See Heinrich Harrer, *The White Spider: The Story of the North Face of the Eiger,* trans. H. Merrick (New York: E. P. Dutton, 1960), 187-225. The reflection of Hellepart that I have translated is absent in the above English edition, but present in Harrer's new revised German edition, *Die Weisse Spinne: Das Grosse Buch vom Eiger* (Berlin: Ullstein, 1999), 191-223. Stefano Longhi, Claudio Corti's climbing partner, had fallen to a ledge some 120 feet below Corti. Following Corti's rescue, inclement weather necessitated the postponement of Longhi's rescue until the next day. Unfortunately, he died during the night. Longhi's body dangled from the North Face of the Eiger for the next two years.

into a wonderful end. We have talked at length about sin in this chapter, because our culture is in denial about sin, despite the fact that sin, as G. K. Chesterton noted, is the only empirically provable doctrine of the Christian faith. The gospel insists on the severity of sin not to produce gloom and dread, but to establish the certainty of joy. The book of Hebrews speaks of the victory of Jesus Christ over sin as "so great a salvation" (2:3). Jesus Christ is the author, pioneer, and perfecter of this salvation (Hebrews 2:10). He is the one sufficient and final savior of humanity (2 Timothy 2:10; 3:15; Hebrews 9:23-28). Jesus is the means of saving grace who forever alters the status, experience, and destiny of believers with God. The victory that Jesus accomplished leads humanity in a triumphal procession to God, in which sin and death are vanquished and mortal life is transformed by the resurrected Christ into eternal life (2 Corinthians 2:14-16). There he oversees the Book of Life (Revelation 13:8). The purpose of the atoning work of Jesus Christ is to prepare believers here and now for a new and eternal existence not limited to earthly life, for "citizenship in heaven." Jesus promises to "transform the body of our humiliation that it may be conformed to the body of his glory, by the power that also enables him to make all things subject to himself" (Philippians 3:20-21).

CHAPTER NINE

The Gospel and Postmodernism

The Hourglass of Salvation

We noted earlier that it is impossible to reduce Christianity to a single phrase or concept, but it is possible to summarize the Bible in a single sentence. The Bible is the story of God's self-revelation through the chosen people of Israel, and God's redemption of them and all peoples through Jesus Christ. Most of the great religious texts of the world, even those far shorter than the Bible, cannot be distilled in this way. The Bible, however, has a grand narrative, and it can even be diagrammed. The architecture of salvation follows a historical process roughly analogous to an hourglass. The process begins at the top of the hourglass at the widest point with the formation of a people who were descendants of Abraham, a Chaldean expatriate who emigrated from the city of Ur to Canaan sometime in the eighteenth century B.C., or earlier. This people — for long centuries little more than a displaced tribe — became the point of contact of God's revelatory activity. As the revelation progressed and became more specific, the hourglass narrowed. The revelation of God's moral will in Torah began the narrowing process, along with the institution of the sacrificial cult of priests and tabernacle. The formation of leaders in judges and kings and prophets narrowed the process still further. The neck of the hourglass, the point of greatest specificity, represents God's final and clearest focus in Jesus of Nazareth. Jesus summed up the whole story, or better, *centered* it. Jesus was Israel reduced to one.

From Jesus the process reversed itself, widening outward to include all who through faith receive the salvation freely offered in him, for "Jew and Greek, slave and free, male and female, for all of you are one in Christ Jesus" (Galatians 3:28). In the particularity of Jesus of Nazareth, all peoples, indeed all creation, hear their own story told.

The New Testament writers and the Jewish sages before them were confident that in the history of Israel, God was weaving the story of the redemption of the world. Like any family tree, there were inevitable gaps and lacunae. But the overall shape of the tree was clear, as the apostle Paul noted in Galatians 3:16, "Now the promises were made to Abraham and to his offspring; it does not say, 'And to offsprings,' as of many; but it says, 'And to your offspring,' that is, to one person, who is Christ." The unexpected emphasis on "offspring" in the singular shows Paul's conviction that God's self-revelation in the history of Israel narrowed to a single point in Jesus Christ.

When one reads the New Testament — and this is especially true if one comes to it from the Old Testament — one encounters an unshakable conviction on the part of its writers that in Jesus Christ the story of Israel has achieved a consummating fulfillment. All the writers of the New Testament are seized by this prodigious reality. What overwhelms them is not something they have discovered, like clues that lead detectives to the solution of a crime. Their wonderment results from a secret that was *revealed* to them, causing them to see and understand the whole history of Israel in a new light. The apostle Paul voiced this new understanding in 1 Corinthians 15:3-8, reminding his readers that Jesus was the fulfillment of the Old Testament Scriptures. Similarly, when a Roman centurion asked about salvation, the apostle Peter told the hourglass story I just outlined, from Israel to Jesus (Acts 10:36-43). The Jesus-event was not a capricious bolt of lightning, but rather the consummation and key of the divine plan within the long history of God's chosen people.

From Matthew to Revelation the New Testament quakes and reverberates with the conviction that the final chapter of the grand narrative of God has been written. Jesus Christ is not another hero in the honor roll of faith, not even the greatest hero, nor a theophany or avatar of God. Jesus Christ is the neck of the hourglass, the one perfect self-disclosure of God, through whom God acted conclusively for the salvation of the world.

The Postmodern Dilemma

There are scores of "hourglass" summaries of the grand narrative in the New Testament and in the creeds of Christianity. One of the earliest and most definitive is quoted by the apostle Paul:

> God highly exalted [Jesus]
> and gave him the name
> that is above every name, so that at the name of Jesus
> every knee should bend,
> in heaven and on earth and under the earth,
> and every tongue should confess
> that Jesus Christ is Lord,
> to the glory of God the Father.   (Philippians 2:9-11)

Definitive statements like this are not warmly tolerated in a postmodern era, however. They fall under a cloud of suspicion, thought to claim too much for too many. I believe that the influence of postmodernism is one of the chief reasons why many Christians today are hesitant to express their faith in a publicly significant way. In most cases, it seems to me, the influence of postmodernism is covert rather than overt, causing Christians to censor themselves. And so the purpose of this chapter is to attempt to shed light on this obscure but influential phenomenon we call "postmodernism," and to consider its significance for Christianity.

Postmodernism is a cultural catchword that is no easier to define than is a word like "art" or "poetry." A barebones description would be this: postmodernism is a theory of knowledge asserting that there is no real knowledge of an external objective world perceivable to the human senses. As a theory, postmodernism arose late in the twentieth century, but it is dependent on the conviction of Friedrich Nietzsche, the late nineteenth-century philosopher, that there are no facts, only interpretations. The most essential tenet of postmodernism is its denial of universals. In this respect postmodernism stands in a tradition of Western philosophy influenced by Immanuel Kant, the eighteenth-century philosopher, who taught that universal categories exist in the human mind but not in the external fabric of nature. Data, Kant believed, have no meaning unless the receiving mind processes them according to patterns inherent in the mind itself. The idea that data themselves have no inherent meaning does not begin with Kant, however. Already in the fourteenth century, William of Ockham, a medieval nominalist, denied the existence of universals in nature.

Of course "postmodernism" literally means "after modernism." When one understands "modern" in the sense of trust in Western values, then "postmodern" is an intellectual revolt against that trust. Twentieth-century experiments in totalitarianism laid an ax at the root of modernism. After the Nuremberg rallies and Auschwitz, Stalinist collectivization and the Gulag, the Cultural Revolution and Tiananmen Square, anything presuming absolute authority, dominance, or determinative value has become suspect. One postmodernist describes the norms and categories of the Western intellectual tradition in terms of "terrorism":

> Post-modernism signals the death of such "meta-narratives" whose secretly terroristic function is to ground and legitimate the illusion of a "universal" human history. We are now in the process of awakening from the nightmare of modernity, with its manipulative reason and fetish of the totality, into the laid-back pluralism of the post-modern, that heterogeneous range of life-styles and language games which has renounced the nostalgic urge to totalize and legitimate itself.[1]

1. See the review by Terry Eagleton ("Awakening from Modernity," *Times Literary Supplement* 4377 [20 February 1987]: 194) of Jean-François Lyotard's *The Postmodern Condition: A Report on Knowledge,* trans. G. Bennington and B. Massumi (Minneapolis: University of Minneapolis Press, 1984). Quoted in Stanley J. Grenz, "The Universality of the 'Jesus-Story' and the 'Incredulity toward Metanarratives,'" *No Other Gods Before Me?,* ed. John G. Stackhouse Jr. (Grand Rapids: Baker Academic Books, 2001), 94.

The word "metanarrative" in this biting denunciation refers to an umbrella of European and Judeo-Christian values that, in the minds of postmodern thinkers, are bankrupt. In addition to the catastrophic forms of totalitarianism mentioned above, postmodernists decry movements and ideologies such as trust in scientific progress; capitalist economic forces and globalization; the technological values of Western society; the imposition of Western values, democracy, and Americanization on other peoples; and categorical religious and moral claims, including those of Christianity. The implicit and often unconscious trust that our culture places in these metanarratives, these overarching values, gives them unwarranted and oppressive power, according to postmodernists.

The problem with metanarratives is twofold. First, postmodernists deny that they have any inherent existence. There is no world-story; there are no universal truths. The world consists of a variety of individual and autonomous fiefdoms that, like mismatched pieces of a puzzle, do not fit together to form a coherent pattern. Each of the fiefdoms has its own narrative. Like a view through a keyhole, for instance, each narrative provides a glimpse of reality, but never a complete picture of it. The first critique, in other words, is that metanarratives are illusory. A second critique has to do with their effects. Postmodernists argue that metanarratives are illusory values that are used by powerful groups and cultures to oppress other, less powerful ones. Metanarratives drown out other voices and stories, especially those of minority peoples and those not in concert with the dominant chorus.

The oppression decried by postmodernists is not primarily the hot-metal oppression of guns and tanks, but the oppression that is subtly undergirded by cultural ideas and assumptions, the intellectual archetypes that justify and lead to military and political domination. All cultures enshrine oppressive assumptions, especially as expressed in language, literature, and the writing of history. Since values and value judgments are culturally bound, postmodernism results in a form of cultural relativism. There are no values, according to postmodernists, that are universally valid for all peoples in all times. Hence the truths that are held, whether by individuals or by cultures, are valid within their respective cultures and tribes, but not beyond them. Such truths are like national currencies: they are valid only in the country of issue. Dollars can be spent in North America, but not in Japan; yen in Japan, but not in Switzerland. All cultures have their particular validity, and all beliefs bearing the imprimatur of the culture are valid. But no belief can claim universal objective truth, or superiority over others. No one size fits all. Postmodernists can and do speak of truths and hard realities, but only as they exist within local and culturally conditioned geographies. When such truths exceed their allotted jurisdiction and presume to the status of metanarratives they become as oppressive — and doomed — as the Berlin Wall in Cold War-era Germany.

When the postmodernist agenda is applied to the reading of literature or historical texts, it is called "deconstruction." Not destruction — as in the eradication of something — but deconstruction, the exposing and dismantling of the "social constructs" embedded in texts. Postmodernists believe that social constructs are the aqueducts of power. Power is an expression of special interests, whether politics, race, class, religion, or gender. When a text is used to support a prevailing power structure it is called a "hegemonic reading," an interpretation favoring those in power. Texts are simply expressions of social constructs and cannot claim universal truth. They have no fixed meaning, but are fluid and polyvalent. Cultural conditions and assumptions embedded in texts distort the way we see reality in the same way that water flowing over an object distorts our view of the shape of the object. Meaning is not determined by what the author intended (for that is merely a construct in the mind of the reader), but by what the reader imputes to the text.[2] Each interpretation is as valid as another, apart from which a given text has no meaning.[3] Since readers and not authors produce meaning in texts, one could say that in a truly postmodern world the name of the reader ought to appear on the cover of a book rather than the name of the author!

2. Tim Meadowcroft, "Relevance as a Mediating Category in the Reading of Biblical Texts: Venturing Beyond the Hermeneutical Circle," *Journal of the Evangelical Theological Society* 45/4 (2003): 619-20.

3. See William G. Dever, "Save Us from Postmodern Malarkey," *Biblical Archaeology Review* 26/2 (2002): 30. Also Gavin Hyman, *The Predicament of Postmodern Theology: Radical Orthodoxy or Nihilist Textualism?* (Louisville: Westminster/John Knox, 2001).

Is Postmodernism a *Postmortem* of Christianity?

How does postmodernism affect belief in Jesus as savior? Let me begin by mentioning ways that aspects of postmodernism may affect Christianity positively. First of all, postmodern historians often point out that the authorized biography of the American "story" has been the story of English and northern European peoples, transmitted in the English language. Postmodernism endeavors to augment this story by hearing and valuing the stories of other Americans — African Americans, Latin Americans, Asian Americans, Native Americans, and others. Postmodernism offers the potential to do the same for Christianity — to flesh out our understanding of our own faith by giving ear to voices that have long been outside the mainstream, such as those of women.

Likewise, postmodernism's sensitivity to power, particularly as transmitted through assumptions of cultural superiority, offers a timely caution light to America as it exercises its role as sole superpower in an unstable post–Cold War era. In a related vein, postmodernism's agenda of freeing the world from captivity to Western cultural norms can have a positive effect on Christian missions. Postmodernism helps to clarify the distinction between Christian and Western: people can be authentically Christian without becoming Western — and they can certainly be Western without being Christian! Postmodernism can encourage Christians to affirm the indigenization of the gospel in other cultures, as they affirm its indigenization in Western culture.

Postmodernism also blunts the Enlightenment bias against Christianity that we discussed in Chapter 1. As long as "real" truth is determined by empiricism, rationalism, and the scientific method alone, other truth claims, including those of Christianity, will be relegated to "non-accredited" status. But postmodernism argues for the epistemological validity of forms of knowing other than strictly empirical and scientific knowledge, including religious forms of knowing. Postmodernism thus extends an invitation to Christianity to take a seat at the table of a postmodern world. This is, to be sure, a double-edged sword, for postmodernism invites virtually all other beliefs to the table as well. Nevertheless, it is not surprising that some Christian thinkers are sympathetic to postmodernism, and will probably continue to be so as Christianity experiences a cultural disenfranchisement in the West, a demotion from center page to margin, from guardian of the social order and chaplain at court to prophet outside the gate.

The foregoing aspects of postmodernism are indeed gains. A categorical embracing of postmodernism, however, would result in several long-term losses. One major problem with postmodernism is its denial of inherent meanings in stories and texts. To say that a story or text is capable of more than one interpretation is not to say it is capable of any interpretation, as postmodernism does. It is, after all, the presumption of meaning that attracts us to art, music, or literature. If we truly thought there were no inherent meanings in texts, if meaning were solely a form of cultural or individual projection, then a given story or painting or song would hold no more potential interest for us than a paint spill. The textual nihilism inherent in postmodernism reduces texts to mirrors of self-projection. And if this were what texts really are, then the New Testament and the proclamation of the Christian gospel would lose all value as sources of knowledge about God and salvation, because they would only tell us what we want to hear.

The pessimism about inherent meaning in texts is an outflow of pessimism about the existence of any absolute values or beings in the universe apart from human beings. Philosopher Jacques Derrida, considered by many the dean of postmodernists, says that if he were sure there were a True Presence apart from himself, that Presence would hold no interest for him. Similarly, he claims to pray only because he does not know to whom he prays. For Derrida, religious belief and prayer are meaningful only because they are founded on skepticism and hopelessness.[4] For Derrida, God seems to be like a piece of abstract art that is capable of many interpretations, or of no interpretation at all. Perhaps Derrida's views are a protest against a type of arrogant religious certainty that lacks charity and humility and a sense of the spiritual. Whatever their origin, I do not think Derrida speaks for many people at this point. As a theology professor and pastor, I spend much of my life talk-

4. Address to the American Academy of Religion in Toronto, November 24, 2002.

ing to people about God, and I do not know many people who are interested in believing in and praying to a God whose existence is a matter of indifference to them. Praying to an uncertain God is as appealing to most people as the thought of jumping out of an airplane with an uncertain parachute.

Beyond its inherent textual nihilism, postmodernism collides with the central claim of Christianity that Jesus Christ is the savior of the *world* (John 4:42). The rejection of universal truth is a second major pitfall of postmodernism. If truth is something each society fashions in order to shape its identity, then there is no truly universal truth. We began this chapter by noting the grand narrative of the Bible, summarized, for example, in John 3:16, "God so loved the world that he gave his only Son, that whoever believes in him would not die but have eternal life." This is in no uncertain terms a metanarrative, for the gospel explicitly claims that the one God who created everything is the one God who in the particularity of the Christ-event made provision for the redemption of *all* people in *all* times.[5]

As we noted above, postmodernists can and do make truth claims. The statement, "Jesus Christ is the savior *for us*," can be made by a postmodernist. The key to understanding this statement from a postmodernist perspective is the italicized portion, *for us*. Such a statement does not intend to make a universal claim, but a parochial one limited to the speaker or the speaker's party. A universal statement like "Jesus Christ is the savior of the world," would be as untenable from a postmodernist perspective as would an expectation that the laws or currency of one country should be valid in all countries. Thus postmodernism embraces faith and moral claims, but it diminishes them almost to a level of personal preference.

A third problem with postmodernism concerns "hegemonic readings," that is, the belief that the interpretation and use of texts support prevailing power structures. Certainly, texts can be used to support unjust power structures, including Christian texts. The support of racial slavery and the subjugation of women through the use of the Bible are ex-

5. See Grenz, "The Universality of the 'Jesus-Story,'" 85-111.

amples of such hegemonic readings. The use of the Bible to justify ravaging the natural world is a further example. It is possible to use any text for ends contrary to its intended purposes. The above examples are misuses of the Bible rather than interpretations that correspond with its spirit and teaching. The assertion of postmodernism that Christianity supports the dominant and unjust policies of Western culture is equally mistaken, in my view. The New Testament is not a product of the values of Western culture, nor does it advocate them. The argument that Christianity undergirds Western imperialism is anachronistic, for the concept of Western culture did not arise, at the earliest, until Constantine fused church and state together, some three centuries after the New Testament period.

The early church proclaimed the gospel of Jesus Christ not from a position of power, nor in support of a position of power. The gospel was first proclaimed by a tiny minority — no more than two or three thousand people at first — on the eastern fringe of the Roman Empire. Its earliest symbols were loaves and fish, a vine and grapes, a lamb, a dove, an olive branch, a boat and anchor, a basin and towel, a veiled woman praying with raised hands, the Good Shepherd. These were not symbols of power and dominance, but of deliverance, security, kinship, healing, and service. The cross was conspicuously absent from early Christian art until after the legalization of Christianity in the fourth century under Constantine. A shameful symbol of suffering and criminal death did not appeal to people who were themselves oppressed.[6] A sword occasionally appeared in early Christian art, but only as a symbol of the incisiveness and effectiveness of the word of God (Ephesians 6:17; Hebrews 4:12), not as one of military might.

The proclamation of the gospel and the missionary outreach of the early church were not pretexts for the legitimation of self-power, as postmodernism insinuates. The New Testament church had no power to

---

6. G. F. Snyder, "Early Christian Art," *Anchor Bible* 1.454-61. Further on the disenfranchisement of earliest Christianity within its host culture, note Origen's admission that Jesus was an unesteemed man among unesteemed people. "Now, our Jesus is reproached for being born in a village, and not a Greek one at that. He did not belong to any nation widely esteemed, but was despised as the son of a poor laboring woman" (*Against Celsus* 1.29).

legitimize. The Christian gospel is the story of a man who suffered the most shameful and excruciating of deaths — crucifixion as a common criminal at the hands of Rome. It was first proclaimed and received by people who were for the most part not educated or powerful or of noble position (1 Corinthians 1:26). From its origin and in its essence Christianity was a proclamation to the disempowered by one who chose to be disempowered. "For you know the generous act of our Lord Jesus Christ, that though he was rich, yet for your sakes he became poor, so that by his poverty you might become rich" (2 Corinthians 8:9). The gospel is not a hegemonic reading of any class or culture or ideology. It is a declaration of freedom from the constraints of class, culture, and ideology.

The Drama of Salvation

We have argued that Jesus is rightly understood as the embodiment of the being and mission of God. The success of this argument depends on recognizing that Jesus was more than a prophet, priest, king, or revealer of God. He was, rather, one-of-a-kind, in a class by himself. Nevertheless, the establishment of his uniqueness does not say all that must be said of Jesus. There are unique, powerful occurrences in nature or history that are not worthy of second thoughts, and certainly not of belief and worship. The eruption of Krakatoa in 1883 was one of the most unique phenomena of recorded history. The explosion blasted the mountain of Krakatoa out of the sea, forming a crater on the ocean floor. It sent towering tidal waves racing across the Pacific at hundreds of miles per hour, killed thousands of people, and launched cirrus ash clouds that blackened the city of London, halfway around the globe. The eruption of Krakatoa was a unique historical event. But who admires it? Power that is phenomenal yet purposeless does not evoke belief or allegiance.

The salvation that the New Testament proclaims in Jesus is unique, but unlike Krakatoa it is not simply episodic. Krakatoa cannot be diagrammed, but salvation can be. The sending of Jesus fits with a divine strategy and plan, like the artistic immensity of a gothic cathedral or the intricacy of a camera. Jesus Christ is the culmination of a history of speech in the divine drama. In about A.D. 58, as he awaited an uncertain fate in a Roman prison, the apostle Paul testified to this grand design: "I stand here on trial on account of my hope in the promise made by God to our ancestors, a promise that our twelve tribes hope to attain, as they earnestly worship day and night," declared Paul to Herod Agrippa II. "It is for this hope, your Excellency, that I am accused by Jews!" (Acts 26:6-8). For Paul and his fellow Jews, history was a standing hope of the fulfillment of the promises of God. This hope was nourished above all by the prophets (see, for example, Jeremiah 31:31-34; Ezekiel 36:24-32), and supremely fulfilled in the sending of the Messiah. "All the prophets testify about [Jesus Christ] that everyone who believes in him receives forgiveness of sins through his name," declared the apostle Peter to the Gentile Cornelius (Acts 10:43). The prophets had not been granted detailed knowledge of the whole plan. They were like people who saw a huge construction project still in progress. Nevertheless, their witness allowed those afterward to recognize Jesus as the Messiah of God (1 Peter 1:9-12). Jesus was the final affirmation of all the promises of God to Israel (1 Corinthians 1:19-22; Acts 13:32-33).

The story of the Bible is the story of an unfolding drama in which God intervened from time to time by sending special actors on stage. The actors were sometimes assigned minor roles and were not fully recognized until later. Especially in the case of the prophets, their roles often entailed disgrace and suffering. The ancient Hebrews often referred to such interventions by the verb *paqad,* which carried the sense of something appointed by God.[7] The exodus of Israel from oppression of Egypt was the classic intervention: "When [the people of Israel] heard that the LORD had given heed (*paqad*) to the Israelites and that he had seen their misery, they bowed down and worshiped" (Exodus 4:31). The story of the vineyard in Isaiah 5 is likewise an allegory of God's repeated interventions in Israel to produce a people who were like a fruitful vineyard. "What more was there to do for my vineyard that I have not done in it?" declares God to Israel (v. 4).

The New Testament is fully alert to this *modus operandi,* seeing in Je-

---

7. *Theological Dictionary of the Old Testament,* s.v. *paqad.*

sus the consummate intervention of God. At the birth of John the Baptizer, his father Zechariah sang, "Blessed be the Lord God of Israel, for he has looked favorably on his people and redeemed them" (Luke 1:68). The word for "looked favorably" in this passage is the Greek equivalent of the Hebrew *paqad*. Later in Luke, when Jesus performed a miracle in a Galilean village and the Jewish peasants exclaimed, "A great prophet has risen among us!, and God has looked favorably on his people!" (7:16), they recognized that God had again "visited" Israel. The magisterial prologue to the Epistle to the Hebrews declares that in Jesus, the Son of God, God spoke the last word. "Long ago God spoke to our ancestors in many and various ways by the prophets, but in these last days he has spoken to us by a Son whom he appointed" (Hebrews 1:1-2). In many and various ways the Bible clearly recounts the architectural design of salvation from Abraham to Christ.

Jesus was aware of the grand narrative and of his particular role in it. When an anxious John the Baptist, languishing in prison under Herod Antipas, inquired whether Jesus was the one to come, Jesus sent the messengers back to John: "Go and tell John what you hear and see: the blind receive their sight, the lame walk, the lepers are cleansed, the deaf hear, the dead are raised, and the poor have good news brought to them" (Matthew 11:6; also Luke 7:22). From our perspective this seems a somewhat evasive reply. But in the Jewish culture of Jesus' day a deed done rather than a word spoken was truly the proof of the pudding. In his reply to John's messengers, Jesus cited his *works* — the very works that the Messiah, anointed by the Spirit of God, would perform (Isaiah 29:18; 61:1-3) — to settle John's anxieties.

Jesus' awareness of playing the decisive role in the drama of salvation is apparent in the most revealing passage in the Synoptic Gospels. "All things have been handed over to me by my Father; and no one knows who the Son is except the Father, or who the Father is except the Son and anyone to whom the Son chooses to reveal him" (Luke 10:22). This remarkable testimony, which we discussed in Chapter 5, does not simply attest to Jesus' unique and unparalleled relationship with the Father. It also attests to his anchor role in the divine relay race, as the following verse testifies. "Blessed are the eyes that see what you see! For I tell you that many prophets and kings desired to see what you see, but did not see it, and to hear what you hear, but did not hear it" (Luke 10:23-24; also Matthew 13:16-17). Israel's prophets and kings had prepared the way for something that superseded them — the sending of the Son.

The Sending of the Son

The load-bearing term for the divine intervention in Jesus is the New Testament concept of "sending." In the Parable of the Vineyard, for example, Jesus told of a landowner who planted a vineyard and let it out to tenants. At harvest time the landowner sent his servants to collect his produce. But in the absence of the landowner, the tenants became claim jumpers. When the owner's servants arrived, they paid their rent in blows. The landowner played the final card in his hand. He "still had one other, a beloved son. Finally he *sent* him to them, saying, 'They will respect my son.' But the tenants said to one another, 'This is the heir; come, let us kill him, and the inheritance will be ours'" (Mark 12:6-7// Matthew 21:37-38). Jesus formulated this parable after the allegory in Isaiah 5, noted above. The description of the landowner's son as the last and only beloved son who is the heir is a self-description of Jesus. No one in Israel, not even the prophets, spoke of themselves as playing such a decisive role. Such terms befit the Messiah — and only the Messiah. They are Jesus' testimony to his central role in the divine economy.

The concept of Jesus as the sent Messiah is deeply etched in the Pauline Epistles and the Gospel of John. After Paul's lament about the human failure to fulfill God's law in Romans 7, he makes an almost rhapsodic transition to Jesus Christ in Romans 8. Despite the weakness of the human will and the inability of Torah to produce human morality, Paul declares that "God has done what the law, weakened by the flesh, could not do: by sending his own Son in the likeness of sinful flesh, and to deal with sin, he condemned sin in the flesh" (v. 3). The sending of Jesus was God's final answer to the problem of human inadequacy, weakness, and sin. Paul repeats the idea similarly in Galatians 4: "But when the fullness of time had come, God sent his Son, born of a woman, born under the law, in order to redeem those who were under the law, so that we might receive adoption as children" (vv. 4-5). God's earlier appointments in Israel had been partial and provisional until the fullness of time, when in a consummating act God sent not a prophet, priest, or king; not a friend of God, envoy of God, or servant of God; not an angel of God, spirit of God, or apparition of God, but *God's Son*, God's incarnational likeness.

Nowhere is the concept of Jesus as the true emissary of the Father clearer than in the Gospel of John. In no fewer than forty instances John declares that Jesus was sent by the Father.[8] The sending of the Son comprises the essence of the Father's work. Indeed, John declares that there is no other work for a person to do than to believe that the Father has sent the Son (6:29; 11:42). Jesus is the authentic reflection of the true God who sent him (John 7:28-29, 33; 8:16, 26); hence, whoever sees Jesus sees the Father (12:45). The Father sent the Son so that people will believe in God (12:44), and whoever knows the Son sent by the Father has eternal life (5:24; 6:39, 44; 17:3). The God who sent Jesus is the true God (7:28; 8:26), and as the true God he witnesses to Jesus (5:37; 8:18, 42) and is with Jesus (8:29). Consequently, Jesus was sent by the Father to do his will (4:34; 5:30; 6:38). No one can do the will of God as Jesus does (9:4), by teaching the will of God (7:16) and speaking the words of God (3:34). Jesus has been sent by the Father not to judge the world but save it (3:17), and introduce the life of God into the world (6:57). The Son surpasses all previous emissaries, including John the Baptizer (John 5:36-38). In truth, whoever receives Jesus, receives the true God who sent him (John 13:20).

The Anointed One

The Hebrew word *Messiah* and the Greek word *Christ* both mean "anointed one." The latter term has become so identified with Jesus that if you did not know that *Christ* was a title you would mistake it for Jesus' last name! In the earliest Christian preaching Jesus was already being

8. See, for example, 5:23, 36, 38; 7:29, 33; 8:16, 42; 12:49; 14:24, 26; 15:21; 16:5, 7; 17:8, 18, 21, 23, 25.

called Messiah (Acts 4:26; 5:42). The title denoted that the one antici-
pated by God in earlier covenants had appeared to consummate the plan
of salvation. In an early sermon in the temple of Jerusalem, the apostle
Peter declared that Jesus was like the proverbial building block that, although initially rejected, later became the capstone of the edifice (Acts
4:10-11). The concrete image of the rejected building block, taken from
Psalm 118:22, signifies that Jesus was the material completion of Israel's
central place and act of worship.

In 1 Peter 2:24-25 we see Jesus further defined. Here Jesus is likened to
perhaps the most enigmatic and sublime figure in all the Old Testament,
the Servant of the Lord. The sacrificial death of Jesus on the cross is described and interpreted by selected phraseology from Isaiah 53: "he himself bore our sins in his body," "by his wounds you have been healed," "for
you were going astray like sheep." These inimitable descriptions of the
suffering Servant of the Lord are applied directly to Jesus' death on the
cross. The Servant of the Lord is the *only* figure in the Old Testament
whose death was endowed with vicarious significance. This otherwise
unknown figure was understood by the early church as a forerunner and
anticipation of the Lamb of God who came in Jesus, whose sufferings and
death would make vicarious payment for the sins of the world.

In still another Messianic echo, the final chapter of the New Testament quotes a resurrected and ascended Jesus declaring, "I am the root
and the descendant of David, the bright morning star" (Revelation
22:16). The images of "root" and "descendant of David" (Isaiah 11:1), and
"bright morning star" (Numbers 24:17), are quintessential Messianic images in the Old Testament. They declare Jesus' identification with the
source of the metaphors in the Old Testament, and his consummation of
them in the New.

In proclaiming Jesus as the Christ, the early church loaded the title
with options far in excess of its basic meaning. This enhancement appears to have originated in Jesus himself. Following a series of contro-
versies during his last days in Jerusalem, Jesus pressed the learned inter-
preters of the law about the meaning of the title "Christ." Citing Psalm
110, the standard proof text vindicating the Davidic lineage of the Messiah, Jesus argued that the Messiah was not defined by David, but rather

that David was defined by the Messiah (Mark 12:35-37; Matthew 22:41-45; Luke 20:41-44). That is, we do not understand the Messiah by first understanding King David. Rather, we understand King David as an illustration of the Old Testament concept of Messiah.

The Power of History

We have spoken in this chapter of the gospel as a historical drama. A drama is a designed uniqueness as opposed to a random uniqueness (remember Krakatoa), and hence a higher order of power and persuasion. If a drama is historical rather than imaginative, it assumes an even higher degree of power and persuasion. The gospel is the drama or story of a self-revelation of God *in history,* and its historical nature lends an evidential or axiomatic quality to the revelation itself.

I once witnessed a strangely effective appeal to this axiomatic power of history. In the 1990s I received a grant from the German government to investigate the fate of Professor Ernst Lohmeyer, a prominent German theologian and president of the University of Greifswald who mysteriously disappeared in 1946. The challenge to unravel the long-suppressed fate of a preeminent German intellectual promised — and delivered — the sensation of a historical thriller. While in Greifswald I worked alone in the archives of the University — alone, that is, except for two women who read large, handwritten folio volumes from 8 a.m. until 5 p.m. daily, with an hour off for lunch. After observing them for several days, and trying but failing to engage them in conversation, I asked the archivist what they were doing, and why they would not speak to me. "They are not allowed to speak to you," the archivist said. "They are serving a sentence." Now, I know people who regard libraries as places of punishment, but I had never known a person to have been *sentenced* to one! The archivist explained, "The two women were both school principals when the Wall came down in 1989. They refused to give up teaching Marxism-Leninism, and they were tried in court. The judge who heard their case saw in them good educators, despite their misguided politics. He sentenced them both to a year in the archive, researching the histories of their respective schools. The judge hopes that real history will dispel bad ideology."[9]

There is the axiomatic power of history. And in this instance, as I later learned, its power was effective. The historical investigation of one of the women caused her to change her political ideology, and she was favorably restored to her post as principal.

One God, One Redeemer

In this chapter we have examined the story of salvation in the context of postmodernism's parochial view of truth claims. And while it seems clear that we can learn some useful things from postmodernism, the New Testament presents a univocal testimony to a purposeful activity of God in history that has universal significance. In the final analysis, the singularity of salvation is "in character" with the nature of God. The nature of God, in fact, offers a final clue to the nature of salvation, for the Bible witnesses that God is one (Deuteronomy 6:4; Romans 3:30). By "one," the Bible means first, that there is only one God; and second, that the nature of the one God is a unified nature. This is the reason the God revealed in Scripture abhors being identified with or likened to other gods and goddesses. There can never be any other god like this God. "Before me no God was formed, nor shall there be any after me. I, I am the LORD, and besides me there is no savior. . . . I am God, and also henceforth I am He; there is no one who can deliver from my hand; I work and who can hinder it?" (Isaiah 43:10-13).

Who God is, determines the way God acts. Form determines function. If there were many gods, we might suspect that there should be many ways of salvation. But if there is only one God, and if God's nature is one, then it is inconsistent to suppose that there should be or even

9. For "the rest of the story" on Lohmeyer, see J. R. Edwards, "Ernst Lohmeyer — ein Schlusskapitel," *Evangelische Theologie* 56/4 (1996): 320-42. Briefly, Lohmeyer was murdered by the NKVD (the forerunner of the Soviet KGB) on September 19, 1946, on fabricated charges of being a war criminal. His refusal to surrender the University of Greifswald to Soviet control was the real reason for his execution, however.

could be many ways of salvation. It is entirely "in character" for a God of singular nature to enact the divine will in a singular way. Being one rather than many, God should elect to save the world in one way, through one individual. This is precisely the scriptural testimony: "There is one God; there is also one mediator between God and humankind, Christ Jesus, himself human, who gave himself a ransom for all" (1 Timothy 2:5). Would a God who provided for the salvation of the world in a unique, costly, and sacrificial death of his Son be willing to accept any other means — and especially any lesser means — of salvation? If lesser means would have sufficed, why the scandalous sacrifice of his Son? Reason concurs with revelation. We should expect that the very particular love of God demonstrated in Jesus Christ would be expressed in a very particular way in the world. One God, one nature of the one God, one saving will for the world, "one mediator between God and humankind, Christ Jesus."

CHAPTER TEN

Does an Exclusive Savior Threaten World Peace?

The Agenda of Soteriological Pluralism

There seem to be two major concerns looming on the horizon at the beginning of the Third Millennium. The first is that the world, despite its diversity, is more accessible and interconnected and interdependent than ever before. The picture of earth that was beamed from the moon in the 1960s — a globe of living blue suspended in dark space — is an icon of this reality. That icon is materializing in countless ways — through world travel and trade, economic globalization, the Internet, and new political alliances like the European Union. But an interdependent world is also a more vulnerable world. When the stock market sneezes in New York or Tokyo or Brussels, people in Mombassa and Santiago and Bombay catch colds. An interdependent world is like a body — and the whole body aches when a thumb is smashed in the door.

This leads to a second major awareness, which is that religion is here to stay. Many advocates of scientific materialism and secularism in the last century expected that they would live to witness religion's inglorious funeral. Thinkers such as Frazer and Marx and Freud believed religion was a developmental state on the human odyssey from magic to science. A leading twentieth-century New Testament scholar in Germany blithely asserted that anyone who flipped on an electrical light switch could no longer intellectually believe in the miracles recorded in the New Testament. Even the Hollywood actor Bruce Willis remarked that "organized religions were important when we didn't know why the sun moved, why weather changed, why hurricanes occurred. Modern religion is the end trail of modern mythology."[1] The idea here is that a mature scientific worldview would cause religion to wither like an appendage that had grown useless. Yet the members of this tribe have been in for a great surprise. Neither electrons nor evolution have caused people to outgrow religious belief. Religion has adamantly reasserted itself as an undeniable constituent of human life and society.

And so we are faced with a dilemma: how can the increasing interdependence of the world and the persistence of religious truth claims be harmonized? Universal religious claims, especially as they appear in the West, are not obviously compatible with the many and diverse cultures, nations, and social systems of the world. Can people who profess one God, one way of salvation, and one moral code live responsibly, respectfully, and non-coercively among peoples who believe none of those things? And if so, how?

A solution commonly advanced to attempt to reconcile these two realities is known as soteriological pluralism. "Soteriology" refers to the theological doctrine of salvation, and "soteriological pluralism" refers to the proposal that there are a variety of means of attaining salvation. Recent findings of the Pew Forum on Religion and Public Life illustrate the degree to which soteriological pluralism has changed traditional religious beliefs, including Christian ones. The study indicates that nearly two thirds of Americans consider religion to be very important in their lives, and nearly as many see religious faith as essential to a strong American society. Religion is not conceived of exclusively, however, for a full seventy-five percent of Americans believe that many religions can lead to eternal life, compared with only eighteen percent who believe their own religion is the "one true faith." Even those who characterize themselves as highly committed to their religion are only slightly less willing to see salvation in inclusive terms; nearly fifty percent of the

---

1. *Los Angeles Times Magazine* (January 11, 2004): 8.

most strongly committed white evangelical Protestants believe that their faith is not the only path to salvation.[2]

A statement from a Christian missionary of Asian ethnicity speaks to the erosion of commitment to the saving uniqueness of Christ:

> Many today are connecting evangelism with colonialism, and they are connecting the doctrine of uniqueness with the idea of Western superiority. In this environment I am finding that many sensitive Western Christians, trying to respond Christianly to the allegations about a Western sense of superiority and arrogance, are really struggling with the doctrine of the absolute uniqueness of Christ. Some Evangelicals seem to have settled for an understanding of uniqueness that is somewhat less absolute than what Evangelicals have generally held.[3]

I am well aware of the evils that have been perpetrated in the name of Christianity, from the Crusades to the Spanish subjugation of Native American peoples to the bombing of African American churches in the American South. I cannot imagine how such atrocities served the gospel, for what denies the spirit of Christ also denies the gospel of Christ. Connecting evangelism and colonialism inevitably jades believers and nonbelievers alike to the gospel. Yet in light of the mistaken belief that they are somehow connected, many Christians have given up "really struggling" with the issue at all. To claim uniqueness and sole sufficiency for one particular savior in a world as diverse and disparate as ours seems to many people, Christian or otherwise, foolish and perhaps even blasphemous.

---

2. *Bible Review* 23/3 (2002): 14-15. For the complete November 2001 report, see www.people-press.org/reports.

3. Personal correspondence. The name and location of the missionary are withheld to protect his security.

Why the Rush to Soteriological Pluralism?

We shall devote the second half of this chapter to the question whether or not the New Testament and historic Christian faith can be interpreted as soteriologically pluralistic. But I want to hold this question in abeyance for the moment and ask first why the idea of many ways of salvation is asserting itself so insistently today. After all, the claims of the gospel and the complexity of the world have been common knowledge for a long time. Why at the present time are people "really struggling with the doctrine of the absolute uniqueness of Christ," to quote the Asian missionary?

There is no doubt that postmodernism, discussed in the last chapter, is partly responsible for the issue surfacing in the present form at the present time. But I see something further at work, and a story may help to illustrate it. In May of 1996 fifty-five mountaineers were inching their way up the steep Lohtse face of Mount Everest. This was the largest number of climbers ever to attempt to scale Everest at the same time, and their great numbers gave many of them a sense of security. The really experienced climbers among them, however, knew that the sense of safety was not only illusory but very dangerous, for the single length of rope to which they were all attached was anchored to only a few precarious ice-screws. The fall of even a single climber could have swept all of them off the mountain.

The mountaineers' predicament symbolizes our own. We are being made aware today that our interconnectedness has left us more vulnerable rather than more secure. It is our foreboding and fear that lie behind our suspicion of the idea that anyone or anything is the world's sole savior. The problem appears to be existential rather than theological. We fear that the misuse of one religion or ideology will lead to violence, and that the violence of one jeopardizes the peace and unity of all. This foreboding bears down on the shoulders of Christians, whose summary confession is that Jesus is *the* savior of the world. If Jesus can be demoted from the sole savior of the world to one savior among others, that is one less match to ignite the powder keg.

Students of history probably agree that the present world is not more violent or more cruel than it has been in the past. But the means of violence are more powerful today than ever before. Given the interdependence of peoples and nations and social systems, modern means of violence are capable of unprecedented degrees of disruption and devastation. The twentieth century is a grim witness to such capabilities, with its staggering 120 million war dead. Our existential angst over environmental devastation, nuclear destruction, economic globalization, and disease warn us not to be indifferent to religious claims. A theologian from India speaks for many when he says, "Since this is a threat to all humanity, to claim that one religious tradition has the *only* answer to such a global problem seems preposterous."[4]

It is not coincidental that the appeal of soteriological pluralism began asserting itself in earnest during the nuclear arms race and the collapse of the Soviet Union. The end of the Cold War has failed to relax global tensions. The proliferation of nuclear warheads and the mass marketing of sophisticated conventional weaponry have refracted the threat that formerly was lodged in the Soviet Union into scores of smaller rogue regimes and tyrannies. The West formerly had one target in its crosshairs. The target was large, stationary, known, and generally predictable. Since the end of the Cold War this threat has been shunted into many smaller, moving, unknown, and hard-to-see threats. In the post–World War II era the West learned to live with a known adversary with an enormous military arsenal; since 1990 it has not yet learned how to live with many unknown enemies that possess fewer and less powerful weapons (at this time), but are more willing to use them.

Of course, it would be a mistake to speak of the West or of the United States as wearing the white hat in all this. As one of the world's leading weapons producers, energy consumers, and environmental polluters, the United States contributes significantly to the problem of international destabilization. Polls of people outside the United States indicate that a large part of the world sees America as one of the chief threats to world peace and unity. Americans themselves usually differ-

---

4. Stanley Samartha, "Mission in a Religiously Plural World," *International Review of Mission* 78/307 (July 1988): 315.

entiate between American democracy and Christian faith, but they are often unaware that many peoples and countries fail to make such a distinction. Especially in Islamic countries, America is considered a "Christian nation," and a rejection of what is seen as American imperialism entails a rejection of Christianity as well. Many Christians who are sensitive to the problem of American arrogance and heavy-handedness in the world, and who wish to alleviate it, are tempted to do so by compromising the uniqueness and superiority of Christ.

Geopolitical destabilization and insecurity have propelled peacemaking to the top of the world's agenda. International tensions are of course not exclusively military; they are fueled by causes as diverse as ethnic tensions, access to land, natural resources, food production, the AIDS virus, and economic inequities. But they are also fueled by religion, and increasingly so. The terror attacks of September 11, 2001, were a violent reminder to Americans that the Crusades of the Middle Ages, the religious wars in sixteenth- and seventeenth-century Europe, and the religious violence of the Middle East, India, Pakistan, Indonesia, Northern Ireland, and Rwanda, are neither relics of the past nor consigned to distant parts of the globe. An increasingly interconnected world is an increasingly vulnerable world. The disruption of any of its parts, regardless of the reason, threatens the whole. In an effort to increase prospects of world peace, a growing chorus of voices is lobbying for the denial of exclusive truth claims that can and do fuel aggression. Here is the voice of an American theologian:

> I have come to believe that this exclusivist tendency in my own faith tradition — and in other faith traditions — is a serious barrier to genuine peace-making in a world of religious pluralism. For Christianity, the claim that salvation is possible only in Jesus Christ is, in the end, dismissive of other religious traditions and inherently divisive. If Christians are to be instruments of the peace of God, we must develop a new Christian theology of religions that will enable us to see God's revelation in Jesus Christ while at the same time rejecting any claim to exclusivism.[5]

5. Joseph C. Hough, Jr., "Ways of Knowing God," *Bible Review* 23/3 (2002): 16.

Of course, 9-11 sparked a religious frenzy in the media. Talk about God and theology were, for once, not merely tolerated but sought after. But the ubiquity of theological advisors and apologists was equaled by a rush to public prayer that was purged of any reference that might give offense to a nation in mourning or to Jews or Muslims or to persons of other faiths or no faith. Like the mountaineers on the Lohtse face who suddenly realized the precariousness of their situation, 9-11 seemed to crystallize "the new environment," as it was called. People were publicly admonished to give up traditions that divide and impede world unity. Christians, in particular, were advised to develop a "new theology" that would preserve God's mercy and redemption in Christ without denying the possibility that God has revealed salvation to other persons in different times and places. Christians were put on notice to "reinterpret their traditions to embrace modernity and pluralism." They were told to acknowledge other cultures' "visions of the transcendent," just as they acknowledged those cultures' law codes and social customs. From a historical and international perspective this sudden angst did not seem entirely rational to me. Compared with the carnage of Tannenberg or the Somme, of Stalingrad or Hiroshima, there was nothing particularly unusual about 9-11 — except that the death tolls and rubble heaps were in America.

9-11 was a violent reminder to Americans of the potential of religion to be used to justify harm, and the need to harness it for peace. After the attacks, pastors and religion professors around the country were solicited for public opinions. Never had our guild so flourished, not even after the fall of the Berlin Wall in 1989. Religion *per se*, however, was not the issue. The issue was religion as a means to *peace*. I stopped getting calls from reporters about the time that church attendance returned to normal. Nevertheless, there was an ironic twist in this for me, as there may have been for others: in our era, which has methodically banished religion from the public square and relegated it to the sidelines of private opinion, I have in the past argued for the public significance of Christianity. After 9-11, I found myself inisting that the public significance of religion certainly does not include religious fanaticism and heinous acts of aggression. And that, of course, is the knife-edge of the dilemma.

How can Christianity claim exclusive salvation in Jesus Christ and not result in coercive acts of supremacy? This is the question to which we turn in the second half of this chapter.

Grace: A Privilege of the Few, or a Gift to All?

The pluralism that we described above intends to do to exclusive religious claims what antitrust and deregulation laws do in the public sector. In both instances the objective is to break down monolithic entities — whether religions or public corporations — into smaller, less powerful, and more manageable entities. The intention, in other words, is to prevent totality or collectivity and to foster diversification instead. When we enter the New Testament world, however, we discover nearly the opposite concern. The world to which the gospel was first proclaimed, as we noted in Chapter 7, was fragmented, parochial, and unequal. Torah was a means of righteousness if one was an observant Jew. But most of the world was Gentile, not Jewish. Those Gentiles who were Roman citizens enjoyed a relatively large number of civil rights. But most of the world did not enjoy Roman citizenship. The various mystery cults offered emotional and psychological benefits to their devotees. But those benefits were inaccessible to most of the world. The aristocratic classes enjoyed privileges that the large slave and servant classes did not enjoy, and never could. The vagaries of social status or wealth or place of birth or ethnicity determined the precincts of privilege and discrimination in life.

The hope of the ancient world (at least for the have-nots) was this: could the privileges enjoyed by the few be extended to *all* people? This is nearly the opposite of our situation today. Modern pluralism fears the universal, whereas the vast majority of the first-century world longed for it. The Christian gospel spoke to this hope as did no other ancient philosophy or cult or promise. The New Testament declares the universal significance of Jesus as savior for all people, for Jews and Gentiles, for every tribe and tongue and nation. Indeed, the significance of Jesus as savior extends beyond humanity to *all creation* in heaven and earth, seen and unseen. If you read through the New Testament and note every text that relates to Jesus as savior, you will discover that by far the greatest number fall into the category of universal significance. The entire New Testament declares and repeats that in the particularity of Jesus, Israel reduced to one, that salvation has been accomplished for and is now offered to all creation.

Those Who Were Far Off Have Been Brought Near

Historically speaking, the most significant issue faced by the fledgling Christian movement was "the Gentile question." Our word "Gentile" is related to the Greek *ta ethnē*, which to the Jewish people of Jesus' day referred to non-Jews in the land of Israel as well as to "the nations" beyond Israel. "Gentile" thus carried both ethnic and geographical connotations. The Gentile question, then, was this: was the salvation promised in Jesus of Nazareth properly confined within the banks of Israel, or should it overflow to those beyond Israel's ethnic and geographical borders? The question was answered in favor of the latter. The answer, at first simply called "the Way," distinguished Christianity from all known forms of Judaism — whether Pharisaic, Sadducean, Zealot, Herodian, Essene, or the folk religion of the "people of the land." And it became the irrevocable first step in separating the Christian movement from all forms of Judaism. Chapters 10-15 of the book of Acts depict some of the historical events that marked the separation; in Galatians and Romans, the apostle Paul describes some of its theological causes. The historical mitosis of early Christianity from its various Jewish siblings was longer, less even, and more painful than the abbreviated New Testament record indicates. For example, the Judaizers mentioned in Galatians were unable to accept it. From the church fathers we learn of Ebionites and Nazaraeans who were caught between the separating camps of nascent Christianity and Pharisaic Judaism. Their allegiance to both Jesus and Jewish Torah relegated them to a no-man's-land in which they eventually withered and died. Yet despite all we do not know and will never know about the process, there could never have been any real doubt about how the early church would decide the Gentile question. The conviction that Jesus was the incarnation of the God who created the world determined the conclusion that Jesus was the savior of the world.

If Jesus were a local avatar — a specialty player in the divine economy — then his significance would be local and specialized. Moses had been one such player, sent to redeem Israel from Egypt. Moses had little or no significance for the larger world beyond Israel. But if Jesus was God incarnate, the very embodiment of the one God, then his significance was as universal as was that of the one God. The conclusion that Jesus was of the essence of the one God cast the deciding vote in favor of the inclusion of Gentiles as well as Jews in salvation. No other conclusion did justice to the early Christian understanding and experience of Jesus.

We noted in the last chapter that oneness entails universality. The question whether reality is one or many has a long and distinguished history in both Western and Eastern thinking, and it has nearly always been decided in favor of one. Science teaches that all living organisms are made up of variants of the same cell structure. Health could be defined as singleness of purpose within an organism: when a cell deviates from that purpose and proliferates randomly, it forms a tumor that will, unless arrested, kill the organism. The principle of unity of purpose applies to marriage, vocation, and most forms of human achievement. Eastern thinking, it is true, often favors the concept of "many" rather than "one." Nevertheless, Eastern thinking as represented in Hinduism also teaches that the center of each individual and the center of ultimate reality are one. The oneness of Jesus with God that is repeatedly affirmed in the New Testament can be seen as an archetype of the deep structure of the universe.[6] The language of the New Testament testifies to this reality. "In no [New Testament] passage does the predicate *theos* [God] designate Jesus as 'God' alongside the one God, but only as God *from* the one God."[7] Jesus is necessarily the one savior of all that God has created. So Gentiles are, along with Jews, fellow heirs of salvation.

---

6. John 1:18; 20:28; Romans 9:5; Titus 2:13; Hebrews 1:8ff.; James 1:1; 2 Peter 1:1; 1 John 5:20; Jude 5.

7. M. Karrer, *Jesus Christus im Neuen Testament* (Göttingen: Vandenhoeck & Ruprecht, 1998), 330.

The signature account in the New Testament of the salvation of Gentiles is the story of the conversion of Cornelius, a Roman centurion. Cornelius is the quintessential righteous Gentile — devout, God-fearing, prayerful, a benefactor of the needy, a doer of good (Acts 10:2, 35). Despite these virtues, however, Cornelius is made aware of his need for something beyond them. In a vision, God directs Cornelius to summon the apostle Peter. This produces a conflict of interest for Peter, a Jew who observes kosher (the distinction between clean and unclean things). The divine command violates the religious and social rules of both Jews and Gentiles. Cornelius is directed to a man from whom he should expect no help, and Peter is directed to one to whom he should show no sympathy. When the Christian missionary and righteous pagan finally meet, the divine conspiracy becomes apparent. Both must graduate in their understanding of God's universal love. "You know," exclaims Peter, "the message [God] sent to the people of Israel, preaching peace by Jesus Christ — he is Lord of all" (10:36). That is a revolutionary proclamation. In Jesus Christ, the promises to Israel are extended to *all* people, for Jesus is Lord of *all* people. Peter cannot believe he is saying it. Cornelius cannot believe he is hearing it. Yet the descent of the Holy Spirit on the believing Gentile confirms it.

Peter's encounter with Cornelius was a watershed in early Christianity. The significance of the lesson not to "call anyone profane or unclean" (Acts 10:28) is nearly impossible to overestimate. No other sect of Judaism, and no other cult or philosophy of the Greco-Roman world, aspired to such inclusivity. The story was so important that it is repeated in Chapter 11 of Acts. The Cornelius episode entered the bloodstream of the early church, and has never left it. It illumined something that in the long history of Israel had lain in the shadows: the offer of salvation to all peoples. The lesson learned from Cornelius became repeated in a vast array of New Testament formulae. A vision and commission similar to Peter's was also given to Paul (Galatians 1:15-16). "Go," commanded God, "for I will send you far away to the Gentiles" (Acts 22:21) to bring the gospel of salvation (20:21; 26:18). The universality of salvation became the driving thrust of Paul's letter to the heart of the Roman Empire, "The power of God for salvation to everyone who has faith, to the Jew first and also to the Greek" (Romans 1:16; 3:29-30; 1 Corinthians 1:18, 21). "Neither circumcision nor uncircumcision is anything; but a new creation is everything," wrote Paul to the Galatians (6:15; 5:6).

The new creation in Jesus reconciled the deep and theretofore unbridgeable division that defined Jews and Gentiles. Like Jews, Gentiles are also saved "through the grace of the Lord Jesus" (Acts 15:11). The mission expansion of early Christianity expressly included Gentiles (11:14-23; 13:46-47; 14:27; 18:4; 19:10). Nor were Gentiles an afterthought of God, an addendum to a salvation more or less complete without them. Rather, from both Jews and Gentiles God ordained to raise up a whole new people whose chief distinction is neither Judaism nor paganism (Romans 9:24-26). The inclusion of Gentiles in the saving economy of God was a mystery that, although hidden from former generations, had its inception in the eternal purpose of God, "before the foundation of the world" (Ephesians 1:3-5). "Gentiles have become fellow-heirs, members of the same body, and sharers in the promise of Jesus Christ in the gospel" (3:5-6). Jesus Christ was sent to minister to both Jews and Gentiles (Romans 15:8-9). Hence, of necessity all people — Jews and Greeks, slave and free, male and female — may be baptized by the Holy Spirit into the one body of Jesus Christ (Galatians 3:28; 1 Corinthians 12:12-18; Colossians 3:11).

The inclusion of Gentiles in salvation was not a maverick innovation of the apostle Paul.[8] To be sure, Paul considered himself the apostle to the Gentiles (Galatians 2:9), but Paul recognized already in the call of Abraham nearly two thousand years earlier the inevitability of the salvation of Gentiles. Abraham was justified, after all, before he was circum-

---

8. One recalls the attempt of F. C. Baur (1792-1860) to explain the New Testament and development of early Christianity as the result of a bitter strife between Jewish and Gentile Christianities, as represented in Peter and Paul, respectively. Baur viewed the development of Christianity as a classic example of Hegelian dialectic: Peter as the thesis, Paul as the antithesis, and their synthesis in second-century Roman Catholicism. Subsequent scholarship has found Baur's Hegelian straightjacket an ill fit for early Christianity. The inclusion of the Gentiles in salvation, which Baur mistakenly attributed to the genius of Paul, is certainly presupposed in significant Old Testament texts and in the ministry of Jesus.

cised, and before the giving of Torah (Genesis 15:6). He was justified, in other words, when he was still a Gentile. Abraham was thus the ancestor of *all* the faithful, circumcised and uncircumcised (Romans 4:11-12; Galatians 3:13-14).

Although the Old Testament is the story of God's overtures to Israel, those overtures were never limited to Israel. The prophets, above all, understood this. Amos saw a vision of "all the nations" coming to Yahweh (Amos 9:12), and Isaiah saw repeated extensions of the good news to Gentiles — to the tents of Kedar (that is, to Arabian tribes, 42:11), to the coastlands and peoples far away (49:1), and, through the Servant of the Lord, to "many nations" (49:6; 52:15). Micah saw a vision of all nations streaming to the restored temple in Jerusalem to learn of God (4:1-5). Zechariah foresaw the final triumph, where "the LORD will become king over all the earth; on that day the LORD will be one and his name one" (14:9). These visions of the inclusion of Gentiles in salvation were given classic expression by the prophet Jonah, who was forced to concede that the grace that embraced a truculent Israel could and also would embrace Israel's pagan archenemy, Assyria.

The intimations of Gentile salvation in the ministry of Jesus are equally evident. On occasion Jesus itinerated in Gentile regions, there healing a menacing demoniac (Mark 5:1-20), expelling a demon from a Gentile woman's daughter (Mark 7:24-30), and healing a deaf Gentile in the Decapolis (Mark 7:31-37). As though recalling the purified temple in Jerusalem that would draw "many nations" in worship (Micah 4:1-2), Jesus cleared the temple of moneychangers whose business prevented it from being "a house of prayer for all nations" (Mark 11:17). Further, in the Parable of the Mustard Seed, Jesus spoke of the birds of the air making nests in the shade of the mustard bush (Mark 4:32). This picturesque image probably connoted the inclusion of Gentiles within the people of Israel, for the nesting of birds in the branches of trees recalls several Old Testament passages alluding to the incorporation of Gentiles in God's chosen people (for example, Psalm 104:12; Ezekiel 17:23; 31:6; Daniel 4:9-21). Jesus' final commission in Matthew's Gospel is, appropriately, to "make disciples of all nations" (28:19).

The considered judgment of the early church was that God "had opened a door of faith to the Gentiles" (Acts 14:27). Peoples and nations who had known nothing of salvation found themselves surprisingly assured of it (Romans 9:30). About the year A.D. 50, the leaders of the early church gathered in Jerusalem and made what was surely the most formative decision in Christian history. Speaking for the council, the apostle James quoted Amos 9:11-12 (quoted above) in support of the decision "not to trouble those Gentiles who are turning to God" (Acts 15:19; similarly Galatians 2:2-10). As we have noted, there was no precedent for this momentous decision either in the practices of contemporary Judaism or in the Greco-Roman world. The testimonies by Peter and Paul of what God had done in their ministries caused the early church to reflect anew on the hints of the salvation of Gentiles latent in the Old Testament. Experience coupled with reflection on Scripture led the church to see the Gentile mission as the leading of the Holy Spirit (Acts 15:28). Some early Christians, like the aforementioned Ebionites and Nazaraeans, could not take this step. Others, like Peter, took it but had second thoughts. In Galatians 2:11-14, Paul rebukes Peter for gravitating back to old distinctions between Jews and Gentiles that jeopardized the one gospel for both. The step to include Gentiles deepened and widened the breach between the fledgling church and normative Judaism (Acts 28:28; 1 Thessalonians 2:16). We cannot today fully appreciate the grief of separation that step most certainly caused. The church took it only reluctantly, not wishing to alienate Jews who saw things otherwise. But it could not refrain from taking the step and still be faithful to God, who in Jesus Christ, provided a means of salvation for *all peoples.*

Jesus, Redeemer of All Creation!

To contemporary readers, "Jews" and "Gentiles" connote historic ethnic groups divided by customs of ritual cleanness, circumcision, Sabbath, food observances, and so forth. If that is the limit of our understanding, then the foregoing texts might simply suggest the reconciliation of two historic ethnic divisions. The texts do, of course, declare the reconciliation of Jews and Gentiles, but they imply far more than that. As we noted at the beginning of the last section, "Gentiles" incorporates by definition both ethnic and geographical connotations. When the New Testament states that God calls both Jews and Gentiles (Romans 9:24) it means, by logical necessity, that God calls *all humanity.*

A large and diverse body of evidence in the New Testament supports this conclusion. Indeed, the evidence shows Jesus to be not only the savior of all humanity, but of all creation, including superhuman powers. Some of the evidence is metaphorical. Jesus is called the headwater of the river of life (Revelation 22:1-3), the "gospel of life" (2 Timothy 1:1; Acts 5:20), and "the true light, which enlightens everyone" (John 1:9; Matthew 5:15). These are foundational and universal images. Light, in particular, is a cosmic image. It cannot be divided or constrained, just as Jesus cannot be divided or constrained, but rather is "Lord of all" (Acts 10:36). The "all," as we have seen above, includes all nations (Matthew 24:14; Mark 11:17; Luke 24:47; Romans 1:13; Revelation 12:5), and all human beings (John 1:16-17; 10:1; 11:51-52; 12:19; 18:14; Acts 2:21, 38-40; 3:21; 3:23; 4:12).

The single most important image by which Paul signifies all humanity is in his use of Adam-Christ typology (Romans 5, 1 Corinthians 15). Both Adam and Christ represent all of humanity, and what Adam corrupted, Christ redeemed. "As all die in Adam, all will be made alive in Christ" (1 Corinthians 15:21). "The first man, Adam, became a living being; the last Adam became a life-giving spirit" (15:45). The logic of this typology is inescapable: Christ has redeemed the same lot that Adam corrupted — all humanity. The world is Christ's parish, as Paul, in obvious but effective redundancy, reminds his readers in Colossians 1:28: "It is [Jesus Christ] whom we proclaim, warning *everyone* and teaching *everyone* in all wisdom, so that we may present *everyone* mature in Christ."

The rightful destination and goal of the gospel is "the world." Jesus commands his disciples to go into all the world and proclaim the gospel to all creation (Matthew 28:19; Mark 14:9; 16:15). In the last day, the Son of Man will gather the elect from the four corners of earth under heaven for final judgment (Mark 13:27; Matthew 24:30-31; Luke 12:8-9). The book of Revelation sees an angel descending from heaven and bringing the eternal gospel "to every nation and tribe and language and people" (1:7; 14:6).

The redundancy is purposeful: it means that no place, no people, and no person is excluded from the promises of the gospel.

But the "world" includes more than the habitation of humanity. It includes the unseen metaphysical world as well as the known empirical world. Not a few New Testament texts refer to Jesus Christ as the author and savior of "all things." The Greek noun *ta panta* connotes, philosophically speaking, total reality. The Epistle to the Hebrews speaks of Jesus Christ as the author of "all things" (2:10), the heir of "all things" (1:2), the one who bears and sustains "all things" (1:3), and the one to whom "all things" are subjected (2:6-8). If you did not know the subject of this last sentence, you would automatically supply "God." Only God can do "all things." The subject, however, is *Jesus*. The Pauline literature repeats this cosmic declaration. Jesus Christ is the one in whom "all things" exist and consist (Colossians 3:11) and who sums up "all things" in himself (Ephesians 1:10). In one of the most comprehensive passage in the New Testament on the person and work of Christ, Colossians 1:13-20 refers to Jesus Christ as the one who is before "all things," through whom "all things" were created, and in whom they are sustained, and who has reconciled "all things" to himself by the blood of his cross, producing peace for things in heaven and on earth (also Matthew 28:16-20).

The New Testament does not give a comprehensive description of the relationship of Jesus Christ to non- or superhuman creatures. Despite the unknowns and ambiguities, however, one thing is confessed: Jesus Christ will reign supreme over "all things," for by his cross he has done what is necessary to reconcile all creation (Colossians 1:21-23). The effects of Jesus' saving activity will extend to all creation (Acts 17:24-31). The apostle Paul reminds the Romans that the redemption for which humanity longs is mirrored in creation itself, which groans and awaits with eagerness the redemption promised in Jesus Christ (Romans 8:18-25).

Included within "all creation" are unseen but powerful spiritual forces and realities. The death of Christ has vanquished "the elemental spirits of the universe" (Colossians 2:20) that once plagued humanity. The wealth of the mystery of the eternal gospel of Christ has been revealed not only to humanity, but "to the rulers and authorities in the heavenly places" (Ephesians 3:10; also 3:14-19; 4:7-10). The resurrected

Christ is now seated above every rule and authority and name, in both the present and future age (1:20-23). The apostle Paul declares in his famous hymn on the Incarnation in Philippians 2:5-11 that at the name of Jesus every knee in heaven and on earth and under the earth will bow, and every tongue will confess Christ to the glory of God. Because Christ is Lord of all and Lord in all, Paul reminds Christians that even now they share in the effects of Christ's sovereignty: "For all things are yours, whether Paul or Apollos or Cephas or the world or life or death or the present or the future — all things belong to you, and you belong to Christ, and Christ belongs to God" (1 Corinthians 3:21-22). The Latin word *universus,* from which we get "universe" and "universal," means "combined into one." The gospel is "universal" in the sense that all things find their center in Christ. But it is also "omniversal," to coin a term, extending outward to encompass all reality in heaven and on earth.

Jesus, the Peacemaker of God

We began this chapter by noting today's apprehensions about single answers and sole saviors. We have shown in this chapter that the New Testament unambiguously affirms Jesus Christ to be the one through whom God created and redeemed *ta panta,* all things. If coercion (or worse, tyranny) lies behind such authority, then the claim of Jesus' supremacy will doubtless raise our apprehensions.

This is a legitimate concern. In order to respond to it let us return briefly to Acts 10 where Peter declared to Cornelius, the Roman centurion, that Jesus is "Lord of all." Here is the sentence in which that phrase occurs, "You know the message [God] sent to the people of Israel, preaching peace by Jesus Christ — he is Lord of all" (Acts 10:36). The point to note is that the omnipotence of Christ is presented in the context of the *peace* of Christ. Jews and Gentiles were separated by an ugly divide, a wall of hostility, as Ephesians 2:14 called it. Nothing in the world could overcome the long-standing antagonism between Jews and Gentiles until the reconciling peace that was effected and offered in Jesus Christ. The proclamation of the gospel to Cornelius did not raise his angst, as it is sometimes feared it will do today. It did not introduce a condition of hostility; it removed one. Let us conclude this chapter by considering the meaning of the peace that Peter proclaimed to Cornelius, and also by considering its significance for our Third-Millennium angst.

We must begin by drawing an important distinction between the contemporary understanding of peace and the biblical one. The modern world views peace as an absence of conflict, as a state of tolerance that allows people to "live and let live." In this view, peace is a condition of non-hostility. This is an anemic peace from a New Testament perspective, however. The New Testament understands peace not merely as the absence of something, but as the presence of something; it is a state that produces well-being, and allows creatures to fulfill their God-intended purpose. Above all, peace is a state of reconciliation with God and others (Romans 5:1).

The New Testament gives at least three meanings to its understanding of peace. Most importantly, both the Hebrew and Greek words for "peace" (*shalom* and *eirēnē*, respectively) describe a condition or state established by God, not by people (Luke 1:79; 2:14; 19:38; 1 Corinthians 7:15; 14:33). "For the kingdom of God is not food and drink but righteousness and peace and joy in the Holy Spirit" (Romans 14:17). That is to say, the peace presented in the Bible is not primarily the result of human effort. It is not something humanity achieves, but something humanity receives. In the Bible, you *announce* peace, you do not make it. In Ephesians 4:3 believers are admonished "to maintain the unity of the Spirit in the bond of peace," not to make either peace or unity. In a few instances English Bibles enjoin believers to "make peace" (e.g., Mark 9:50; Romans 12:18; 2 Corinthians 13:11; 1 Thessalonians 5:13), but the Greek word behind this rendering, *eirēneuein*, is better understood as "being peaceable." The same is true of "Blessed are the peacemakers" in the Beatitudes (Matthew 5:9), which means those who *do* or *enact* peace, rather than those who effect a state of peace.

The Greek verb "to make peace" (*eirēnopoiein*) occurs only once in the New Testament, where it refers to the peace made by the blood of Christ, which reconciled humanity to God (Colossians 1:20). This introduces the second foundational sense of peace in the New Testament. Jesus is both the means of peace with God (Romans 5:1) and with one another (Ephesians 6:15). Jesus is the mission of God, and that mission is reconciliation and peace. Hence we find many references in the New Testament to the peace that comes through Christ Jesus (John 14:27; Acts 10:36; Ephesians 2:17; Hebrews 7:2; 13:20; Revelation 12).

The third characteristic of peace is that neither *shalom* nor *eirēnē* refers to peace as a mental state or attitude.[9] Rather, almost without exception peace is a tangible condition that is corporate rather than merely individual. Peace can be political, as it often is in the prophets. It can also include material prosperity, as it often does in the Old Testament. Or, as in the case of Peter and Cornelius, peace can be a declaration that a state of hatred and discrimination is over and a state of reconciliation is begun. Peace is not something people think or feel. It is something they experience. The peace that attends the proclamation of the gospel is thus the announcement of a condition produced and delivered by God, not by human effort; it is a condition effected by the work of Jesus and declared in his name; and finally, it is communal rather than private or primarily emotional, affecting in material ways the relations of Christians with the world.[10]

With this in mind, consider the following testimony to peace in the New Testament. Peace (usually accompanied by the word "grace") occurs in the salutation of every epistle in the New Testament with the exception of James and the three Epistles of John. It characterizes the gospel of Jesus Christ because it characterizes the nature of God. God is a God of "love and peace" (2 Corinthians 13:11; Hebrews 13:20), "not of disorder" (1 Corinthians 14:33). The bond that God wills for humanity is not one of coercion or injustice or power or supremacy, but "the unity of the Spirit in the bond of peace" (Ephesians 4:3; also 1 Thessalonians 5:23; 2 Thessalonians 3:16). Because peace is the nature of God (Romans 16:20; 1 Thessalonians 5:23; Hebrews 13:20; 2 Peter 3:14), it is also enjoined as a defining characteristic of Christian life and community (1 Corinthians

9. One exception to this is Romans 15:13.
10. *Theological Dictionary of the New Testament,* s.v. *eirēnē.*

7:17; Galatians 5:22; 6:16; 2 Timothy 2:22; Hebrews 12:14; James 2:16; 3:18; 1 Peter 3:11; 5:14). When Paul enjoins the Romans to pursue those things that lead to peace (14:19), he means the peace of Christ that rules in their hearts and that produces oneness among believers, just as God is one (Colossians 3:15).

Walls are symbols of division. One such wall existed in the temple of Jerusalem, separating the Court of Gentiles from inner precincts of the temple open to Jews. At various intervals along the temple wall, a warning was posted in Hebrew, Greek, and Latin: "No foreigner is to enter within the balustrade and embankment around the sanctuary. Whoever is caught will have himself to blame for his ensuing death."[11] The temple wall that separated Jews and Gentiles into two hostile camps has been forever removed in Jesus. "He is our peace," declares the Epistle to the Ephesians. "In his flesh [Jesus] has made both [Jews and Gentiles] into one and has broken down the dividing wall, that is, the hostility between us" (2:14).

All the verbs in Ephesians 2:14-20 are in the past tense. The removal of the wall of hostility, the making of two hostile peoples into one reconciled people, the drawing near of those once far off — all these are the results of Christ's reconciling work. They are accomplished facts, not outstanding moral imperatives remaining to be accomplished by humanity. Hence, they are part of the gospel announcement; they are not conditions that Christians impose on people in order to be made right with God.

Soviet Communism used to speak a great deal about peace, as do most forms of totalitarianism and absolutism. But the peace was conditional, predicated on following the communist agenda. It said, in effect, "Everyone has a right to my opinion." Do it my way, and all will be well; do it your way, and there will be force to reckon with. That is a form of coercion; it binds people and holds them hostage.

This is precisely what the gospel does not say. The gospel declares a

11. See Josephus, *Wars of the Jews* 5.194-95; and *Antiquities* 15.419 (and note *d* in the Loeb Classical Library edition, trans. R. Markus [London: Heinemann/Cambridge: Harvard University Press, 1969], 202-3).

de facto, unconditional peace already in effect because of the atoning work of Christ. It proclaims peace to everyone, everywhere, to those far off and to those near. This puts to rest the fear that an exclusive savior necessarily results in coercion and supremacy. The peace announced in the gospel is not achieved by an imposition of power on others, but by the self-sacrifice of Jesus.[12] There is no passage in the New Testament that justifies doing ill or evil to others in the name of Christ, or for the purpose of converting them. No command to do so, no condoning of doing so, no tolerance for doing so. The will of God in Christ for humanity is not separation or superiority, not arrogance or judgment, not fear, violence, or death. "Christ has abolished the law with its commandments and ordinances, that he might create in himself one new humanity in place of the two, thus making peace" (Ephesians 2:15). In other words, Christ has already created the conditions of peace; Christians are to live in light of that peace.[13] The gospel does not destabilize and threaten the world. It reconciles the world.

12. Celsus, the second-century despiser of Christianity, mocked God for not getting revenge on those who crucified Jesus. Origen, however, defended the gospel by reminding Celsus that Christians are meek and peaceful; they bless rather than curse (*Against Celsus* 8.41).

13. Again, notes Origen, "Jesus is not the leader of any seditious movement, but the promoter of peace. . . . It would be those of this world, not those of God, who would wage war" (*Against Celsus* 8.14).

CHAPTER 11

How Should Christians Think
about Other Religions?

Your Call, Sir!

Oprah Winfrey, the popular talk show host, once remarked, "One of the biggest mistakes we make is to believe there is only one way. There are many diverse paths leading to God."[1] These words seem to be the modern mantra about religions.

It is not surprising that people think this way. There is a strong commitment today to the idea that all religions teach the goodness of God and the moral accountability of humanity. These two tenets of belief cut through the superstitions and fanaticism that are played out in the name of religion. The idea of the essential equality — and perhaps even unity — of all religions seems to be not only compelling but also necessary.

There are several reasons why we want to harmonize different religions. The first was discussed in the last chapter — the danger of religious differences. The differences among religions seem largely responsible for the havoc and mayhem wreaked in the name of religion. Discount the differences and you go a long way toward enhancing the public good of religion. Many people imagine that the religions of the world are close enough in their essentials to achieve a similar effect.

A second reason stems from the intellectual relativism of our day. If beliefs about matters of ultimate reality such as morality and religion are

---

1. Quoted in *Christianity Today* (April 1, 2002): 45.

considered largely matters of opinion rather than objective realities, then it is safer to trust the intuitions of the herd than the particular doctrines of a given religion. When we must make decisions about controversial matters, in other words, the lowest common denominator has more persuasive force than the particulars of a given religion. The trunk values common to all religions seem more important than the branch values taught by individual religions.

A third reason to favor a generic religious approach is the modern aversion to elitism. There is something strongly attractive about the doctrine of universal salvation, that in the end all people make it — or can make it if they choose to. The idea that one group of people — regardless of who is a part of that group — controls the toll road to heaven is offensive and alienating. And the doctrine of eternal damnation for those who do not know the road or cannot pay the toll strikes us as monstrous.

The first two assumptions above are essentially knowledge-based; they can be either verified or falsified by a comparative study of various religions. The third assumption is of a different order, however. It is a *conviction* that no religion should presume saving uniqueness, and that doing so is elitist, arrogant, and perhaps even nefarious. A contemporary philosopher, Thomas Nagel, gives an eloquent apology for one version of this conviction:

> In speaking of the fear of religion, . . . I [am not] referring to the association of many religious beliefs with superstition and the acceptance of evident empirical falsehoods. I am talking about something much deeper — namely, the fear of religion itself. I speak from experience, being strongly subject to this fear myself: I want atheism to be true and am made uneasy by the fact that some of the most intelligent and well-informed people I know are religious believers. It isn't just that I don't believe in God and, naturally, hope that I'm right in my belief. It's that I hope there is no God! I don't want there to be a God; I don't want the universe to be like that.[2]

2. *The Last Word* (New York: Oxford University Press, 1997), 130.

Nagel's honesty is refreshing. I think he is right that in the final analysis our insistence on the essential unity of different religions is not based on comparative data but on the *desire* that they be alike. We don't want the universe to be otherwise.

These sentiments seem to be as widely held and passionately embraced in the church as they are on the opinion page of the newspaper, and our attraction to them is entirely understandable. As a college student I took a course on Asian literature and I can still recall the magnetism of the Eastern genius for integrating logical polarities. I have since come to believe that such integration is not possible. Nevertheless, in my attempts to convince people of its impossibility I have often felt somewhat like the seaman second class in the following story: A Navy captain at the helm of his ship at night saw a light on the horizon that was on a collision course with his vessel. He sent a message, "Change your course ten degrees west." A reply came back, "Change *your* course ten degrees west." The captain sent a second message, "I am a captain in the United States Navy. I order you to change your course." A second reply came back, "I am a seaman second class. Change your course now." The captain sent a final message, "I command a battleship. I'm not changing course." A third reply came back, "I oversee a lighthouse. Your call, sir."

I see my task somewhat like that of the seaman second class. People want to be the captain of their ship on the issue of the essential equality of all religions. I cannot pontificate on such matters, but I can set forth the evidence and reasoning for what I understand to be the relationship of Christianity to other religions. On the basis of it I shall echo the seaman second class: "Your call, sir."

Are They Really the Same?

The modern West's encounter with other religions began with the age of exploration in the sixteenth century. It was the outreach of foreign missions in the nineteenth century, however, enabled and accelerated by modern communication and transportation systems, that threw open the gates to cultures and religions long sequestered. The increase in knowledge that resulted from the missionary encounter with other religions has greatly affected our understanding of other religions as well as of Christianity.

There are certainly points of contact between Christianity and other religions, particularly in the field of ethics. All religions agree that some acts are prohibited and others commended, and most summarize their ethical principles in something approximating what Christians call the Golden Rule, even though there are differences in how those principles are understood and practiced. The religions of the world agree, in other words, on absolute moral categories. Most religions agree on broad fields of ethical behavior, including honoring parents, and usually elders, and sometimes ancestors. Most religions agree that parents have duties to their children and posterity. They teach laws of righteousness that include truthfulness, honesty, and justice. They teach the idea of good faith, and that there are duties in life that supersede the fulfillment of personal pleasures. Nearly all religions teach that compassion and mercy are among the highest ethical requirements, especially to the defenseless, weak, needy, and poor. The obligation to share, particularly with those who have less, is central to nearly all religions. Religions may differ on whom one may kill or how many wives a man may have, but no religion teaches that one may kill or marry whomever one wishes.

Some people infer from agreements such as these that all religions are basically the same. That is an unwarranted conclusion, however, as the following example illustrates. Suppose three people are discussing the attributes of a model citizen. One of the three is a Muslim, another is committed to communism, and the third to democracy. We have no trouble imagining that all three would agree that workers should not steal from their employers, that citizens should pay their taxes and devote a portion of their time and energy to public service, and that the government should establish museums, libraries, schools, and so forth. But despite these similarities, we know that the differences among Muslim societies like Saudi Arabia or Pakistan, and communist countries like the former East Germany or Cuba, and modern democracies like Denmark or the Netherlands are qualitative and profound. The actual values and commitments that produce such societies are so different that none of the three persons in the conversation would likely choose to live in a society dominated by the other two.

In a similar way, the ethical overlap of the world's various religions tells us very little about the essence and ethos of each religion. A given religion's tenets and character, the qualities that attract people to it and keep them in it, will differ greatly from those of other religions. In fact, the general agreement in ethical matters among the various religions seems all but incidental to their ultimate concerns. The ultimate concerns of religions turn on the important questions in life; the problems that need to be overcome — and how to overcome them — in order to achieve a complete and pleasing life; the relation of humanity to the world, others, and God; the possibility of life after death; and so on. In such matters, the world's religions differ markedly.

We obviously cannot examine the tenets of all religions, or even of the major religions of the world. But we can take two religious systems — Christianity and Hinduism — and compare them at key points. I believe that Christianity and Hinduism occupy the pole positions on the religious spectrum, between which nearly all other religions can be located. Think of the following comparison as the opposite ends of a continuum of all religions.

	Christianity	Hinduism
Ultimate Reality:	God	Nirvana
Object of Religion:	Salvation	Enlightenment
Destiny of Self/Soul:	Redemption and transformation through Jesus Christ	Extinguishment and non-existence of the self
Time:	History is purposeful and goal-directed	History is cyclical and endless
Suffering:	Suffering may be redemptive	Suffering is evil
Love:	Sacrificial self-giving	Detached benevolence
Saving Knowledge:	Must be revealed by God	Inherent in each individual

All of this suggests how wide of the mark Oprah Winfrey and others are who imagine all religions to be equal paths to God. Indeed, God is not the goal of Hinduism at all; Nirvana is. Where Christians envision a personal relationship with a divine being, Hindus seek a state of the soul in which there is no knowing, desire, suffering, or individual consciousness.[3] And so where Christians see the chief flaw of humanity as sin — that is, as an infraction against God's will — Hindus see it as ignorance. Thus, their essential goals are different: Christians think of salvation as reconciliation with God; Hindus understand enlightenment as the product of a journey inward, of self-understanding. The differences go on, and it respects neither Christianity nor Hinduism to suggest that the two are basically the same.

The statement that all religions are basically the same is usually heard from people who are not adherents of any religion. Yet this presumption to know the meaning of a belief system better than those who live and die by it is, in the words of the Christian theologian Alister McGrath, "intellectual Stalinism."[4] To outsiders (and this includes most scholars of religion), Islam is the religion of Muslims. It can be studied as objectively as one studies shipping or agriculture. But to Muslims, Islam is the Truth. Assumed within that claim is that other religions are not true, at least not to the same degree. The same could be said of most every religion. Actual Christians, Buddhists, animists, Taoists, and so on maintain that their traditions are not clones of one another, but rather perceptions of and responses to reality that are fundamentally different

---

3. The Buddhist and Christian perspectives on suffering further illustrate the differences between the two religions. Both Buddhism and Christianity acknowledge the problem of suffering, which Buddhists typically attribute to *dukkha*, meaning "dislocation" or "out of kilter"; and which Christians generally attribute to sin. Buddhists, however, see suffering as "in character" with the universe, whereas Christians regard suffering as an intruder. The Buddhist response implies that the world is fundamentally and irretrievably flawed, and consequently must be escaped; the Christian response suggests that the world was created good, but is infected by a flaw that can and has been remedied in the cross of Christ.

4. Quoted from *Four Views on Salvation in a Pluralistic World*, ed. Dennis L. Okholm and Timothy R. Phillips (Grand Rapids: Zondervan, 1996), 206-8.

from one another. To assert that all religions are basically the same, or that one route to the summit is as good as another, is like saying that all sports are basically the same. Bullfighters and bowlers are unlikely to agree. Only a non-athlete can assert such a thing.

What Does the Bible Say about Other Religions?

The Bible does not directly address the question why so many religions exist. The Old Testament, for instance, does not seem compelled to resolve the question of monotheism versus monolatry. Monotheism — the belief that there is only one God — is clearly assumed in some Old Testament passages (for example, Isaiah 43:10-11; 45:14). Other Old Testament texts, however, seem to assume monolatry — the belief that there are many gods, but that Yahweh alone is worthy to be worshipped among them (for example, Exodus 20:3; Psalm 16:4). Both the Old and New Testaments acknowledge that there are many different religious systems, "many gods and many lords," as the apostle Paul said (1 Corinthians 8:5). The Bible is generally indifferent to the origin of other religions, and to some extent to their significance. Among all these unresolved questions, however, both Testaments affirm and teach the absolute supremacy of God. The Old Testament teaches that Yahweh alone is worthy of supreme worship and glory, regardless of whether other gods exist; and the New Testament teaches that this same God is the one true God, who is the Father of Jesus Christ, the sole savior of the world.

The biblical ambiguity toward other religions stems from the fact that the Bible differentiates among various forms of religious expression. Some are judged quite negatively, whereas others are judged more positively. At the negative end of the spectrum are the Canaanite fertility cults, specifically those of Baal, Astarte, Moloch, and Chemosh, that practiced sacred prostitution and child sacrifice. I want to describe Canaanite religion in some detail because I see parallels between it and the modern tendency we discussed in Chapter 8 to shift the focus of Christianity from transcendence to immanence.

The discovery of several ancient documents at the Syrian archaeological site of Ras Shamra in 1929 opened up detailed information about Canaanite religious practices. The basic premise of Canaanite religion revolved around powers of fertility in the soil. Land was believed to be the sphere of divine power. The lord or owner of the land — the deity Baal — was the source behind its fertility. The rains that fell and aroused the mysterious powers of the soil were believed to emanate from the sexual intercourse between Baal and his consort in heaven. The sacred marriage in heaven ensured fertility and prosperity on earth.[5] Conditions on earth, in other words, were believed to mirror those in heaven. Rain and productivity indicated divine pleasure; drought and calamity indicated divine displeasure. Nor were humans mere spectators of this divine-terrestrial exchange of power. By ritual enactments of this divine drama, either by sexual intercourse or human sacrifice, devotees could assist in integrating the cosmic will into the life cycle of nature.

This linkage of nature and God in the Canaanite fertility cults is the subject of unrelieved repudiation in the Old Testament. The prophets, in particular, believed nature to be a very unreliable indicator of God, and assumptions about God on the basis of nature resulted in disastrous consequences. Nature, of course, is God's handiwork, and as such it reflects God to some extent, if indirectly. But nature is not an extension of God, as in pantheism, for nature, like humanity, is tainted by sin. In contrast to what was taught in Canaanite fertility cults, springtime does not necessarily indicate God's pleasure, nor earthquakes God's displeasure. And since God and nature are not one and the same, God cannot be manipulated by nature rituals. Quite the opposite, in fact: King Manasseh's fifty-five-year indulgence in Canaanite fertility religion aroused God's wrath and was viewed by the prophets as instrumental in the destruction of the Kingdom of Judah (2 Kings 23:26-27).

Practitioners of Canaanite religion worshipped a divine force pulsat-

---

5. On Canaanite religion, see H. and H. A. Frankfort, J. A. Wilson, and T. Jacobsen, *Before Philosophy: The Intellectual Adventure of Ancient Man* (Baltimore: Penguin Books, 1973), 137-234; B. Anderson, *Understanding the Old Testament*, 4th ed. (Englewood Cliffs, N.J.: Prentice-Hall, 1986), 183-93.

ing through nature. The primary expressions of this force in Canaanite religion, as in nearly all nature cults, were sex and death. The shift in much contemporary Christian theology from transcendence to immanence, from the redeeming work of God through Christ to the expression of God in the created order of nature, is a step in the direction of a religious expression that was strongly condemned by the great prophets of Israel. We have seen throughout this book that the Bible locates the redeeming work of God not in nature, but in *history*. The grand narrative of salvation is not an analysis of recurrent patterns of nature, but a historical story of God's interventions in history to redeem the world.

Canaanite fertility cults are categorically rejected in the Old Testament not only because of their cruelty, but because the close identification of God with nature inevitably results in idolatry — the replacement of God by images believed to embody God. The uncompromising renunciation of Canaanite religion is not the Bible's sole response to other religions, however. In some instances religious practices are rejected not for their wickedness but for their worthlessness. Paul and Barnabas appealed to worshippers of Greek gods and goddesses to "turn from these worthless images to the living God" (Acts 14:15). The Greek word for "worthless," *mataios,* means "futile," "useless," or "fruitless." Similarly, Paul wrote to the Corinthians, "What pagans sacrifice, they sacrifice to demons and not to God. I do not want you to be partners with demons. You cannot drink the cup of the Lord and the cup of demons. You cannot partake of the table of the Lord and the table of demons" (1 Corinthians 10:14-22). Paul's concern not to contaminate "the cup of the Lord" with "the cup of demons" derives from the practice of stocking markets in Corinth with meat that had been sacrificed to pagan deities in the city's temples. A bull or a ram was a big-ticket item, and devotees of the cults at which they were sacrificed often tried to recoup part of the expense by selling in the marketplace the remainder of the carcass that was not consumed in the temple. Buying and eating such meat from the marketplace did not overly concern Paul, since in his judgment the deities to which they were sacrificed were illusory. "We know that 'no idol in the world really exists,' and that 'there is no God but one,'" said Paul (8:4). But participation in those sacrificial cults by Christians was idolatry, and thus something from which Corinthian believers should flee.[6]

A similar view is apparent in Psalm 135. "The idols of the nations are silver and gold," says the psalmist,

> the work of human hands.
> They have mouths, but they do not speak;
>   they have eyes, but they do not see;
> they have ears, but they do not hear,
>   and there is no breath in their mouths.
> Those who make them
>   and all who trust them
>   shall become like them.   (vv. 15-18)

Here, too, the problem is not so much wickedness, as it is in the case of Canaanite fertility cults, but folly. Idols are mere products of human creation and, as gods, worthless. The error in worshiping them is folly — although not innocuous folly. Those who worship idols become like them, and to pattern oneself after a material object is to cease to pattern oneself after the image of God.

Two second-century church fathers, Irenaeus and Clement of Alexandria, likewise characterized both paganism and Gnosticism as folly. Their judgments alternate between disdain and guarded sympathy. That is, they regarded paganism as noxious and demon-ridden, and yet they also saw in it a broken reflection of something true and God-given. Irenaeus condemned several Gnostic teachers, among them Valentinus, Saturninus, Basilides, and Carpocrates, as irrational and blasphemous heretics who deceived and destroyed those who were snared by them (*Against Heresies* 2.31.1-2). Similarly, the shameless schemes of the Greek gods and goddesses and the foolishness of the mystery religions were heaped with scorn by Clement of Alexandria because they trafficked in vain fables, deception and seduction, and overall absurdity. Clement likened paganism to a siren's song that would shipwreck anyone lured by its melodies. Let the Greeks, like Odysseus, "shun this billow; it vomits

---

6. See B. Witherington III, "Why Not Idol Meat?", *Bible Review* 10/3 (1994): 38ff.

forth fire; it is a wicked island, heaped with bones and corpses, and in it sings a fair courtesan. . . . Leave her to prey on the dead. . . . Sail past the song; it works death."[7]

Paganism is thus rejected by the psalmist, Paul, Irenaeus, and Clement (and many others) more for its folly than for moral depravity. While it may be well-intentioned, and may be attractive to many people, it is a perversion of true worship, beneath the dignity of both God and humanity. But even a perversion is a twisting of something that originally was rightly formed, just as cancer is an aberrant growth of a healthy cell. In this perspective, the problem with some religions is not, as in the case of Canaanite fertility cults, wickedness, but simply folly.

A third perspective on non-Christian religious practices is also evident, one which we might call foreshadowing. In Galatians 4:1-7 the Apostle Paul reflects on how the sending of Jesus "in the fullness of time" caused people to mature and come of age. The Epistle to the Galatians was addressed to a mixed congregation of Jewish and Gentile Christians, and we may assume that Paul intended the analogy to incorporate both groups of peoples. Prior to the revelation of Jesus Christ, people were, spiritually speaking, relegated to infancy. Paul describes them metaphorically as "minors," still "under guardians and trustees." Unlike normal infancy, however, from which children naturally emerge to become adults, Paul implies that the world was confined to an infantile status for a prescribed time. It was inhibited from coming to faith, "enslaved to the elemental spirits of the world." Release came not by a process of natural maturation, but by an occurrence extrinsic to it. "When the fullness of time had come, God sent his Son . . . so that we might receive adoption as children." The Incarnation, in other words, changed the status of people. Those who receive Jesus Christ in faith are emancipated from slavery to become fully endowed children, who know God as *Abba,* as intimate and loving Father.

Paul portrays salvation as a historical process leading from infancy

---

7. Clement, *Exhortation to the Greeks* 12. Origen likewise said that those who visited pagan temples oare gave themselves to mages and sacred seasons were "blinded" (*Against Celsus* 3.77).

to adulthood. Several church fathers developed a similar understanding of salvation as a progressive historical process that was summed up and completed in Jesus Christ. Irenaeus, whom we examined above, reasoned that God's purposeful activity was not present only in the history of Israel (although it was present there more clearly than elsewhere), but also in Greco-Roman history, and in human history in general. For Irenaeus salvation was a process of "education" in the true sense of the word, leading humanity from lower to successively higher stages of understanding of God. Irenaeus saw history as a series of beginnings and fulfillments, initial types and ultimate consummations, an Old Testament and New Testament, a First Adam and a Last Adam. Each stage of revelation superseded the previous one in ordered regularity until God brought the process to its climactic goal and completion. In the sending of Jesus Christ, Irenaeus saw the triumphant summation of the entire process. In his well-known reliance on Ephesians 1:10, where God sums up all things in Christ, Irenaeus speaks of the "recapitulation" of not just Jewish history, but of all human experience.[8]

Clement of Alexandria echoed Irenaeus. By the year 200 early Christians were adapting pagan artistic images for Christian purposes. The vine of Dionysus was employed to signify the vine of Christ in John 15:1-8; a sun god, Helios or Apollos, was reinterpreted as the resurrected Jesus Christ, the sun of righteousness who radiates salvation to all the world; Orpheus, the mythic minstrel, was transformed into Jesus Christ as the prince of peace from Isaiah 11.[9] Clement saw these and other pagan images, as Paul saw Adam in Romans 5, as types that were perfected

8. Irenaeus, *Against Heresies* 3.18.7; 5.19.1. Similarly, Eusebius, *Preparation of the Gospel* 1.1; and Clement of Alexandria, *Miscellanies* 1.5. Origen, *Against Celsus* 6.3-4. See W. H. C. Frend, *The Rise of Christianity* (Philadelphia: Fortress Press, 1984), 247-48. In *The Spirit of Early Christian Thought* (New Haven: Yale University Press, 2003), Robert Wilken notes that early Christians did not think of the time before Christ as Muslims thought of the time betore Muhammad, as *al Jahiliyyah*, "the time of ignorance." Rather, God's revelatory work was already present and at work; it was not a time of darkness, but a long dawn that would yield to the sunrise of the gospel (318).

9. See R. Jensen, "How the Early Church Pictured the Divine," *Bible Review* 18/5 (2002): 42ff.; A. D. McKenzie, "Adapting Pagan Images," *Bible Review* 19/1 (2003): 8ff.

and fulfilled in Christ. At the conclusion of his *Exhortation to the Greeks,* Clement appealed to his Hellenistic pagan readers to grow up, to stop dabbling in practices, whether worthless or dangerous, that were broken reflections of the true and saving God. Clement echoes the apostle Paul's summons to the Greeks in Athens to embrace the Unknown God whom they intuited but did not know (Acts 17:23). Clement envisions God calling to the world and saying, "Come to Me, that you may be put in your rank under the one God and the one Word of God. . . . I want to impart to you this grace, bestowing on you the perfect gift of immortality; and I confer on you both the Word and the knowledge of God, My complete self. . . . I desire to restore you to the original model, that you may become also like Me" (chapter 12). There was a pattern, an "original model," for Clement, from which humanity was cut, but to which it no longer conformed. Like Paul and Irenaeus before him, Clement appealed to his pagan hearers to be restored to the original model and become what they were created to be, knowledgeable heirs of the one true God. It was inherently reasonable that they should "ascend to God," as he says, to mature and graduate to their created destiny.

The idea of recapitulation prevailed into the fourth century. Eusebius of Caesarea (260-340) argued in his lengthy *Preparation for the Gospel* that Plato and the Greek philosophers did not oppose the understanding of salvation adumbrated in the Old Testament, but in general agreed with it. Eusebius reasoned that the God who created all peoples of the world had in the gospel of Jesus Christ befriended them, calling Greek and barbarians, men, women, and children, rich and poor, wise and simple, slaves and free to accept the gift of grace proffered in Jesus Christ.

The idea of recapitulation was not an innovation of the early church. In his dialogue with the woman at the well, Jesus hinted that the gospel was foreshadowed in the incompleteness of a prior tradition. The woman was a Samaritan, a member of a faith tradition closely related to Judaism, "You worship what you do not know," says Jesus. "We worship what we know, for salvation is from the Jews" (John 4:22). The substance of these words seems to be echoed in the apostle Paul's words to the Athenians. Noting an altar to an unknown god in the religiously pluralistic environment of Athens, Paul announced, "What therefore you worship as unknown, this I proclaim to you" (Acts 17:23). To be sure, both statements convey that something is defective in the worship of Samaria and Athens. Both worship in ignorance as opposed to knowledge. Nevertheless, neither Jesus nor Paul says that the woman and the Athenians do not worship. They do worship, but not knowledgeably. Although neither form of worship is endorsed, both forms are accorded a measure of initial legitimacy — a step on the wrong foot in the right direction, as it were.

Likewise, in Romans 10:4 Paul states that "Christ is the end of the law." This controversial passage occupies a disproportionate amount of space in nearly all commentaries. Even if one takes the severely critical view that Christ dismissed or discarded the law, the law still must be understood to play a preparatory function leading to Christ. My own interpretation is that the word "end" is better understood to mean "fulfillment" rather than "termination."[10] This is also the sense of Galatians 3:24, in which Paul speaks of the law as a *paidagogos,* a Greek word that referred to a slave hired to take children, as a school bus does today, to their master at school. The law, in this analogy, leads people to Christ, in a similar way, for instance, that courtship leads to marriage, or pregnancy to birth (similarly, Galatians 3:15-18).

We may summarize our survey of the Bible's attitudes toward other religions by saying that judgments vary from case to case. Cults that resulted in moral depravity and idolatry were wholly rejected as evil. Other cults were judged as falsifications of true worship, sometimes ridiculous and pernicious falsifications. Their adherents, nevertheless, were not condemned, and certainly not annihilated, but persuaded to abandon their folly and embrace the true God. Finally, some religions are seen as playing a foreshadowing role for the gospel of Jesus Christ. The primary example of a foreshadowing religion is Judaism, to which we now turn.

---

10. See J. R. Edwards, *Romans,* New International Bible Commentary (Peabody, Mass.: Hendrickson, 1992), 247-51.

Are There Two Saving Covenants:
One for Jews and One for Christians?

This brings us to a question of increasing urgency today. Are Jews, the closest siblings to Christianity, in a valid and saving covenant with God *apart from the gospel?* Since Judaism and Christianity are organically related, it would seem that Jews and Christians should more easily understand one another than other religions. In reality, their proximity and similarities are like two magnets: the more closely they are brought together, the more strongly they seem to repel one another. In nearly two thousand years of living together, Jews and Christians have defied all social logic and become foreigners rather than neighbors. Frustrated, even wounded, that most Jews did not accept Jesus Christ, Christians have punished them and persecuted them, and in the darkest chapters in their history have justified their cruelty and violence theologically. Out of defense, certainly, Jews have wounded Christians in a different way, by treating them with indifference, succeeding almost in denying their existence while being surrounded by them. From the parting of the ways between Judaism and Christianity in the late first century until the twenty-first century, the story of Christians and Jews has been a story of much darkness, and often on the part of Christians, of much shame.

Fortunately, the twentieth century has witnessed some rays of light in this darkness. In 1928 Joseph Klausner, a Jew, wrote a book entitled *Jesus of Nazareth.* A book about Jesus was certainly not new, but a book about Jesus by a Jew who did not seek to vilify him, but rather to understand him and even claim him as a Jewish prophet, was a first in nearly two thousand years of Jewish history. Klausner could not have foreseen that his book would open a floodgate of Jewish scholarly interest in Jesus that continues unabated to this day.

The Holocaust (or the *Shoah,* as Jews call it), the systematic hunting, seizure, transportation, incarceration, and murder of some six million European Jews by the German Nazi Party and its supporters during World War II, has been not only one of the deepest tragedies of Jewish history, but also one of the deepest tragedies of human history. As the dominant religion in Western culture, Christianity has had to confess a share of responsibility in the Holocaust. Believing Christians, certainly, were not directly responsible for the Holocaust, but centuries of a lack of charity and of negative stereotyping of Jews by Christians helped to produce a mental and emotional climate that allowed persons of evil intent to plan and execute mass murder with shockingly little opposition. The horror of the Holocaust has forced the church to acknowledge its complicity in what became Hitler's "Final Solution," and seek to become a neighbor instead of an alien, even a brother's keeper of Jews.

Other changes in the twentieth century have been more ambiguous. The founding of the State of Israel in 1948, while providing the first autonomous homeland for Jews since the Maccabean Period in the first-century B.C., has been a source of controversy for both Jews and Christians. Orthodox Jews, who await the founding of the New Jerusalem by the Messiah, have traditionally opposed Zionism, if not the actual State of Israel. Fundamentalist Christians, on the other hand, who regard the rebuilding of the Jerusalem temple as a prerequisite for the Second Coming of Christ, have staunchly supported the Zionist cause. Moderate and liberal Christians, while usually affirming the right of the State of Israel to exist, have been critical of the injustices imposed on displaced Palestinians by Zionism.

Another factor affecting contemporary Jewish-Christian relations is the steady conversion of Jews to Christianity. The great parachurch initiatives that characterized the postwar era included several that targeted Jews. Considering the very low numbers of (free will) conversions of Jews to Christianity in the past two millennia, the influence of specialized missions to Jews and the numbers of converts is remarkable. Not surprisingly, Christian missions to Jews have aroused sharp antagonism from the Jewish community.

It is hazardous to try to speak for another faith tradition, and this is especially true when a Christian tries to speak for Jews. I think it fair to say, however, that as a rule Jews do not consider Christians to belong to the people of God but rather to "the nations."[11] The emphasis in Judaism

---

11. P. Lenhardt, *Auftrag und Unmöglichkeit eines legitimen christlichen Zeugnisses gegenüber den Juden. Eine Untersuchung zum theologischen Stand des Verhältnisses von Kirche*

(and also in Islam) on orthopraxy (correct behavior) as opposed to the emphasis on orthodoxy (correct belief) in Christianity is a beginning point of departure between the two faiths. From a Jewish perspective, God spoke for the first and last time at Sinai. The result, Torah, is for Jews the supreme and final statement of God's will. The Christian replacement of Torah by Christ — particularly a Christ who is a metaphysical Son of God whose death atones for the sins of the world — is a virtually insurmountable barrier to Jews. Jews do not consider Christianity a valid extension of their religion, which generally means that they consider Christianity a heretical departure or an autonomous religious system. Not all Jews will share Jacob Neusner's judgment that Judaism and Christianity "really are totally alien to one another,"[12] but most Jews certainly see categorical differences between Christianity and Judaism.

Christian perspectives of Judaism, on the other hand, can be said to fall into three general camps. The traditional Christian position has been to regard Judaism as a religion whose essence and existence have been superseded by the gospel. This view is still generally maintained by Christian fundamentalists and some conservative Christians. It believes that Judaism has no further role to play in the unfolding of God's work, except perhaps to rebuild the temple in Jerusalem as a preparation for the Second Coming of Christ.

The supersessionist view is currently under strong attack. The Holocaust has forced thinking Christians and Christian communions to reconsider the relationship of Christianity and Judaism. Mainline Protestants and Roman Catholics, especially, are devoting renewed attention to a biblical and theological understanding of Judaism. The most pronounced result of this rethinking is a reinterpretation of the apostle Paul that argues for a "two-covenant theology." This is the second major Christian perspective on Judaism. According to this understanding, the Torah-covenant of God with Israel remains valid for the salvation of

---

und jüdischem Volk, Studien zu jüdischem Volk und christlichen Gemeinde (Berlin: Institute Kirche und Judentum, 1980), 1.

12. "How Judaism and Christianity Can Talk to One Another," *Bible Review* 6/6 (1990): 35.

Jews, whereas the gospel of Jesus Christ is the means by which Gentiles are saved. There is, in other words, *one* salvation of Jews and Christians via *two* separate covenants. The foundational assumption of two-covenant theology is that Paul considered himself the apostle to the Gentiles (see, for example, Galatians 1:15-16), and that his doctrines of justification by faith and union with Christ were directed to Gentiles, not Jews. Statements like those in Romans 3:31 — "Do we then overthrow the law by this faith? By no means! On the contrary, we uphold the law" — are taken to affirm Torah as a valid means of salvation for Jews. Two-covenant theology argues that the gospel of Jesus Christ has not completed, and certainly not replaced or superseded, the Torah-covenant of God with Israel. That covenant first instituted at Sinai remains valid for Jews of all time. The Torah covenant has, however, been augmented by a new covenant, the gospel of Jesus Christ, by which Gentiles may be saved.

Two-covenant theology is currently advocated by many academic theologians, and is often assumed in Jewish-Christian dialogue.[13] In my judgment, however, it rests on an impossibly selective reading of the New Testament, and of the apostle Paul in particular. It is true that Paul considered himself the apostle to the Gentiles, but only in the sense that the gospel he was extending to the nations was the same gospel that originated from Israel and was intended for Israel. It is also true that Paul affirms the law in Romans 3:31, but he affirms the law because it revealed sin, not because it saved. Paul states on many occasions, as he does at the beginning of Romans, that "the gospel is the power of God for salvation to everyone who has faith, to the Jew first and also to the Greek" (Romans 1:16). At no place either in Paul's letters or in the New Testament is there a statement to the effect that Jews are saved apart from Jesus Christ. Paul indeed affirms that Jews are heirs of God's gifts and revelation in the history of salvation. They are, according to Romans 9:4-5, recipients of God's adoption, glory, covenants, the law, worship, and the promises. Conspicuously absent in this list, however, is *salvation*. If Jews

13. Initial formulators of the theory are John Gager, Lloyd Gaston, Krister Stendahl, Heikki Räisänen, Hans Küng, and others.

apart from Christ were in a saving covenant, Paul would not have had "great sorrow and unceasing anguish in [his] heart" for them (Romans 9:2). He would not have said, as he does in Romans 10:1, "Brothers and sisters, my heart's desire and prayer to God for them [that is, the Jews] is that they may be saved." The law that was given by God to Jews was intended to lead to Christ, "For Christ is the end of the law so that there may be righteousness for everyone who believes" (Romans 10:4). Romans 9–11 is the most sustained treatise in the Scriptures on the question of why the Jews for whom the gospel was intended have failed to receive it. At its conclusion Paul concedes that as far as the gospel is concerned, "they [again, the Jews] are the enemies of God" (Romans 11:28). That statement surely cannot be interpreted to mean that Jews are in a saving covenant with God.

Despite the harshness of that statement, Paul maintains vigorously that Jews who have not believed in the gospel are *not* rejected by God, nor have they forfeited a special place in the divine economy. In Romans 11:1-2, Paul says, "Has God rejected his people? By no means!" In Romans 11:28, the passage where Paul calls Jews enemies of God on account of the gospel, he adds that they remain beloved of God because of God's ancestral election of them.

Paul's understanding of the relationship of unsaved Jews to the gospel comes to clearest expression in his metaphor of the olive tree in Romans 11:17-24. In the metaphor, the "root" that supports the branches is a reference to the history of salvation leading from Abraham to Jesus Christ. Jews who failed to respond to the gospel are likened to branches that were cut off, and believing Gentiles to branches that were grafted into their place. It is Paul's belief and hope, however, that unbelieving Jews will be regrafted back onto the saving root "if they do not persist in unbelief" (Romans 11:23). The point of the metaphor of the olive tree is that both Jews and Gentiles must be grafted onto the "root" in order to be saved, and in both instances this grafting is the result of God's sheer grace. Paul is perplexed, as Christians ever after have been, by the failure of Jews to receive the gospel. He sees their failure as a "hardening" that was the result both of God's will (11:25) and theirs (9:30–10:3). His perplexity is outweighed, however, by the assurance that God's calling of the Jews is irrevocable (11:29), and that finally "all Israel will be saved." The statement that all Israel will be saved is not expressed in isolation apart from Jesus Christ, but as the conclusion of the metaphor of the olive tree. As if to leave no doubt about who will be the savior of Jews, Paul states in the following verse that their savior will be the Deliverer from Zion (11:27), that is, Jesus Christ, who is the subject of the gospel (11:28).

The most dedicated discussion of the gospel and the Jews in the New Testament in Romans 9–11 thus declares that God has not rejected the Jews, but is working through the gospel for their salvation. That means that neither supersessionism nor two-covenant theology properly reflects New Testament teaching about Jews and the gospel. A third position, which I call teleological, reflects a more faithful understanding of the relationship of Christianity and Judaism, in my judgment. According to Paul, Judaism has not been superseded in the sense that it has been discarded. Judaism continues to play a role in God's abiding purpose. In a mysterious way that Paul himself did not fully understand, God continues to work through Judaism, even though it has not (yet) arrived at its intended fulfillment in Jesus Christ. Moreover, both Paul and the New Testament affirm that the divine purpose in the sweep of Israel's history is the full engrafting of Israel into Jesus Christ. Christ is the point of destination of the law (Romans 10:4), and the one to whom the law delivers believers (Galatians 3:24). "Teleological" means the direction and arrival of something at its proper destination. The proper destination of all creation, Jews included, is Jesus Christ, who fulfills all things.

Should Christians share the gospel with Jews? According to the New Testament witness, the answer must be yes. If Jesus is the good news of salvation for the world, no people, Jews included, should be excluded. But let me add that the gospel of Christ must be shared in the spirit of Christ. Here is a real-life example of the gospel of Christ shared in the spirit of Christ. It is told by Elie Wiesel, a Jew, about a conversation with Francois Mauriac, a French Catholic:

"You told me that I had to speak, to write," said Wiesel.

"Yes," said Mauriac, "I suggested that. You belong to a people who has survived by and through the Word."

"What word?"

"The Lord's Word," returned Mauriac.

"And the Lord needs men to communicate His will?" queried Wiesel.

"It would seem so," said Mauriac. "Otherwise He would not have done it. The Jewish people have been invested with His word, have they not?"

"We are supposed to testify for Him," conceded Wiesel. "But how? Christians say, through suffering. We say, through faith."

"But is that enough?" pressed Mauriac. "You are not the only ones to have suffered, nor to have rejected heresy. In what way are the Jewish people different from others?"

"All peoples are different, each in their own way."

"Only the Jewish people," Mauriac reminded Wiesel, "offered the world and its history the man capable and desirous of saving them from themselves."

"Jesus of Nazareth?" asked Wiesel. "I know you believe that. But for me — forgive me for repeating it — he is not the Savior."

"For me He is. I recognize it by His suffering, His agony. I belong to Him because He is Love," said Mauriac.

"The Jew in me is obliged to say that he belongs only to God. And God is one," responded Wiesel.

"Any Christian believer would say the same," added Mauriac. "For us too, God is God, and He is one. But Jesus is His son."

"All human beings are His sons," replied Wiesel.

"In that case, how do you explain the existence of evil?" pressed Mauriac. The Nazi hangmen? Those who massacred the Jewish children you know? Were they, too, God's sons?"

"That is for God to answer," replied Wiesel.

"Sometimes God prefers to ask questions," Mauriac said.

"The answer is beyond me, *Maitre.* But I do know that the Nazi killers and torturers were baptized," added Wiesel.

There was a long silence, after which Mauriac said, "Let us not blame Jesus for that." He lowered his voice. "It is not His fault if we betray His love for us."

"I'm not blaming Jesus. He was crucified by the Romans, and now it is Christians who torment him by committing evil in his name."[14]

From beginning to end, this conversation is a testimony to Christ. It is a testimony, first of all, in what Mauriac does not say. He allows Wiesel the last word, even when that word is not entirely charitable. Mauriac combines humility with courage, neither denying the evils that have been done in the name of Jesus, nor attributing them to Jesus. There is not a word of condemnation for Wiesel or denigration of Judaism. Mauriac speaks of Judaism with both knowledge and respect. He knows the best in Judaism, and he presses Wiesel to live up to it. I admire the courage with which Mauriac raises the name of Jesus Christ not as a sword against Judaism but as the rightful goal of it. Wiesel is able to hear Mauriac — and yes, even disagree with him — because he knows that Mauriac has no intention of using his faith against him. On the contrary, it is because Mauriac loves Jesus that he defends Jews; because he suffers at Jesus' suffering that he seeks to assuage the suffering of Jews; because he believes Jesus is the truth that he risks broaching its significance for those who do not know it or who deny it.

---

14. Elie Wiesel, *All Rivers Run to the Sea: Memoirs* (Thorndike, Me.: Thorndike Press, 1996), 470-72. I had a similar conversation with Elie Wiesel. An essay written by one of my students, Kimlyn Bender, won the Elie Wiesel Ethics Prize. Mr. Bender was invited to the Yale Club in New York City to receive the prize in June of 1992, and I accompanied him. At one point in the conversation I said to Mr. Wiesel that I admired his writings but was bothered by the theme "never forget, never forgive." He agreed that the theme appeared in many of his writings. "Could you forgive the Germans?" I asked. "Yes," he replied promptly. Not prepared for the haste of his response, I paused and then asked, *"Have you forgiven them?"* "No." "Why not?" I asked. "Because they have never asked for forgiveness," said Wiesel. I asked Mr. Wiesel if I might carry the conversation a step further. He invited me to do so. "Isn't that the point of the cross of Jesus Christ?" I said. "He died for the sins of the world before the world deserved it, or asked for it, or even desired it. Isn't the forgiveness of Jesus Christ unconditional?" Wiesel looked at me and said, "That is why you are a Christian and I am a Jew."

Can People Be Saved Without Having Heard the Gospel?

A common and perplexing question in Christianity is how the God and Father of Jesus Christ could reject people from eternal life who through no fault of their own have not heard the gospel. This question has attended the Christian faith throughout its history, but its urgency seems to be heightened in the modern world. As both the globe and the influence of the church in the Western world shrink, we are becoming increasingly aware that many people live and die without having heard the gospel of Jesus Christ, or without having heard it in a way that would lead them to faith.

One possible solution to the dilemma is that those who have not known Jesus Christ in this life may by the grace of God be granted the opportunity of hearing and responding to the gospel after they die. This is, to be sure, a theological hypothesis, for the Scriptures do not specifically raise this question or provide definitive guidance on it.[15] Nevertheless, the hypothesis is attractive in several respects and seems to be gaining currency today. The hypothesis acknowledges that a great many people in the world have never been exposed to an adequate exposition of the gospel of Jesus Christ. On the other hand, it maintains that the salvation of such people, even if after death, depends solely on Jesus Christ. The hypothesis, in other words, is true to the nature of the world as we

---

15. New Testament passages that conceivably broach the issue are 1 Thessalonians 4:13-18, 1 Peter 3:19-20, and more especially 1 Peter 4:6. The last passage, however, is unclear whether the gospel was preached to the dead, or to those who have died. See E. G. Selwyn, *The First Epistle of St. Peter* (New York: Macmillan, 1969), 337-39. The Roman Catholic Church has come close to making the hypothesis into dogma. *The Documents of Vatican II* (1963-1965, Book II, Chapter 16) contain the following statement, which has been repeated and affirmed in *A Catechism of the Catholic Church* (1992, Paragraph 847): "Those who, through no fault of their own, do not know the Gospel of Christ or his Church, but who nevertheless seek God with a sincere heart, and, moved by grace, try in their actions to do his will as they know it through the dictates of their conscience — those too may achieve eternal salvation." For a thorough and thoughtful discussion of the possibility of salvation after death, see R. Todd Mangum, "Is There a Reformed Way to Get the Benefits of the Atonement to 'Those Who Have Not Heard?'" *Journal of the Evangelical Theological Society* 47/1 (2004), 121-36.

know it, and also to the clear teaching of Scripture that no one comes to the Father except through Jesus Christ. True, the hypothesis is innovative in suggesting that the grace of God in Christ may be accessed after death. But may it not be permissible to suppose that the same grace of God that saves a defiant humanity in this life (Romans 5:8-10) would grant to a desirous humanity what it was denied in life? In a rather unique way, the hypothesis seems to accord with the spirit of Christ as attested in Scripture.

Yet despite the attractiveness of this hypothesis, it seems to me inadvisable to teach it in the church or to base policy decisions on it. The practical implications of this hypothesis would surely militate against evangelism. The purpose of dogmatic theology, that is, theology in the service of the doctrine and mission of the church, is not speculation. The purpose of theology and doctrine is the responsible interpretation of Holy Scripture, and lack of clear attestation in Scripture to the possibility of saving grace being extended to those who have died outside the faith should place this issue outside the parameters of normative church teaching. It is surely irresponsible from a pastoral perspective to encourage people to contemplate decisions of eternal consequence on a hypothetical possibility. The church has never been briefed on a Plan B of salvation. Even the carefully nuanced articulation of the hypothesis in the Catholic Church (see note 15) is not without theological problems. The suggestion that people may "achieve eternal salvation" on the basis of "a sincere heart" or "the dictates of their conscience" seems to verge on attributing salvation to human effort, that is, to ascribe to human virtue what the gospel ascribes solely to the grace of God. An implication of salvation by human merit rather than by the completed work of Jesus Christ is a false gospel (Galatians 1:6).

Let us hope that those who have died without having heard the gospel may, by God's grace, be offered the possibility of responding to the gospel. But let us also be aware that a formal reliance on this hypothesis would likely endanger the proclamation and mission of the church. And let the church preach with fervency the one way it knows for certain, that there is salvation in no other name than the name of Jesus (Acts 4:12). To quote the apostle Paul, "Now is the day of salvation!" (2 Corinthians 6:2).

"Removing the Veil"

When we review the interface of biblical faith vis-à-vis other religions in the ancient world two things become apparent. The first is a challenge to an overly narrow and rigid conception of Christianity that would reject all other faiths as demonic and evil. We have seen that early Christians did not adopt a one-size-fits-all judgment of other religions. They weighed and analyzed others' beliefs and practices in light of the standard of the character of God as revealed in the gospel. In that same standard they judged them in truth and charity.

On the other hand, we do not find any support for an uncritical pluralism that supposes all religions to be inherently equal. The commonly held view that all religions are merely variant streams of one transcendent source is wholly absent from the New Testament and early church. Judaism, as we have seen, is generally seen in the New Testament and early church as a trajectory leading to the gospel of Jesus Christ. But even Judaism did not lead inevitably to Christ; many Jews rejected that trajectory and refused to acknowledge Jesus Christ as Lord. Nor is Judaism endowed by the writers of the New Testament with saving efficacy. The apostle Paul declares that Jesus Christ is necessary to remove the veil so that Jews can see the true intent and meaning of Torah.

> We act . . . not like Moses, who put a veil over his face to keep the people of Israel from gazing at the end of the glory that was being set aside. But their minds were hardened. Indeed, to this very day, when they hear the reading of the old covenant, that same veil is still there, since only in Christ is it set aside. Indeed, to this very day whenever Moses is read, a veil lies over their minds; but when one turns to the Lord, the veil is removed. (2 Corinthians 3:13-16)

Only "when one turns to the Lord, [is] the veil removed." If this divine transformation of heart and mind is necessary in Judaism, the closest analogy to the Christian faith, how much more so must it be necessary in other faiths more distant from Christianity? When God removes the veil, says Paul, humanity is enabled to see the glory of the Lord and to be "transformed into the same image from one degree of glory to another" (2 Corinthians 3:18). Jesus Christ makes clear and understandable "the end" (v. 13) or purpose of Judaism. And not only Judaism, but the end and purpose of all other faiths as well. It is the Lord, who is also the Spirit, who removes the veil of confusion, ignorance, and resistance, and who gives freedom to see the transforming glory of God in the face of Christ.

CHAPTER 12

The Mystery of the Incarnation

The most unique and essential characteristic of Christianity is the Incarnation. Christianity teaches that Jesus Christ was the true God in truly human form, who gave his life as an effective sacrifice for the sins of the world and whose historical resurrection from the dead is an anticipation of the resurrection of those who trust in him. No other religion — ancient or modern, local or universal — makes anything approximating the claim that God, without sacrificing his divine nature, has become a full and complete human being. The Incarnation reverses the traffic pattern of all other religions: it is not we who, by morality or enlightenment or some other means, mount the ladder to heaven, but God who comes to us in our weakness and unworthiness. According to the New Testament, our knowledge of God is not derived from intermediaries, whether prophets, priests, visions, oracles, avatars, or spirit-persons, but immediately from Jesus Christ, who was not only sent by God but who *was* God. Christianity claims to rest on a personal self-disclosure of God in human form.

Because the Incarnation distinguishes Christianity distinctly from other religions, it opens Christianity to charges of supremacy in the modern mind. If Christianity is unique in the way described above, then it offers a personal revelation of God not offered in other religions. This claim is offensive in a world in which pluralism is highly valued. In an effort to lessen or alleviate the supposed exclusivity of Christianity and to enhance its compatibility with other religions, the uniqueness of Jesus is sometimes scaled down to the status of prophet or revealer, similar to Moses or Muhammad, Buddha or Black Elk. In an effort not to offend believers of other faiths, some Christians surrender that which is most distinctive about Christianity in order to identify with that which is most common in other religions. I have no doubts that most people who do this are motivated by good will, hoping for what might be called benevolent universalism. The cost, however, jeopardizes the heart of the Christian faith. The quest for a lowest common denominator on which all religions can agree and perhaps eventually unite inevitably compromises the particularity of the Incarnation.

The goal of true interfaith dialogue is better understanding among religions, the dismantling of stereotypes, and the recognition of common ground and cooperation in common endeavors. These goals seem to me entirely worthy — indeed I should say obligatory — of any Christian who claims to be motivated by the twin commitments to truth and love, as Paul enjoins all Christians to be in Ephesians 4:15. When a history of injustices and even crimes colors the dialogue, however, as is the case in Jewish-Christian dialogue, then rare qualities are required of participants on both sides of the table. Injustices must be named and confessed. Christians, in particular, must be willing to confess and repent of complicity in many forms of anti-Semitism in past generations. But they cannot be expected either to retract or repent of the essence of the gospel, and certainly not of their belief in the Incarnation. To expect that would be like expecting children to repent of being children because they behave selfishly or even cruelly. They may repent of their selfishness or their cruelty, but they cannot — indeed should not — repent of being children. Christianity, likewise, may repent of the evils done in the name of the faith, but to repent of the faith itself would be to perpetrate another injustice — against itself.

The Incarnation and the Meaning of Life

In the last chapter we saw that the earliest Christian tradition displayed a range of judgments about other faiths and religions. Some religions were judged to be grave distortions of the truth; others seemed to be "preparing" for Christianity in various ways. Whether distant or near, however, no other faith was judged viable on its own. No way other than the gospel leads to salvation. Through the lens of the gospel we can see the God-breathed characteristics that are present and intimated in other religions. In some cases those characteristics are few, in others many — but in all cases they are corrected and completed in Christ. The New Testament speaks of this "God-quality" in the cosmos as *mystērion*, a word translated either as "secret" or "mystery." The apostle Paul speaks of the mystery thus:

> We speak God's wisdom, secret and hidden, which God decreed before the ages for our glory. None of the rulers of this age understood this, for if they had, they would not have crucified the Lord of glory. But as it is written, "What no eye has seen, nor ear heard, nor the human heart conceived, . . . God has prepared for those who love him." (1 Corinthians 2:7-9; also Ephesians 3:9)

The word translated "secret" in the above quotation is *mystērion* in Greek. It refers to the unfathomable wisdom of God that, although hidden from human understanding, is destined to reveal God's glory. The *mystērion* of God is the determinative character of God implanted in the world, the divine genetic code that is at work in creation, destined to achieve God's saving purposes.

The *mystērion* contains and reveals the very will of God (Ephesians 1:9), and as such it cannot remain forever concealed. The apostle Paul declares that in a unique event in history God disclosed his character in the revelation of Jesus Christ. Prior to that event God's character and will had been perceived in nature, apprehended at least in part by human reason, and more fully revealed in the history of Israel, particularly through the Law and Prophets. But this knowledge was mainly knowledge *about* God. Until the veil was removed in Jesus Christ, people could not truly and intimately know God as God willed to be known. The *mystērion* became known in the same way an iceberg becomes known. The crest of the iceberg visible above the surface of the sea reveals the mass and movement of something submerged in the depths beneath. Something similar occurs in Jesus Christ, who makes visible God's will and purpose in creation. But where the greater part of the iceberg hides forever beneath the surface, in Jesus Christ the greater part of the *mystērion* rises above the surface. The overtures of God that have been unrecognized or unappreciated throughout history and nature are fully identified and summed up in Jesus Christ, who is the fulfillment of God's will and purpose in creation.

The proclamation of Jesus Christ is "the revelation of the *mystērion* that was kept secret for long ages, but is now disclosed . . . and made known to all the nations" (Romans 16:25; also Colossians 1:26). The *mystērion* is not like a code that defies cracking. It is not like a black hole in outer space, too dense to be penetrated. The *mystērion* is knowable, even though the initial and earlier parts of it, especially, lay beneath the surface of human understanding. The capacity of the *mystērion* to be known depends on a revelation of God, not on human intelligence or ingenuity. In the fullness of time, God made known the divine will (Ephesians 1:9) in the sending of the Son, Jesus Christ, the *mystērion* of God (Colossians 2:2; also 1:27). The heart of the *mystērion* of God is the proclamation of the cross of Christ. The crucified savior, whose death effects forgiveness of sins and reconciles the world to God, is the clearest revelation of the divine *mystērion* (1 Corinthians 1:23; 2:1-5). The *mystērion* is the cosmic plan of salvation revealed in Jesus Christ.[1]

Speaking of the *mystērion*, the apostle Paul declares that the purpose of God in Jesus Christ is "to gather up all things in him, things in heaven and things on earth" (Ephesians 1:10). We have already seen how Irenaeus founded his concept of "recapitulation" on this passage. The concept of recapitulation suggests earlier intimations and inklings being finally summed up and plainly identified for what they are. Jesus Christ is like a great magnet, as it were, who draws to himself all things in creation and history that respond to his pull. The gospel of Jesus Christ is

1. See *Theological Dictionary of the New Testament*, s.v. *mystērion*; also J. Paillard, *In Praise of the Inexpressible: Paul's Experience of the Divine Mystery*, trans. R. J. Erickson (Peabody: Hendrickson, 2004), 75-92.

like a Geiger counter, detecting and revealing the divine radiations, whether strong or faint, emanating from the rocks of the universe.

The idea of recapitulation as expressed in Ephesians 1:10 declares that nature and history emit a code, the *mystērion*, but that the key to understanding the code remained outstanding until the sending of Jesus Christ. God has left "fingerprints" in creation, as the apostle Paul indicates in Romans 1:18-32. Those fingerprints include the purposefulness of creation, the various ways in which creation reflects an artful and purposeful creator, the innate moral sense of humanity, and so forth. On the basis of the fingerprints, it is reasonable to conclude that all creatures have at least some intimation of and inclination for God. To my mind, this is the most satisfying explanation for two recurrent facts of historical anthropology: that all peoples in all times have had both a concept of the sacred and some way of revering it. Yet these "fingerprints" or intimations are only partial. In themselves they are incomplete and insufficient. They are whispers too faint to be fully discerned, lights too dim to illumine the way. But they are whispers and lights nonetheless. And however untutored, human beings have always felt compelled to respond to them, albeit in sometimes stammering and faltering ways.[2] Even in their crudest and cruelest forms, the religions and cultic practices of humanity are responses, however imperfect, to the *mystērion* of God implanted in the universe. The knife that slays the sacrificial victim, whether on a Canaanite or an Incan altar, knows that the stairway to God is broken and cannot be restored apart from a propitiatory death. The sages and gurus who declare that the divine is compassion and peace, not arbitrary power and revenge, are rightly on the scent of the *mystērion* of God.

---

2. In *Church Dogmatics* IV.3/1 (ed. G. Bromiley, T. F. Torrance [Edinburgh: T&T Clark, 1961]), Karl Barth speaks of "true words spoken in the secular world" that are understandable in light of the true Word of God in Jesus Christ. God has acted and continues to act outside the spheres of Bible and church, but only in Jesus Christ is that activity and speech understood for what it is (116-18).

A Puzzle

Imagine the religions of the world as a group of people trying to assemble a puzzle. Each religion has puzzle pieces before it, and each is trying to fit the pieces into a meaningful pattern. There are two problems, however. The first is that the box top with the picture of the puzzle on it is missing. All religions, in other words, are trying to assemble a pattern about which they are ultimately ignorant. The second problem is that not all the puzzle pieces fit the puzzle. Many pieces, indeed most of them, do not fit the puzzle at all. They are pieces belonging to other puzzles that have no relation to the puzzle needing to be assembled. The alien pieces must be discarded, of course, but without the box top it is difficult to know the right pieces of the puzzle from the wrong ones.

What are the various puzzle pieces that other religions possess? Hindus have a sense of the descent of various deities to earth to minister to specific needs. Buddhists stress the centrality of love, or better perhaps, benevolence, in their tradition. And both Hindus and Buddhists stress the knowing of self, human consciousness, and the powers inherent in the mind. These are true pieces of the puzzle. Jews and Muslims have other pieces. Both traditions lay great emphasis on social morality, such as almsgiving to the poor, the transformation of society according to the will of God, and the requirements of justice. In addition, Judaism has an expectation of the advent of the Messiah. These are true pieces as well. Taoists have pieces related to the humble and mysterious *tao*, the rhythmic pattern of the universe. Confucians possess pieces related to honor and respect for elders and those in authority. Animists, who sense the energy of the divine pulsating through nature, possess pieces that recognize the divine power inherent in creation. What Jesus said to the woman at the well and what Paul said to the Athenians — that they worship that which they do not know — could also be said of the various religions. Each possesses pieces of the puzzle, but none knows the pattern. The pattern of the puzzle is not contained in any piece, or in many pieces.

The pattern of the puzzle cannot be known until the final *mystērion* is revealed. The Incarnation of Jesus Christ is the *mystērion*, the box top of the puzzle, as it were. The gospel gives the whole picture, the pattern of the inchoate pieces that in other religions is unknown and incomplete. All things in heaven and on earth have been gathered up in Christ (Ephesians 1:10).

Some, of course, will object that the Christian claim to possess the box top is precisely the problem. The claim of any religion to possess *the* box top will inevitably lead to arrogance, dominance, and eventually the misuse of power. I shall speak further to this objection in my comments about "particularity" at the end of the chapter. Here I wish to say that wherever the gospel is truly present in the hearts of Christians and churches and missions it leads not to arrogance but to humility, not to dominance but to the desire to serve, not to the misuse of power but to the willingness to suffer.

True Christians know that it is not to their credit that they possess the box top. They do not have it because they are smarter or more worthy than others. They have not invented the box top or discovered it on their own. For all we know, it is because they are the most unworthy that they have been given it. They possess the box top solely as stewards, and they are responsible to share it with others working on the puzzle.

The puzzle analogy does not imply that everything in all religions and cultures points to Christ. We noted above that all peoples and cultures have many alien pieces from many different puzzles that do not fit the pattern. There are customs and aspects of every religion and culture that are incompatible with the gospel. These cannot be made to fit into the true puzzle and they must be discarded if the proper pieces are to be assembled. As Irenaeus asserted, Jesus Christ sums up and recapitulates in himself those elements of history and culture that are reflections of himself. Many elements, indeed the vast majority, are not reflections of God. A magnet attracts only metallic substances, a Geiger counter detects only ionizing radiations. Everything else is passed over.

A Parable

How can Christians share the box top of the puzzle? Consider the following parable from the Swiss New Testament scholar Eduard Schweizer.

Suppose that my father died when I was twenty years old, just as my younger brother was born. The main difference between my brother and me is that I knew our father and he did not. I would gladly tell him whatever he wanted to know about our father. But my having known our father most certainly would not mean that I was necessarily the better son.[3]

The elder son in the parable is not entitled to speak to the younger brother because he is the better son. He may not be. It may be that the boy who never knew his father is actually the more exemplary son. We all know people — people of other religions or perhaps of no religion — who are better than some people who call themselves Christians. The parable relieves us of assuming that witness to Jesus Christ presumes moral superiority.

At the same time, the elder son bears a responsibility to his younger brother. His responsibility is not grounded in his moral superiority, but in his relationship with the father. He knew the father personally and his younger brother did not. There is a difference between knowing about God and knowing God. Many people know something about God; adherents of other religions often know a great deal about God, in fact. But knowing God personally is a different matter. The younger son may know quite a lot about his father, but that cannot replace the elder brother's firsthand knowledge of his father.

The New Testament is replete with statements that Jesus is the one complete revelation of the Father, and that those who know Jesus know God. "Whoever has seen me has seen the Father" (John 14:9). "[Jesus] is the image of the invisible God" (Colossians 1:15). Jesus is a window of revelation to God that is not replicated anywhere else in creation. The knowledge *of* God and the reconciliation *to* God that is offered to the world in Jesus ushers believers into a unique relationship *with* God. Be-

---

3. E. Schweizer, *Jesus, das Gleichnis Gottes: Was wissen wir wirklich vom Leben Jesu?* (Göttingen: Vandenhoeck & Ruprecht, 1995), 114 (footnote 190). The English translation entitled, *Jesus, the Parable of God* (Princeton: Princeton Theological Monograph, 1994), 111, footnote 190 omits the third sentence of the quotation and distorts Schweizer's intention.

lievers in the gospel are responsible to that knowledge, as Peter testified to the pagan soldier Cornelius, "[God] commanded us to preach to the people and to testify that [Jesus Christ] is the one ordained by God as judge of the living and the dead" (Acts 10:42). Believers are saved not because of their merits, but solely because of God's grace; as a consequence, believers bear witness not to their merits but to God's grace in Christ. They bear witness to the *mystērion* of God revealed in Jesus Christ. Listen to Schweizer's concluding words on the parable:

> In my view, God's hard and unshakable love is nowhere better known than in Jesus Christ. Therefore, I want to tell Christians and non-Christians about him. . . . At the end of time, when we really see the face of God (and I believe the face will have the features of Jesus) we will then all be saved only through the love of God that took form in Jesus.[4]

The Scandal of Particularity

There is a final aspect of Schweizer's parable that I wish to emphasize. It concerns the subject of mission and evangelism. It is my sense that the prospect of taking the gospel of Jesus Christ to the world often makes Christians despondent today. Rather than being news of great joy, the gospel is often seen as an imposition on the world. Christian missions and evangelism seem to be associated with a sense of guilt and suspicion: why should God reveal himself in a saving way only in the gospel, and not in other times and places, or in all times and places? We may even convince ourselves that people do not want to hear the gospel. If we view missions and evangelism as an impropriety, perhaps even an offense to others, then we shall also view them as a burden to ourselves.

For moderns, the chief offense of the gospel seems to be in "particularizing" it. If, as Christians maintain, God became a human being in Jesus of Nazareth who lived in first-century Palestine, then what about

4. Schweizer, *Jesus, das Gleichnis Gottes,* 97 (my translation).

people who lived before then, or people ever after who have not had access to that *locus?* The particularity of the Christ event in time and space seems to hinder its universality. It seems to exclude people. The Incarnation, once again, is the cause of offense.

Our initial response to the particularity of the gospel may be like my own instincts the first time I drove over a blind hill in England. Decades of driving in the States had conditioned me to think of the left lane as the wrong lane. As I approached the crest of a hill I was strongly tempted to swerve into the right lane. It took considerable mental discipline to resist my conditioned impulses and stay left. What seemed right to me in this instance was not; in fact, it could be fatally wrong. In a similar way, particularity does not seem right; it seems offensive and wrong, the antithesis of universality. When we think through the issue to its conclusion, however, we discover that particularity is not the problem but the answer. Particularity is the presupposition of universality.

If God is truly to enter into human history as a human being, then God must do so as a particular human being in a particular time and place. The entering of God authentically into human history makes the Christian faith something other than, or more than, an idea, philosophy, myth, or intuition. The Incarnation roots the Christian faith to a historical event, to Jesus Christ "who was crucified under Pontius Pilate," as the Apostles' Creed maintains. The Incarnation reveals that God wills to invade our world, no longer to be held at celestial arm's length, but to intrude and break into the world (John 1:11). The particularity of the Incarnation is not just good news, it is the *best* news. It means that God can now be known as never before. In the Incarnation, a religious longing has become a historical fact.

Historical particularity has a crucial advantage over a universal idea. Think of the search for the cure of diseases like AIDS, cancer, and Parkinson's. Until someone, somewhere actually discovers a cure, no one's life will be saved from such diseases, no matter how fervent the longing for a cure. Historical particularity is the hinge that changes a potentiality into an actuality, a hope into a reality. No one, I think, would regard the discovery of a cure for AIDS in Rochester or Cambridge or Tokyo as exclusive. It would, rather, be a sign that a horrible disease can finally be eradicated, as polio and other diseases have been. The same is true of the Incarnation. Far from excluding people from salvation, the Incarnation means that all people can now experience what they have always longed for.[5]

And thus the third point of the parable. The elder brother should scarcely be despondent about telling his younger brother about their father. He is not reporting something foreign or disagreeable. He is telling the younger brother about his own father. He rightly assumes that the younger brother wants to know about his father, for in learning of his father he learns of himself. The assurance that God is the Father and Christ the saving elder brother of those to whom we share the gospel makes a big difference in how we conceive of evangelism and missions. Evangelism and missions are not religious spam. They are not bothersome activities, like telephone solicitations or children selling candy for a school fundraiser. True Christian witness is making known to non-Christian neighbors that they are also created by God, made in God's very image, and that by faith in Christ they too may become God's children.

It would be a cruelty if a cure for a dreaded disease were discovered, but not delivered to those suffering from the disease. "If the claim of Christ's Lordship is true, it is true for all and must not be concealed from any."[6] The gospel is the *mystery* of the cosmos revealed. Those who hear and believe it are under a divine mandate to make it known. The God who sent the Son into the world to die for the sins of the world now sends believers in the Son into the world. They bear the good news that the God who is the world's only creator is also its only redeemer in Jesus Christ.

---

5. Already in the third century Origen defended the particularity of the Incarnation, saying that Jesus Christ appeared in "one corner of the world" so that he might heal "people in every country, for He came as the Savior of *all* people" (*Against Celsus* 4.4 [emphsis in original]).

6. Lesslie Newbigin, *Truth to Tell: The Gospel as Public Truth* (Grand Rapids: Eerdmans, 1991), 34-35.

Index of Subjects

Index of Scripture and Other Ancient Texts